# Tracing the Melanesian Person

This book is available as a free fully-searchable pdf from

**www.adelaide.edu.au/press**

# Tracing the Melanesian Person:

## Emotions and Relationships in Lihir

by

Susan R Hemer

*Discipline of Anthropology and Development Studies*
*School of Humanities and Social Sciences*
*The University of Adelaide*

UNIVERSITY OF ADELAIDE PRESS

THE UNIVERSITY *of* ADELAIDE

Published in Adelaide by

University of Adelaide Press
The University of Adelaide
Level 1, 230 North Terrace
South Australia 5005
press@adelaide.edu.au
www.adelaide.edu.au/press

The University of Adelaide Press publishes externally refereed scholarly books by staff of the University of Adelaide. It aims to maximise the accessibility to its best research by publishing works through the internet as free downloads and as high quality printed volumes on demand.

Electronic Index: This book is available from the website as a downloadable PDF with fully searchable text.



For the full Cataloguing-in-Publication data please contact the National Library of Australia: cip@nla.gov.au

ISBN (paperback) 978-1-922064-45-5
ISBN (ebook) 978-1-922064-44-8

Project Editor: Patrick Allington
Cover design: Emma Spoehr
Cover photograph: Norm Hanson
Book design: Zoë Stokes

*Dedicated to the memory of Emma Zanahien, who taught me to approach the world with good humour and love despite hardship, and of Mesulam Aisoli MBE for his wit and enthusiasm for learning.*

# Contents

# List of Maps and Figures

# Acknowledgements

This book would not exist without the knowledge, encouragement and nurturance I received from many people. My greatest debt is to the people of Lihir. *A puet sna e makil yo se muel torme te die. Go i tnien puet te e yo na e nien ka erem puet. Yo nanse mle e pu snieng torme ki giet i anio. Yo kasi ertawet no nanse baliye go i Mahur.* Special thanks go to Wengbeh for her gift of friendship, and to her son Gas, who gave me coconuts. Thanks go to the families of Kso, Wengbeh, Pangpang, Tumdi and Nalo for many hot meals. Also to Pangpang and Atzo for providing accommodation while on Mahur, and to the Tniltalgo clan for building my house. My gratitude goes to the patience and perseverance of Isidore Lakiah, who schooled me in the Lihir language, and to Loeng, who conveyed the nature of Pindik and other customary matters to me. Thanks also to Denita Kaimua for providing me with the first opportunity to laugh on Mahur.

At Samo village thanks are due to the family of Aisoli, who accepted my occasional visits over a period of many years, and who accepted me and my son Oliver as part of their family. On Malie I owe a debt of gratitude to Morpo for his interesting conversations about matters of *kastam*, and to Biorbi and Pulerau for accepting me as part of their family. Also to Moktel for demonstrations of the continuing practice of trepanation.

My time on Lihir was enriched by many of the staff of the Lihir Management Company, particularly members of the Community Relations Department. Especially notable are Mesulam Aisoli, Leonard Lagisa, Martin

Asu, Emma Zanahien, Clothilda Molong and Jacky Membup, both for their encouragement during my doctoral fieldwork, and later as my colleagues and friends.

This book began life as a doctoral thesis first through La Trobe University and later the University of Melbourne. La Trobe University supported me with a generous fieldwork grant, and a context to engage with fellow students. Wendy Mee, Ju-Lan Thung and Yekti Maunati in particular enriched my experience there. I followed my doctoral supervisor, Dr Martha Macintyre, to the newly formed Centre for the Study of Health and Society at the University of Melbourne. I am deeply indebted to her, particularly for the integrity I have seen in her dealings with people both in academia and in the field. Having someone to discuss issues and situations with who worked in the same field site made the experience far richer for me. I am very grateful for her ongoing friendship.

My deep gratitude goes to the original examiners of the thesis, and the reviewers of this manuscript. In particular I would like to extend my thanks to Dorothy Billings for her unique contributions to New Ireland ethnography and for the support she has shown me over the years.

I thank my colleagues at the University of Adelaide, and in anthropology more generally. Nick Bainton followed me to Lihir for his doctorate, and I am very grateful for many conversations over the years, and his astute observations and analysis. More recently, Kirsty Gillespie has provided new insights into Lihir culture through her work on songs and stories. In particular, discussions with Alison Dundon enriched the sometimes isolating process of book writing and reviewing. The many coffees with fellow staff and postgraduate scholars in Adelaide eased the frustrations of writing. Thanks also to Sharon Lewis for many discussions and laughs.

Finally, to my friends and family, who accepted my disappearance to another country for a year with grace, and then later for another two years. Thanks to Melissa, Anne and Lucy for continuing friendship, support and advice. Thanks especially to Catherine: this book would not exist but for her. During my doctoral fieldwork my mother, Jo Hemer, managed my finances and kept a group of friends and family in touch with photocopies of letters. She also kept me supplied with food parcels and a fruity birthday cake. My family gave me life, and gave me the resources to seize the opportunities it presents.

Finally, to John, Oliver, Lucy and Adele, thank you for your love and support during this time. This monograph and the fieldwork on which it is based has been the context for the experience of great love.

# Prologue

## *Yumi lus pinis*

On Wednesday, 6 May 1998, a boat called 'Maria' belonging to the Tnialen clan of Mahur Island went missing. In it were two adult men, Nezik and Ngalbolbeh, and two boys, Gilas (sixteen years old) and Michael (Ngalbolbeh's son, eight years old). The boat had gone to the main island of the Lihir group, Niolam, but did not return late Wednesday afternoon as was expected. People on Mahur, including myself, became increasingly anxious about the welfare of those in the boat as the days passed. Stories were told of other lost boats, prayers were said in church, and dreams and other signs were interpreted for clues as to the fate of those in the boat. Eventually, the following Monday, the boat and all of its occupants returned safely.

This incident became a critical point of reflection and reflexivity for my view of the emotional lives of Mahurians. Some aspects of their reaction to this loss were so familiar, such as their fear and anxiety, while others were incomprehensible to me, for instance, the apparent lack of relief at the return of the boat. Additionally, the loss of this boat corresponded to the time of confirmation in the Catholic Church, which for Catholic Lihirians incorporates the local *kastam* (T.P.) of *pindik*.[1] Confirmation/*pindik* became central in explanations about the loss of this boat, although later less esoteric explanations such as a lack of petrol prevailed.

I employ the loss and return of this boat as a window onto themes about life in Lihir that I explore in this book. The emotional reactions of Mahurians, the importance of Christianity to Lihirians, and my positioning in the flow of life on Mahur are all critical to my argument. Their entailment in the story of this missing boat allows me to pose questions that I address in the body of this work.

## Tripping to Tabar

Ngalbolbeh, Nezik, Gilas and Michael left Mahur Island on Wednesday morning, 6 May, to go to Samo village on the south-west coast of the main island, Niolam. Their aim was to collect Ngalbolbeh's wife's father, Zikmandawit, and take him to Mahur for a major celebration planned for Friday, 8 May: confirmation in the Catholic Church for the grade five school children. Ngalbolbeh's oldest son was to be confirmed, as was Gilas. Those aboard the boat attempted to collect Zikmandawit from Samo village, but he was unwell and did not want to go. He watched them push the boat out and begin the two-hour journey back to Mahur.

Ngalbolbeh and Nezik thought they had enough petrol to make it to Mahur, but they also knew it would be a close call. Ngalbolbeh told Nezik

[1] Throughout this book I indicate Lihirian words by the use of italics, for example, *pindik*, while words in Tok Pisin (a creole widely spoken throughout PNG) are also in italics followed by 'T.P.' in brackets, for example *kastam* (T.P.). In general I use the Mahurian dialect of the Lihir language, which is often known as 'shortcut' due to the dropping of certain vowels in comparison to dialects on the main island of Lihir. I also use the spelling of Lihir and Mahur terms that was used throughout my fieldwork. Recently there has been a decision to drop the use of a 'z' in favour of 'ts', amongst some other changes. This is altering the names of some villages (e.g. Zuen is changing to Tsuen) yet Lihirians recognise both and many favour the former practise. There is little difference in the dialects of the three outer islands, but some Mahurians said they had some difficulty understanding the dialect of Matakues (on the south-eastern side of the main island, Niolam).

to check the petrol when they were at Kunaye village,[2] and if it was low, said they should call in and collect some from Ngalbolbeh's wife's sister. Nezik did check, but felt there was enough petrol to make it to Mahur.

Nezik ran the boat slowly, and by the time they approached Mahur it was dark. They were close enough to see the light of lamps, and hear the beat of kundu drums practising for the confirmation celebrations … and then the petrol ran out. The boat had no oars, torches, canvas or raincoats, life jackets, flares, cooked food or water. Nezik and Ngalbolbeh pulled up the planking in the bottom of the boat and fashioned some oars from this. They then did their best to row to Mahur, but the tide was strong, and after a long effort, they gave up. They anchored for the night using a fishing line off the village of Lakamelen on the south side of Mahur, checked that this anchor would hold, and slept.

Towards dawn the anchor slipped and they began drifting to the western side of Mahur, to the village of Kuelam, where they had left the previous morning. Again they tried to row ashore, but found the tide was too strong. They tried to signal using a mirror, but it was too cloudy. They managed to stay within sight of Kuelam until about 10 a.m., but by this time the tide was pulling them to the northern side of Mahur. If they had followed this current they would have been drifting north with no islands in their path. At this point they realised they were actually in trouble and Nezik commented '*Yumi lus pinis*' (T.P. 'We are lost'). Until this time they had felt they would be seen or would be able to row to Mahur—they had not been afraid until this point. Luckily, the wind was blowing to the Tabar islands[3] and thus they decided their only chance was to head quickly for there. They had to think about young Michael, and the dangers of dehydration. They rigged up a sail from Gilas's *laplap* (T.P. sarong) and set sail.

---

[2] Kunaye is the northern-most village on the main island, Niolam, and is the last point of call before setting out for Mahur.

[3] A group of four islands to the west of the Lihir group. It is only about three hours by boat between Lihir and Tabar, when under engine power.

Night fell. They were very close, and spotted lights on the southernmost island of the Tabar group, Big Tabar. They tried to aim for the lights, but adjacent to Tabar there was a current and they were unable to make it. They paddled, and eventually landed on a small, uninhabited beach at about 8 p.m. Ngalbolbeh carried Michael to a cave for shelter; he had vomited three times from lack of food and water, and was crying for his mother. They made a fire and cooked some *mami*[4] (T.P.) that they had got from Zikmandawit at Samo village, while Ngalbolbeh looked for water. Finding none, he sent Nezik to climb a coconut tree (one of two on the beach), despite it having a *golgol* (*gorgor* T.P.)[5] taboo on it. They got six coconuts, which they shared and ate with the *mami* and then they settled down and slept.

In the morning Ngalbolbeh climbed up the cliff hoping to find nearby inhabitants. He found a road that he followed a little way in both directions, and found a few fallen coconuts. These he took back and they ate them with the last two *mami*. Then they all climbed the cliff and set off to find some people. They wandered into a hamlet where an old man and woman and a young boy were staying. They were startled, and the old woman tried to talk to them in the local Tabar language. Ngalbolbeh and Nezik then explained their story.

They were taken into the main camp where they were fed and looked after. Ngalbolbeh recognised some people from his days in high school on the New Ireland mainland. By this time it was Friday (8 May) and it was obvious that Gilas was going to miss his confirmation, which was to be held that morning. Ngalbolbeh did his best to send word to Mahur that they were safe but this was by a very circuitous radio route, and those of us anxiously waiting on Mahur never received this message.

Thinking that the people of Mahur knew they were safe, Nezik and Ngalbolbeh agreed to stay and have a proper, though small, feast in their

---

[4] Mami is a starchy tuber much like a yam, and is common in Papua New Guinea.

[5] A *golgol* is a piece of plant (generally a form of ginger) tied around a tree to taboo it from use.

honour.[6] The women went to the gardens to get vegetable foods, while the young men went and retrieved the boat from the uninhabited beach, and caught fish for the feast. Meanwhile the four 'trippers' had a proper meal and then slept. That afternoon they feasted and then prepared to leave early the next morning.

Next morning, Saturday, they pushed the boat out and were farewelled by the Tabar people. They started to motor away when something in the boat motor burst into flame. They had to row all the way back to the shore, and were in grave danger of drifting again. The boat motor was fixed, but they hesitated to leave that day, fearful after nearly being lost a second time. Instead, they waited until Monday morning when they were able to be accompanied by Bruno, a Tabar man, with his boat motor as a back-up to their own. They finally arrived back on Mahur on Monday, 11 May at 1.30 p.m.

## Fieldwork on Mahur Island

This incident came about half way through my twelve-month doctoral fieldwork stint in Papua New Guinea. Mahur Island is the northern-most island of a group of four called Lihir, located to the north-east of central New Ireland. The main island of Lihir, Niolam, is the southern-most island in the group, and is home to a large gold mine that began production in 1997.[7] The island group was home to about 10,000 people in 1998, 800 of whom lived on Mahur. The population has since grown in number through natural increase and migration for employment, with about 14,000 Lihirians and 6,000 non-Lihirians resident in the islands in 2008 (Bainton 2010:21).

---

[6] It seems to be the custom on Tabar, as it is in Lihir, to treat visitors extraordinarily well and supply them with all the food, betelnut, tobacco and so on that they want. On Mahur this is called feeding (*pniari*) the visitors (*wasir*). See Chapters 3 and 5 for further discussion of *pniari wasir*.

[7] The Lihir gold mine was constructed by Davey Kinhill Flour Daniel before being managed by Lihir Management Company, a wholly owned subsidiary of Rio Tinto, until 2005. It then operated as Lihir Gold Limited, before being bought by Newcrest Mining Limited in 2011.

These islands were the site of my doctoral fieldwork of fifteen months duration, from November 1997 to October 1998, plus shorter trips of June to July and December 1999. Most of my time I spent on Mahur Island, living in Kuelam village. In addition I spent time living in Samo village on the south-western side of Niolam, and time in the mining town, Londolovit, on the eastern side. I also visited the other two islands in the group, Malie and Masahet. Between 2000 and 2002 I spent more than two years largely on Niolam researching health, education, women's development and the relocation of Kapit village for the mining company. I made short return trips to Lihir in 2003, 2004, 2011 and 2012 to conduct extra fieldwork and maintain relationships.[8]

I went to Lihir initially with the intention of studying emotions, particularly grief. I was interested in how Lihirians spoke about grief, local notions of grieving, whether and how they expressed grief, and whether they had a gendered view of emotions in general. However, on arriving in Lihir I found it extremely difficult to elicit information about grief, which was complicated by the lack of any deaths on Mahur Island, and therefore funerals, for the first four months of my twelve-month fieldwork period. I hoped, given the context of a recent death, that it may be easier for people on Mahur to speak about grieving. Yet I was disappointed when, on the death of two children in a period of a month, people still were not interested in discussing their own or others' emotional reactions. I experienced a period of doubt in my abilities as an ethnographer, believing that the material was there to gather. I decided that I was asking questions in the wrong way, always assuming that people did not understand my intentions, or that I was asking the wrong people. This was partially correct, as I came to understand over the course of the twelve months. The issue was not that there was a pool of information about grief in Lihir that I simply had to tap, but that the people's reticence or even silence was in itself a statement about the nature of grief. Lihirians experienced and expressed grief differently from people in my own

[8] All references in the present tense to Lihir indicate at the time of publication.

society and in ways not susceptible to many of the analytical assumptions of Western studies of grief (Hemer 2010).

I also came to realise that my idea of simply 'studying grief' was naïve. I had assumed, following dominant theory in psychology, that grief was the automatic reaction to the loss of significant others in a person's life. Yet none of these concepts could be assumed in a different cultural context. What was the nature of death in Lihir and the meaning of 'loss'? In what ways were people 'significant' to one another? I broadened my perspective, and the result is this ethnography of the nature of persons, their relationships to one another, and of emotions.

It is attention to the context of emotion that interests me. While it is necessary that the study of emotion in anthropology be approached through language, it should not be limited to this. In the words of one contribution to the literature:

> In the study of emotions anthropologists often analyse these as 'terms and concepts' which are subsequently located within 'webs of significance'. As a consequence the focus tends to become lexical and the studies frequently constitute meta-semantic exercises. Accordingly, it has been argued (Rosenberg 1990:171) that the contextualisation of emotive terms and concepts really amounts to nothing but a reduction of situated discourse to a discourse about situations which eventually may even end up in a discussion on the appositeness of particular terms in given situations. (Rosengren 2000:221)

Given this risk of reductionism, in this book I have chosen not to organise chapters around particular emotions but on other thematic issues.

Thus, the loss of this boat and the reactions to it were central to my study. In another way it was central to me because I was living in the hamlet where Ngalbolbeh and Michael had been resident. They had become my friends and part of my day-to-day life.

## My reaction: a little self-reflection

I first heard about a boat being missing on Thursday afternoon, 7 May. At first it seemed nothing important, and no one seemed particularly worried. Instead, most attention was directed towards the preparations for confirmation to be held the next day. During that particular period I had been spending time in the neighbouring hamlet, and was unaware that the immediately affected families were already worried. It was that night that Lolot[9] went to ask that a radio call be made early Friday morning to the neighbouring island groups of Tabar and Tanga, to check if anyone had seen the boat. Even so, at this stage there was not much talk about this boat, and I assumed, with others, that it had simply gone ashore and spent the night at Masahet or on Niolam.[10]

The following day, Friday, was the day of confirmation, and I was very busy recording this event. At about 2 p.m. the parish priest, Father Steve Boland, and the Bishop of the New Ireland Diocese, Ambrose Kiapseni, left Mahur to go to perform confirmations on the neighbouring island of Masahet. By this stage I was getting a little anxious, especially with the stories Steve Boland told me of other lost boats.

I was connected closely with the family of Ngalbolbeh and Michael: my house on Mahur was located in their hamlet, and I ate with them quite often. I knew Gilas's family less well at the time of confirmation but by the end of my fieldwork Gilas's father was one of my better informants.

By Friday afternoon my worry for them was growing, especially as it became obvious that they were truly missing. Gilas would not have missed his own confirmation without very good reason.

By Saturday I was truly afraid. The time passed with no word except from Tabar and Tanga to say that no one had seen the boat. On Saturday at sunset I went down to sit on the beach. At the time I wrote:

---

[9] Lolot is the sister of Kwildun, whose husband Ngalbolbeh and son Michael were missing.

[10] This is quite a common occurrence if the weather is bad or the sea is rough.

> I can't find peace on the beach tonight. Kwildun stands with Eric [her fifteen-month-old son] and a pipe on the shore—looking out. Each time I look at her I have to fight back tears. Where are the planes to search for them? Where are the boat safety measures (like flares)? … Where is the coastguard? Here the ocean simply swallows people up. If they had touched land there would be word on the radio. There is silence. They are already three days without water. And Michael is so young. This place certainly isn't 'Death Without Weeping'.[11] (Personal Journal 9 May 1998)

As time passed, I became certain that they were properly lost. This would mean either no trace of them would be found, or the boat and possibly some survivors would turn up two or three months later in some distant place like the Solomon Islands or Fiji.[12]

By Monday morning I had basically given up hope that the boat and occupants could all be found safely. At 1.30 p.m. I was just finishing a language class when two boats went past to go ashore at the wharf. I paid little attention until I noticed some of the young children from my hamlet running to the wharf. I asked one what boat it was and she said 'Maria'. In amazement I turned and walked very quickly to the wharf. All four occupants were safe and sound. I was nearly in tears from relief. I expected to see Kwildun at any moment sprinting to the wharf to hug her child to her and check he was still in one piece, but she didn't arrive. The only person who seemed to be amazed was me.

## The families' reactions

Three immediate families were involved in this boat's disappearance. The family that seemed the least involved was that of Nezik. Nezik and Ngalbolbeh

---

[11] Scheper-Hughes (1992).

[12] There are a number of stories of previous boat losses involving Mahurians. For example, one boat drifted for four months before arriving in Tuvalu with half of those originally on board alive. Another boat drifted for a number of months before arriving in the Solomon Islands with only two survivors.

were closely related and called each other *sunglik* ('brother': actually FBS).[13] However, Nezik's family lived on Malie, another small island in the Lihir group, and at first they didn't even know he was missing. Eventually they were told, but I was not able to observe their reactions.

The second family involved was that of Gilas. His father, Bale, was one of the leaders of the customary celebrations for *pindik* in 1998 (Ngalparok, Ngalbolbeh's father, was the other main leader). Bale was withdrawn while the boat was missing, and he and his wife did not go to the wharf on Friday to see the Bishop and Priest off—they stayed in their hamlet and worried (*lil zket*, T.P. *wari*). Later Bale told me that by the end of the time that Gilas was missing they had begun to believe that he would die.

My most detailed knowledge is of the third family immediately affected by this boat loss: the family of Ngalbolbeh and Michael. Ngalbolbeh's father, Ngalparok, was one of my main informants, and I could see that he was very worried. Ngalbolbeh's wife, Kwildun, was one of the owners of the hamlet, Lalakam, where I resided. I knew Kwildun, her sister Lolot, and their children well.

Boats were normally greeted in this hamlet, Lalakam, by shouts from the children as they guessed the identity of the boat. During the five days this boat was missing I never heard one child shout the name of an approaching boat. The atmosphere, even among the young children, was very subdued.

Thursday morning Kwildun was seen sitting on the beach staring out to sea with her children.[14] Her distress was not obvious until Friday, when she did not go to the feasting following confirmation, despite the fact that her oldest son was confirmed that day. On the Saturday and Sunday afternoons she stood on the beach holding her fifteen-month-old child watching as the sun went down—something very unusual for her. Saturday evening I could hear her

[13] The acronym FBS refers to Father's Brother's Son.

[14] This was reported to me by one of the people in the neighbouring hamlet on Saturday—it was made as a comment on Kwildun's distress.

crying (from the neighbouring hamlet). That day her face was a study in fear and distress. She did not finish betelnut when it was given to her. People told me that this was the effects of *lil zket* (T.P. *wari*).

## Lil zket

Lil zket *is a Lihirian term that translates as 'bad feelings' or in the form* a ling sa zket *as 'my insides are bad'. They translate it in Tok Pisin as* wari, *or worry.*[15] *This was the term constantly applied to Kwildun (particularly) and also the family of Gilas.*

Lil zket *is something to be guarded against. Kupulie (a very close informant) said at one point that Kwildun was feeling so much* lil zket *that she was nearly sick from it, and that if it continued she* would *be sick. In previous contexts I had been told that* lil zket *can kill.*

*It was seen as very important to prevent Kwildun from focusing on this* lil zket *or at least not to increase it. People thus went and talked about other subjects, seeing it as crucial not to mention any signs that suggested the boat was permanently lost. The only sign that was told to Kwildun was a positive one. On Thursday Ngalparok had a stone thrown at him—but not by a human being. It was a stone from the beach (rather than from deep under the sea), which suggested that the occupants of the boat had (or would) reach land safely. This stone was said to be thrown by a* kanut *(spirit of a dead person).*

[15] At the time of this boat loss my grasp of the local language was still quite rudimentary, and thus my discussions about what was happening were conducted in Tok Pisin. I also checked all of the emotion terms in the local language.

*On Saturday night, when people noticed Kwildun wasn't finishing betelnut, a few people went and stayed talking in the hamlet till late, and then slept in the family men's house (*a rih*). This was to try and distract her so she could not dwell too much on her missing son and husband.*

By Monday, Kwildun was looking somewhat better. Her sister, Lolot, had a dream the previous night that the boat and its passengers were safe on the Tabar Islands. Early that morning Ngalparok (Ngalbolbeh's father) sent the community boat to go to Tabar to find them.[16] They knew that the prevailing winds on Wednesday and Thursday had been towards Tabar. Thus, Kwildun seemed more relaxed while waiting for them to return, which they did a few hours later.

When the boat arrived Kwildun did not rush to see her husband and son. Neither did Gilas's family, who were all up in the gardens finding food. I went to Lalakam hamlet and reported to Kwildun that her son was fine. She seemed to take it for granted that this would be the case. She calmly told me that there had not been any bad signs to say they were really lost. Such calmness baffled me at the time: I had expected joy and relief and tears.

## Perspectives from the community

While this boat was missing it was the most common topic of conversation. This was not the case at first, as it took a while for the news to spread and for people to begin to be concerned. By Saturday, people were talking about this boat and telling stories of other boat losses, especially to me.

[16] The 'community boat' is a boat that the entire community of Mahur Island owns. This is in contrast to boats owned by clans (like 'Maria', the lost boat) or boats owned and operated by individuals as a business.

The possibility of using divination (called *niakiel*) to find the fate of those in the lost boat was raised, but had not yet been tried when they returned. A pot of seawater is collected from the open ocean, a wild taro leaf (*a kiel*) is put in this, and then these are put in the room of one of the missing persons. The house is then left vacant for the night, and in the morning the pot is examined. If the leaf is torn, the boat has sunk. If there is some sand, bits of food, betelnut or tobacco on the leaf, this means the boat has reached land. If there is no change, they are simply drifting.

The wider community talked about signs regarding the loss of the boat. One young woman, Weinrau, went to the gardens very early Thursday. While in an area of forest belonging to Ngalparok she heard a young boy crying—but no one was there. This was a particularly bad sign about Michael, the youngest 'tripper'. Such signs appeared to be a way of expressing concern for those in the boat. Many people said to me 'I'm just thinking about the two children' (T.P. *Mi tingting tasol long tupela mangi*). At one stage Kupulie sat quietly for a long time, and then said that she hoped that coconuts would float their way.

The community also talked about the lost boat in another way. On Sunday during the church service, this boat was mentioned in prayers at the beginning and during the service. Somewhat surprisingly, the prayers were only for those in the boat—not for their families waiting on Mahur for news.

Also on Sunday there was a meeting held regarding the possibility of a prospecting lease being granted by the government for Mahur Island. One of the major topics of this meeting was instead about the community boat, and the possibility of putting restrictions on it to make it safer. It was decided that this boat should leave the main island by 3.30 p.m., thus arriving on Mahur by about 5 p.m. That way it would be known while there was still daylight if there was a problem. In practise this rarely occurred, but it is an indication of the level of concern in the community that they considered such measures.

Finally, the community talked about the lost boat through the medium of explanations for it being missing. Ngalbolbeh and Nezik had taken the boat 'Maria', belonging to Tnialen clan. This boat was designated to pick up the Bishop and Parish Priest on Thursday in preparation for the confirmation ceremony. There was petrol put aside for this job, and it was this petrol that Ngalbolbeh and Nezik used (intending to replace it later). Many people expressed to me that this was a mistake given that '*pindik*' was involved with confirmation.

**Pindik**

Pindik *is concerned with the growth and teaching of young people. A few people said it was 'like a college'. In the past the initiates were taught such things as garden and fishing techniques and magic—all those things needed for everyday living. More recently* pindik *has dovetailed with confirmation in the Catholic Church, and teaching is about being a good Christian.*

Pindik *has a 'spirit' that is awoken for the teaching of the initiates. This spirit has the power to kill people who disobey the laws that are in place during the time* pindik *is 'awake'. People should not wander around at night or joke about the power of* pindik.

*Before* pindik *is awoken, some structures are built within a coconut leaf fence (*benben*). These structures can take many forms, according to the imagination of the 'boss' of* pindik. *However, the painted designs (circles on a black background representing eyes) remain constant. Once these structures have been built,* pindik *can then be awoken by the one or two men who are the 'bosses' or leaders of* pindik.

*In the past there were five* pindik *groups in Lihir. There were two on Mahur: one for the men and one for women. Then there were three other* pindik *groups for males on the other islands in the Lihir group. While said to be indigenous to Lihir by Lihirians themselves, other groups on New Ireland have had groups or 'cults' that are termed* 'pindik'*, a Tolai word meaning 'secret'. For the Usen Barok,* pindik *is a word that refers to any sort of secret society, each of which then have individual names such as Buai, Tubuan and Taberan (Wagner 1986:122–40). However, for Lihirians it seems that* pindik *refers not to the class of cults or secret societies, but to a specific one.*

Pindik *is now only practised on the two outer islands, Mahur and Masahet, and occurs in conjunction with confirmation in the Catholic Church (Hemer 2011). The coming out celebrations for the initiates happen on the day that the sacrament of confirmation is received. The tunes for singing in the confirmation ceremonies come from* pindik. Pindik/*confirmation is a major event in the Mahur calendar and occurs biannually.*[17]

[17] See Chapter 5 for further discussion of *Pindik*.

Some people said that *pindik* knew this boat and petrol were designated for use on Thursday, and so *pindik* had made them go missing. This understanding was strengthened by the close association the families had with *pindik*. Ngalbolbeh's father and Gilas's father were the two leaders of *pindik* in 1998. One man, Joe, told me before the boat went missing, that while men were inside the *pindik* enclosure they had heard the spirit of a young man (*tombuarien a zik*) walking around in sandshoes, and that this meant this man was going to die. Efforts were made to discover the identity of this spirit, but these were unsuccessful. While the boat was missing, Joe said that the spirit may have been Ngalbolbeh, as he sometimes wore sandshoes.

Another explanation was that even though this boat was called 'Maria', the captains of it would often miss church on Friday and go early to the market on the main island. One woman said that the Virgin Mary had turned her back on this boat that was her namesake due to this behaviour. This explanation and the ones referring to *pindik* are moral commentaries on the actions not only of Ngalbolbeh and Nezik but of the Tnialen clan that owned the boat Maria.

After the boat returned, explanations for its loss took on a much more practical dimension. Those involved ascribed the boat loss to carelessness, lack of experience in judging the amount of petrol needed, and poor driving of the boat (which used more petrol/got them to Mahur at nightfall). Those involved actively denied more esoteric explanations based on *pindik* or the church. Some months after the boat loss, Gilas's father, Bale, asked, 'How would *pindik* affect them? Drink their petrol?'

Added to, and in some cases transforming, community explanations were those of Ngalbolbeh and Nezik. The differences in their commentaries of this event are an example of the continual negotiation and conflict of meaning in Lihirian life. The stories (and accusations) of Ngalbolbeh and Nezik are in the vein of practical explanations. Ngalbolbeh told the story of the boat loss and ascribed it to poor judgement of petrol reserves on both his and Nezik's part. He said Nezik drove the boat poorly, but in the end he (Ngalbolbeh) appeared ashamed and took responsibility for his part, particularly the lack of safety equipment in the boat. Nezik, on the other hand, said it was all Ngalbolbeh's fault for taking authority for the supply of petrol when he was not a 'real' boat captain.

## Conclusions and beginnings: person, emotion and relations

This is in essence a happy story, yet I learned much from the experience about the nature of fear and worry (*lil zket*). Once the boat returned, the interest in it stopped almost immediately. For a long time I believed I learned little of the nature of relief and joy from this incident—except perhaps that they are very low-key, and certainly do not appear in the same form as in Australia. I recognised Mahurians' expressions of distress very easily, and yet their lack of joy and relief left me baffled. Did such reactions not occur in Lihir? Were they in a form that I did not recognise? Or was this particular occasion one that did not lead to such reactions? The answers to these questions require an understanding of the nature of emotions in Lihir, and at the time of the boat loss I was unable to answer them. This book taken as a whole is in part an answer to such questions.

Some Mahurians commented on my reaction to this boat loss. After the boat was found safe and sound, one woman, Zilio, said that I would die quickly from worry (*lil zket*) if I was lost in a boat because I reacted badly to this one. She said I was a person who worried easily (T.P. *wari i stap klostu*). In this, Lihirians can be seen to be evaluating me and my propensity to experience certain emotions. This, for me, raises issues about the application of personality characterisations in Lihir, particularly given the recent literature on 'relational persons' in Melanesia, who are defined by their relations rather than any inherent qualities (Strathern 1988). It also raises questions about Melanesian theory of mind as discussed in a 2008 section of *Anthropological Quarterly* (for example, Keane 2008; Rumsey 2008; Schieffelin 2008). I evaluate these constructions of Melanesian sociality in the Lihir context throughout this work, with the aim of taking seriously the relationships between emotions and personhood.

This prologue mirrors the style and many issues that concern me in this book. My analysis is explicitly partial and positioned. I was positioned during my doctoral fieldwork as a relatively young, single, female student, and on later trips as someone with a partner, someone who did research work for the Lihir Management Company (locally known in T.P. as the *kampani*), and finally as a mother. My understandings of what it means to be a Lihirian person are naturally partial, but particularly so because the depth of linguistic competence, of relationship and insight necessary to get to the heart of person and emotions is difficult to achieve in a few years. My understandings of being

Lihirian are also multiple, like the explanations for the loss of the boat, as Lihirians themselves are positioned.

Like this prologue, this book as a whole is peopled. In analysing the everyday practices of Lihirians I do not abstract relationships and emotions from the people who enact, experience or perform these. For Lihirians themselves, their world is composed of named and individuated people who are known for their capacities and habits. In tracing the nature of Lihirian persons I took inspiration from a local phrase '*a malmalien e makil*', meaning the traces that are left behind when people leave an area: the footprints, dust, and scraps of betelnut skins and food. These can be read to understand who was in a place and what they were doing. In this sense I trace aspects of Lihirian lives with the aim of getting to the heart of what it means to be a Lihirian person.

My ethnographic research centred on the everyday lives and practices of Lihirians. Partially this is the result of accident: when I arrived in Lihir in 1997 it was the end of a long drought. That year there was very little feasting, and the beginning of the next year was occupied with apparently mundane tasks. There were no major court cases and so forth. Hence, my attention turned to the daily practice and work of life in Lihir. What became apparent in those early months was the salience of emotional and moral commentary about others.

While the semantics of emotion are important, in this book I shift attention to the performance of emotion and the contextual analysis of emotion. This work is not structured around individual, named emotions as the subject of chapters, but instead follows broad emotional themes in three parts: connections between people, conflicts, and finally loss and transformation. Lihirians are connected in this book through relationships of kinship and marriage (Chapter 1), through households (Chapter 2), and through movements that connect and separate persons in space (Chapter 3). Yet Lihirians were not only concerned about connections between people, but also moral evaluations and critiques of others, and of disconnections: Chapter 4 explores how Lihirians evaluated the morality of conduct of their fellows through Lihirian virtues, both Christian and local. These appraisals were the basis for conflict where people did not meet these ideals, as discussed in Chapters 5 and 6. Finally, in Chapters 7 and 8 I trace the transformation and dissolution of persons and relations at the end of the life course through death and mortuary rituals.

Emotions are a critically important aspect of this book, and of Lihirian life, but my aim is to move beyond the lexical focus of earlier works on emotion (for example, Lutz 1988; Lutz and Abu-Lughod 1990; Rosaldo 1980). Emotions are embedded in the everyday practices of Lihirians, and particularly implicate constructions of the person and relationships. It is this triplet that I take as critical to an understanding of what it is to be Lihirian: the person, emotions and relations. It is also this triplet taken together which I suggest is crucial for being able to trace the nature of the person more generally in Melanesia.

# PART I

# CONNECTIONS AND RELATIONS

# 1

# Navigating the seas of relationship

## On being Pulerau: entering the field

I arrived in the Lihir group of islands on 15 November 1997. As the plane circled over the four islands I noted that they looked quite green, despite the severe drought in Papua New Guinea of the previous few months, only recently broken. Lihir contrasted with the brown drabness of Port Moresby where I had spent the previous thirty hours, and I immediately decided that I was going to like this place. I stayed that night on the main island of the group, Niolam, in dormitories belonging to the gold mine, and ate at their 'mess'. The food amazed me: a choice of meat or fish, lots of vegetables, a salad bar, cordial, and various types of dessert. Was this fieldwork in remote Papua New Guinea?

A few days later I climbed aboard a small 'banana boat'. These craft, with an outboard motor and a plank in the bottom of the boat to sit on, are either 19 or 23 foot long and are the motor craft of choice for Lihirians. Luckily, at this point I did not realise that these boats generally have no safety equipment and occasionally have holes in the bottom of them. Nor had I yet heard the stories about their quite frequent disappearance.

The trip to the island, Mahur, where I was going to spend most of the rest of my fieldwork period, took one hour that day. The seas were kind to me, and gave me a false impression that was rectified fairly quickly. Occasionally during fieldwork I arrived on the beach battered and saturated after a trip that took over one and a half hours. However, on this first day the sky was blue, with little wind. I left the beach in the company of Christina and her sister Mary, both fluent speakers of English, as it was with their family that I was going to live on Mahur island.

We arrived at the wharf of Kuelam village on Mahur island. I expected more people to greet me, but I later learned it was the time for yam planting, and most people were spending time in their gardens, often sleeping there at night. All my gear was dumped on the wharf, and a group of children gathered to help us carry it to the hamlet where I would be living, at the other end of the village. I was startled to see a young child put a car battery on his shoulder and carry it for the ten minute walk to the other end of the village: I could only just lift it.

I was given a room in a house at the back of Lalakam hamlet, the southern-most hamlet of Kuelam village and owned by Christina and her siblings. This particular house belonged to a bachelor, and I was to use it as a temporary home until my own house was built, while he shifted to sleep in the men's house. In reality it took seven months for my house to be constructed, and thus I spent more time in my 'temporary' house than in my permanent one. However, this gave me a chance to come to know and observe my three neighbouring households in a way that would not have been possible had I lived the entire year in my 'permanent' house.

Over the next few days I fought my rising terror. The place was beautiful, and the people hospitable, but what was I doing here? I felt like an imposter, a feeling exacerbated by the fact that my Tok Pisin was poor, my Lir language non-existent and I could communicate with virtually no one.

After ten days on Mahur I felt I had something of a breakthrough. Christina's classificatory brother, Ziklala, gave me a name, 'Butbut'.[1] This name belonged to a woman of their lineage who had been very interested in culture, and was someone who talked a lot. While this second quality seemed totally inappropriate as I barely spoke at this stage, the name made me feel that I was somewhat accepted. I felt the people had given me a place in this community, and that I could settle down to work.

My terror later returned when after a couple of weeks all of the English speakers with whom I had been spending time left Mahur to return to their places of residence on the main island. I began to spend a little more time with my neighbours. One evening my teenage female neighbour, Zilio, arrived at my house and asked me to go and *lotu* (T.P. worship) with them.[2] Walking through the village, she told me that I was Pulerau: that this was to be my name and that she and I were now cross-cousins. I was somewhat confused by this at first, because I had already been given the name Butbut by Christina's family. However, Zilio explained that this was another name.

Over the next few weeks I came to better understand what this name meant. It turned out to be more than just a name: Pulerau had been a young girl who had drowned in the 1970s and in taking her name I had been given her place in the kinship system, which meant that I now had siblings, a mother, cousins and so on. I also was a member of a clan and lineage. It was primarily through my identity as Pulerau that people traced my fictive kinship and I came to know the meanings of clan and kinship in Lihir.

In this chapter my intention is not to classify the kinship 'system' of Lihir, nor am I going to deal with marriage exchanges or clans as corporate

---

[1] This is not pronounced like 'butt' but is pronounced to rhyme with 'put'.

[2] *Lotu* is a word in Tok Pisin that covers words such as religion and church service. People ask what *lotu* you are (what denomination), and to *lotu* is to conduct or participate in a church service.

groups. Rather, my approach to kinship is from the perspective of the nature and content of these relations. Relationships in Lihir were not predetermined at birth by a set of static kin categorisations and clan membership; people did not passively fill roles given by virtue of their position in a system. Kin relationships need to be explored together with other relationships of marriage, friendship and namesakes in order to illuminate the way Lihirians actively negotiated their relations with others. In this arena I too learned to navigate.

## Clan affiliation

Clans in Lihir are a very complex phenomenon, as is evidenced by the Filer and Jackson report (1986), where they give four possible versions of a clan system. They state that even given much more time they would not be able to come to a consensus about clans in Lihir:

> even if our sources of information were more extensive, we should not expect to be able to arrange them all into one internally consistent model of the clan system as a whole ... the local people's models of the system are as diverse as the interests which they express. (Filer & Jackson 1986:86)[3]

Much of the difficulty with clans appears to occur when Lihir is taken as a whole. On Mahur, clans appeared much simpler. Clans are matrilineal and membership is automatic at birth. There were four clans, which then each had a number of named subdivisions (subclans). Clans are termed *tbawin* on Mahur, and subclans *zre tbawin*. The four clans were arranged into moieties, which appeared to have little purpose in daily life. Some people said that they

---

[3] This report was written as a base line survey in the context of the development of the gold mine. With regard to the clan 'system', note, for example, Filer's discussion of the group called Nayal: 'This group is widely distributed throughout Lihir, and is normally identified as a clan in its own right. N. Bokas (Kunaye) and G. Tukas (Malal) have both suggested that NAYAL is a sub-clan of AHOT, but other informants (in South Niolam) would reverse this relationship, and make NAYAL one of the two or three main division of the MALKOK [*smol pisin*] moiety. In 1985, Balkun (Lataul) argued that TINIENTALGO and NAYAL (in that order) were the two main divisions of this moiety, but other informants would reverse the order of priority. In 1985, some Bulamue men suggested that NAYAL 'covers' NISAL, LALA, NIELIK, MASI, and AHOT.' (Filer 1992: Appendix 3).

used to have to marry someone from the opposite moiety (as Ramstad n.d.a:5 stated was the case in the late 1960s for Kunaye village on Niolam, and occurs in many places on the New Ireland mainland, see for example Clay 1986; Wagner 1986), but there is little evidence that this was ever the case on Mahur. Rather than using the local language, these moieties on Mahur were always referred to in Tok Pisin, as *bik pisin* and *smol pisin*.

The four clans on Mahur were called Nawus and Tnialen (*bik pisin*), and Tniltalgo and Nzol (*smol pisin*).[4] I became affiliated to Nawus clan by virtue of two things. First, the woman with whom I had arrived on Mahur, Christina, was a member of Nawus clan, and so the hamlet I was living in belonged to a Nawus lineage. Second, Pulerau had been a member of Nawus clan, and I 'inherited' my clan membership from her.

While it seems easier to find a clan 'system' on Mahur than in Lihir when taken as a whole, I would argue that to see clans in this way would be a mistake. Difficulties such as those expressed by Filer and Jackson (1986) are a result of their efforts to find the 'Lihirian clan system'. Relationships between clans in Lihir are based on cooperation and exchange in the context of feasting rather than a static hierarchy of six 'major' clans each made up of a number of subclans, which comprise a number of lineages. While the relationships between clans and subclans in one area of Lihir, such as Mahur, may appear to be relatively simple, in another area of Lihir these clans may have a different relationship because these relationships are open to continual renegotiation in feasting.

For example, while Masnahuo is a subclan of Nawus clan on Mahur, in other areas of Lihir it is a clan in its own right. On Mahur, Masnahuo always cooperates in feasting with Nawus, having too few people to hold major feasts on its own. Tnialen clan sometimes cooperates with Nawus, and they are both in the *bik pisin* moiety. On the other hand, Nawus never seems to cooperate with Tniltalgo or with Nzol clans, both *smol pisin* moiety. These

[4] In the mainland Lihir dialect, these were called Unawus, Tinalian, Tiniltalgo and Nisal respectively.

relationships of cooperation in feasting do not hold in other areas of Lihir, and so relationships between clans and subclans are different.

The problem partially appears to be of the chicken-and-egg variety: are the relationships between clans and subclans the way they are because of the way they cooperate and exchange in feasting, or do they cooperate in that way because of pre-given relationships? Lihirians themselves like to propose that there is a 'clan system,' and they readily give versions of it, which, however, cannot be reconciled. Despite this, and the fact that Lihirians say that relationships between clans are based on cooperation in feasting, the idea that there is a 'clan system' remains powerful.

What did clan membership mean to me and to the everyday life of people in Lihir? Initially the most obvious aspect for me was in the context of feasting. In many feasts the distribution of food is based on clan membership. Food is generally divided between men and women, and then this is further divided into four clan groups and then distributed to small groups of people sitting together (three to seven people).[5] I had to be able to recognise my clan group, and then go to sit with them.

Clan membership also regulates marriage, with clans being strictly exogamous. There was a case of endogamy that caused much discussion while I was in the field in 1998 and again in 1999: a young man and woman were not only members of the same clan, but also the same subclan. They were said to love (*leimuli*) each other, and despite not being married she had given birth to three children that people stated were his. The birth of the second child had occasioned much discussion about whether they should be allowed to marry, however the issue was unresolved even after a third child was conceived and stillborn.

The organisation of church services is regulated according to clans. Each week a clan group organised the service, did the Bible readings, led

[5] In some contexts the middle step was left out, and food was divided between men and women, and then straight to the small groups.

the singing and so on. The rotational system ensured that each clan would perform this duty every four weeks. It was not the entire clan that lead the church service. Instead, some people from that clan would meet in the nights before the service, practice the songs they were to use, and decide who was to do each Bible reading. Often the people who chose to do this were the young unmarried members of the clan, both men and women.

I came to know the clans through my positioning as Pulerau, and much of my time I spent with people from Nawus clan—I lived in a Nawus hamlet, and tended to eat with various households that were primarily Nawus. I also had a special relationship with Tniltalgo clan, which was the clan that 'fathered' me: Pulerau's father was from that clan. This clan, Tniltalgo, looked after me: they volunteered to build my house. I also had close relationships with a small segment of Nzol clan (of Alonsiat subclan) who had married Nawus men of the lineage of Pulerau, or had been fathered by them, and I had meals with them sometimes. The clan I had least contact with was Tnialen clan: it took most of the year before I began to make good contacts and find informants in this clan. As I was Pulerau, these people were not in my immediate sphere.

## Lineages

Lineages on Mahur are termed *bior*, and are traced from a female ancestor sometimes only two or three generations above the living adults of the lineage. Thus, lineages are quite shallow genealogically, often being about five generations deep. From my position as Pulerau, there were two or three generations above me, and one or two below me.

Often the lineage appeared to be the landholding unit on Mahur, though people assured me that land was owned by clans. There were a multitude of relationships to land on Mahur, and certain relationships took precedence over others. When asked, people would say that a piece of garden land belonged to a particular clan (one of the four on Mahur), yet this statement disguised the fact that land on Mahur in practice was divided between the three villages first, and then divided between clans. In practice, also, household units often organised by lineage cleared and worked land, so that a number of households within a lineage would garden together. Areas of land were associated with particular lineages within a clan, who had used that land for gardening over generations. While other lineages of the clan had the right to make gardens in that area (or members of the same clan from another area of Mahur or even elsewhere in Lihir), none would do so without asking first, not because that lineage 'owned' that area, but out of 'respect' (*sio*).[6]

Stating, then, that clans are the 'landholding units' (for example) oversimplifies the situation in Lihir, where there are a number of levels of relationship to land. The issue of exactly which group owns land has become a problem mostly in the context of the development of the gold mine on Niolam, which necessitated the documentation of ownership of land within the Special Mining Lease (including the pit and plantsite). In this case, ownership was said to be clan-based, with particular 'executives' of each clan being block controllers. This documentation has perhaps hardened relationships to land in certain areas of Lihir into the binary opposition of ownership:non-ownership, rather than the more flexible relationships that continue on Mahur.

Residential land was also said to belong to clans, but, like garden land, in practice it appeared often to be held by lineages. The village where I was staying, Kuelam, was divided into sixteen hamlet areas called *a den anio* ('a fenced area'), each of which was named. Hamlets in Kuelam are contiguous and divided from each other by a low stone wall (*welot*) or by a picket fence of stakes of the *bumbrier* plant, which continue to grow once cut and planted for the fence. There were five Nawus hamlets, five Nzol hamlets, three Tnialen hamlets, two belonging to Tniltalgo and the final one belonged to the Catholic church (containing the school and church). The hamlet I lived in, Lalakam, was said to be a Nawus hamlet but was actually owned by Masnahuo lineage/

[6] See the discussion of *sio* (respect) in relationships in Chapter 5.

subclan, as they had bought it.[7] The neighbouring hamlet, Liabanis, was used by the Tandum lineage of Nawus, while another Nawus hamlet was used by the third subclan of Nawus. In practice, hamlets become associated with particular subclans or lineages, even though they may be said to be owned by clans.

On a practical level, then, lineages are the most important unit for usage of land, be it for residential or garden purposes. People's practical relationships to land on Mahur are primarily through lineages, even though this may be owned on a clan basis.

In being Pulerau, I was a part of the lineage whose apical ancestor was Liomet (the Tandum lineage)[8] and who were associated mainly with Liabanis hamlet in Kuelam (though many were resident elsewhere). My 'temporary' house at the back of Lalakam hamlet belonged to a bachelor of this lineage, Soklas, who became my 'son' (he was older than me) when I became Pulerau. Three of the four households nearest me (in Liabanis and Lalakam hamlets) were of this lineage. However, it was not with this lineage that I was technically resident. The land in Lalakam belonged to another lineage of Nawus clan (of Masnahuo subclan), some members of which were resident in the fourth household in the vicinity, and it was they who invited me to stay and to build a house on their land. The other households stayed in the Lalakam by the grace of this owning lineage.[9]

At Christmas time in 1997, Nezik, a man of the clan that fathered me (Tniltalgo), asked me why I was living in the hamlet that I was, suggesting instead that I should stay with the woman who was Pulerau's mother, Nalo.

---

[7] Buying land was extremely uncommon at this time on Lihir, and this was the only occasion that I heard of on Mahur. Lalakam hamlet was part of a section of land that had been designated as land for plantations during the time of the Australian administration, and was also the site for the public cemetery and a desalination machine. It had an ambiguous character as both Nawus clan land but also 'public' land, which was unproblematic unless triggered by a need to use the land for some purpose (e.g. for the Aidpost as mentioned in Chapter 6).

[8] Lineages were not named. However, for ease while in the field I began to equate lineages with their oldest female member. To avoid confusion I continue this practice in this book.

[9] I deal with households in my Chapter 2.

She was staying on land that belonged to her deceased husband. Nezik was asking me why I was living so far away from Nalo (who lived at the other end of the village), and with a lineage of Nawus clan that was of a different subclan. He urged me to build my house in the 'right' place, close to Pulerau's mother.

At other times I was identified more with the Masnahuo lineage on Mahur. When I went to Samo village on Niolam, Christina introduced me to people as being part of 'her' group. In feasting on Malie Island, and at Samo and Kunaye villages on Niolam, it was with this lineage that I spent my time and was identified.

On Malie this lineage of Masnahuo subclan was one of the lineages of Nawus clan that held a mortuary feast (Pkekanut) in October 1998. I was identified with the 'feast givers' (*hukarot*) rather than with visitors (*wasir*), despite the fact that it was only my second visit to Malie island. Being part of the feast givers meant I was not identified as Pulerau (and I did not sit with that lineage of Nawus clan), and I was fed from food provided for feast givers.

My navigations between these two lineages of Nawus clan continued right up until the time I left the field. In preparation for my departure, a feast (Niaktip) was organised to rid me of the effects of any powerful Mahurian spirits (*a tndol*). This feast was jointly held by the Tandum and Masnahuo lineages, on Tandum land with bananas bought/grown by Tandum people but with a Masnahuo pig.

Besides being important for people's practical relationship to land, lineages are also important for a sense of a person's rightful place in actual physical space. For a long time I was confused by one woman's comment that she was a woman of Mahur (T.P.: *meri* Mahur), despite the fact that she spent most of her childhood on Masahet island, went to high school on mainland New Ireland, then found work in Port Moresby, married and lived in Madang, and divorced and was living at Samo village on Niolam. She had only spent small amounts of her life on Mahur. When stating she was a '*meri* Mahur' (woman of Mahur), she was stating her rightful place, based on her lineage's origin place at Lalon on Mahur.

While I did hear a number of stories about the origin and migration of clans and lineages, as well as about particular ancestors that Lihirians locate in real time, Mahurians very rarely told stories unrelated to something contemporary or in the recent past. I had to prompt to get stories even about the war or the arrival of white people, and in fifteen months of fieldwork time I heard only two mythical stories. I was never able to elicit myths even in contexts such as the meaning and origin of 'Y'-shaped stiles on men's houses. Gillespie (2011) has recorded a story genre known in Lihir as *pil*, which are short stories recounted in domestic contexts as a source of entertainment and comment on aspects of Lihirian life. Yet like myself, Macintyre reports a similar reluctance of Lihirians to tell mythical stories (pers. comm.). Simon Foale, who worked briefly on Mahur in 1997 collecting ecological information, heard myths relating to specific sites of spirits (*a tndol*, T.P.: *masalai*), suggesting that the Lihirians saw the myths as contextually significant and then recounted them (Foale, pers. comm.). The stories that I heard were about specific named ancestors such as Tgorous, who brought peace to Lihir,[10] or Tumngiet, who went to live in a stone cave on top of the plateau of Mahur. Unlike stories in the 'Culture Hero' mode of elsewhere in the New Guinea islands, these tend to relate to only one event or theme rather than a series of them, and Lihirians locate these in distant but real time (see the 'Culture Hero' genre of stories in Epstein 1969; Foster 1995; Neumann 1992).

Migration stories appear to be situated in the very distant past, and speak of flights to other islands to escape cannibalism, of groups at war, and of marriages and births of children. Often these flights to other areas are from the origin place of the lineage, portrayed as occurring in the very beginning (of time, perhaps? Lihirians do not clarify what they mean by this). The births in these stories represent the continuation of the lineage in a new place, and

[10] See references to Tgorous in Chapters 4 and 6.

the people are generally named. For the stories I checked, the people born in the tale had often only just died, placing such stories also in the recent past.

Some people on Mahur declared a particular lineage as not being Mahurian, because its origin was elsewhere (for example, Masahet island). Coming from Masahet, this lineage had little right to land on Mahur and had to negotiate to temporarily use or buy land from other, land-rich lineages. While they gained some land from transfers from father to son, there was crowding on their residential land in Kuelam. This example highlights the importance of the lineage to the practical usage of land as well as Lihirians' ideas of a person's rightful place being based on lineage. Through practical usage of hamlet and garden land, and ideas of origin, lineages are the primary link between groups of people and place.

## Kinship: terms and relationships

Yngvar Ramstad, an ethnographer who did fieldwork in Lihir in 1968/69,[11] wrote a paper dealing with the relationship between kinship and politics in Lihir in which he examined kinship structurally: in terms of the 'rules and ideals' rather than the nature of actual relationships (Ramstad n.d.a:6). He gave a list of various categories of kin and the behaviour appropriate to these relationships, before giving this summation:

> On Lihir the kinship terminology seems to be a categorization of one's immediate social universe in terms of how individuals actually perceive the quality of their relationship to others and also in terms of what is relevant for men trying to extend their sphere of influence … the quality of the interaction between different categories of kinsmen is caused by a special way of using one's closest kinsfolk in this particular form for political competition. The rules of avoidance and respect and the institutionalised joking has an adaptive value by ritualizing

[11] Yngvar Ramstad did fieldwork on Niolam for his doctoral thesis based at Australian National University. He never completed his thesis in English (though he may have done so in Norwegian) and never published any material about Lihir. He did write a number of unpublished papers about Lihir (Ramstad n.d.a, n.d.b., n.d.c).

> certain solutions to behavioural problems regularly created in these circumstances. (Ramstad n.d.a:25–6)

Ramstad, then, concentrated on the structural aspects of kinship in Lihir, on the rules of conduct and how these facilitated political competition.

In his paper Ramstad also commented on the ethnopsychology in Lihir associated with particular kinship relations, such as attributing 'violent jealousy' to relationships between siblings (ibid.:21). He also suggested that joking between cross-cousins masks 'the suppressed reality of envy and conflict of interests' (ibid.:23). Ramstad gives no evidence for these statements, and does not clarify whether these are his own observations or those of his informants. From his paper I am left with a view of Lihirian representations of kinship as being a political tool and a cover for passionate feelings.

Ramstad's approach gives little indication of the actual content of kinship relationships between particular people in Lihir and in this, I shall argue, suffers from a similar failing as does the literature on personhood. Studies of 'relational' personhood (or dividual, composite and so on) argue that the person in Melanesia is composed of relations, or is an objectification of relations (Battaglia 1990; Leenhardt 1971; Strathern 1988). Such relations must then exist prior to the person, who can only act passively in terms of them. Strathern states that relations can be affirmed or denied through action, but the form of them cannot be changed (1988:261–2). For Strathern, agency and cause are split, an 'other' being the cause of a person's actions (agency) (1988:272–4). Relations are *given* in this view of personhood.

This approach to personhood and relations constructs the person as passively acting in the context of relations whose form is taken for granted. This is simply not the case in Lihir. The kinship terminology a person uses for others in their social universe is somewhat determined by birth,[12] but rather than this being deterministic of relationships, terminology simply defines the

---

[12] Much kin terminology is set from birth as a function of a person's gender and generational level. A few terms change because of marriages that occur, such as when a *koko* (cross-sex cross-cousin) becomes a *tambu* (in-law) through marriage.

boundaries of these relationships which are then continually constructed and renegotiated by the people involved. Given that in Lihir a kin term could be applied to everyone, kinship categorisation explained little about the content of particular relationships. Kinship in Lihir functions somewhat like Bourdieu's *habitus*. It defines an arena of action or limits the amount of choices available to someone but does not determine these choices (Bourdieu 1990).

The kinship terminology I used followed from my position as Pulerau rather than my association with the Masnahuo lineage. In my experience in Lihir, a kinship term could be found for anyone I met. Considering there was a population of about 9000 on the island group as a whole in 1998, this was quite extraordinary. For people with whom I had everyday contact, appropriate kin terms were fairly obvious, being an exact replica of my 'sister' Weinrau's kinship (Pulerau's biological sister). For people who lived distantly from me, kinship terminology was determined by a discussion of clan and lineage, and my relationship to certain people. Once a generational level had been worked out, an appropriate kinship term was found.

Kinship terminology in Lihir shapes the outside boundaries of a relationship by explicitly specifying some rules of conduct. When asked, Lihirians could give a list of rules of conduct appropriate to each kin relationship. *Ksien* (same-sex female siblings) must have a relationship that is polite. *Kasien* (cross-sex siblings) must also be polite, never discuss sexual matters or affairs in one another's presence, and sisters cannot walk past the head of their sleeping brother. Both *puelkan* and *koko* (cross-cousins of same or cross-sex respectively) must have a joking relationship. As with many other ethnographies, I could conclude my discussion of kinship with such a list of appropriate behaviours. However, what interested me in Lihir was the actual content of relationships rather than the terminology and stated rules of conduct.

The relationship between *ksien* was one that captured my attention, and initially made me think about kinship terminology and categorisation as more like *habitus* than like rule. *Ksien* are same-sex female siblings or female parallel cousins, as well as females of the third generational level above or below a female ego. Females of the same clan and same generational level would also be referred to as *ksien* when no other relationship was traceable.[13]

Christina, the eldest female of the family with which I was resident on Mahur, had six sisters and three brothers. While the explicit rules of conduct for sisters in Lihir supposes politeness, Christina had a contentious relationship with most of her sisters. Many of them did not approve of her, as she had split from her abusive husband and was seeing other men, and at one stage some of her sisters beat her. However, in daily life the sisters were polite, sharing food and talking in the evenings. Christina said only one of her sisters had consistently been nice to her, and had never been violent with her. Perhaps because of the fact that most of her sisters disapproved of her conduct, two of them looked after Christina's six children between them. Christina portrayed this as her sisters helping her because she had paid employment, rather than them thinking she was incapable of caring for her children (on women in paid employment in Lihir, garden work and their relationships with family, see Macintyre 2003b; 2006). The relationships between Christina and her *ksien* were thus not determined by rules of kinship, which portray *ksien* as having polite and caring relationships, but were constructed by them according to the situation.

The nature of relationships between various categories of kin was dependent upon a number of things other than simply the terminology given at birth. Personality or character was one factor that influenced relations between kin.[14] In my own household there lived a woman and her *kasien* (MZS), who did not have a harmonious and caring relationship. She would complain about him—his laziness and the fact that he dressed to show off

[13] These last two examples do not really concern me here; Lihirians themselves viewed these types of sisters differently from 'true' *ksien* (i.e. sisters and female parallel cousins).

[14] See my discussion of the applicability of the term 'personality' to the Lihirian person in Chapter 4.

(*mdengniat*). Yet she rarely complained about his older brother, who was the area catechist for Mahur; a conscientious and quietly spoken man who did not shirk his obligations.

Having the right temperament was an important factor in whether a person in Lihir was taught any esoteric knowledge, generally by a grandparent. Anyone who is two generations above a person is called *pupu* (grandparent) and this means that people have many grandparents, and a great many grandchildren. Ngalparok was one of my main male informants, and was in the position of *pupu* to me, which made his teaching of me appropriate. He was also engaged in discovering whether his grandson Marwan had the aptitude to learn from him. Often people would say that knowledge was being lost because young people showed no interest in learning it. The special relationship developing between Ngalparok and Marwan is the ideal grandparent/child relationship, being one that depends not on the kinship categorisation but on the personality and relationship of those involved.

Age was a crucial factor in determining the nature of relationships in Lihir. Accounts of matrilineal societies in Papua New Guinea often state that the mother's brother is critical. It had not really occurred to me before I arrived on Mahur just how many mother's brothers a person may have, especially so given the number of classificatory mother's brothers. In Lihir, a child calls all the mother's sisters and female parallel cousins '*mama*'. All of their brothers and classificatory brothers are then 'mother's brothers' (*mduan*).[15] While it is true that a few of these are critical to a person's life, most are not. Due to the amount of children women sometimes have (up to eight is fairly common, and I know of a number of people with 10 surviving children), a person's *mduan* (MB) may be the same age as they are. This was the case with Kupulie's children, who were mother's brother to her sister's daughter's son. Kupulie's children were 12, six and four years old, and were *mduan* (MMZS) to children aged 13 and five. In this case they played together much like siblings, and

[15] '*Mdiong*' means 'my *mduan*' or 'my mother's brother'.

had none of the authority sometimes accorded *mduan* over their classificatory sister's sons. On the other hand, their *kesnalik* (MZS) had much authority over them, as he was aged in his early thirties.

A number of relationships in Lihir seemed to be more tightly determined by kinship terminology than those I have been discussing, such as the relationships between *tambu* (T.P. in-laws),[16] an avoidance relationship, and cross-cousins, a relationship based on institutionalised joking. *Tambu* relationships involved avoidance of joking and often of the use of names, and were generally said to be more constrained in the past, including not entering each other's houses and not walking passed their head if they were lying down. *Tambu* relationships in Lihir seem now to allow quite a freedom of choice about the nature of the relationship, more than is reported for other areas of New Ireland (Eves 1998; Foster 1995).

Cross-cousin kin categorisation, however, seems to have retained its determining role in relationships into the present. Both *puelkan* (same-sex cross-cousins) and *koko* (cross-sex cross-cousins) are expected to joke with one another. If a person leaves to go to another island for the first time (for example, to neighbouring Tabar, Tanga, mainland New Ireland or mainland Papua New Guinea) his/her cross-cousin is allowed to take his/her pigs and produce. Cross-cousins can also demand things from one another, and the other must comply with this request (this applies as much to large things, such as stereos, as it does to betelnut; see also Wagner 1986 for an account of cross-cousin behaviour). *Koko* (cross-sex cross-cousins) are also not allowed to use each other's names. These relationships are close and *puelkan* often help each other (for example, in clearing a garden or in feasting). So important were these explicit rules when determining conduct that I often would not go to the home of my *puelkan* at night if I was feeling tired and not like joking: Zilio (my *puelkan*) could not suspend the rules of conduct due to my tiredness.

---

16 Lihirians used the Tok Pisin term '*tambu*' to refer to all in-laws, and most had difficulty recalling the appropriate Lihirian term for specific classes of in-laws, such as a *pos* for wife's sister. Hence I use the Tok Pisin term here as it was in daily usage on Mahur.

While the relationship between cross-cousins seemed more determined by categorisation given at birth, this still applied more to some cross-cousins than to others. While the name prohibition for *koko* would often extend as far as people knew the relationships, and joking was somewhat expected even between very distantly related cross-cousins, the situation did become less determined by the categorisation, and more became the choice of the persons involved to sustain such a relationship.

Relationships on Mahur are far more dynamic than dry discussions of kinship and kin terms allow. Mahurians may refer to a kin term to explain a relationship, but this in itself does not determine the relationship. I had to learn to look beyond these statements in understanding the relationships around me. Lihirians were active agents in constructing and renegotiating the relationships to which these kinship terms refer. Christina, Kupulie and their kin developed relationships that suited their situations. Rather than persons being the passive objectification of relations, Lihirians actively create and renew their webs of kin relationship.

## Names and namesakes

One relationship linking persons in Lihir was that of *trongbar*, meaning someone who gives a name. People chose to create and maintain this relationship to another by first giving a name and later 'strengthening the name' through the giving of gifts of food, a baby pig or money. Not only those people who either give a child a name, but also those who have the same local name are *trongbar*, '*trong*' meaning 'my friend' but *trongbar* perhaps best translated as namesake. *Trongbar* who simply have the same name do not exchange gifts, but instead are seen to be identified with each other, and call each other '*trongbar*' to highlight this identification, rather than use the particular name in question.

People in Lihir generally have quite a number of names, including their 'Christian' name (for example, Thomas, Maria, Philomena) as well as at least one local name. At least two names are given soon after birth, the Christian name, a recent invention and often given by the sisters at the mission hospital or by catechists, and one or more local names. The close relatives of the child choose the local names, which are sometimes created to reflect a particular incident at the time of the child's birth. For example, one child was called Potkrim ('Indian giving,' giving and then taking back) because the pig given as part of the bride price payment for the child's *mama* (MZ) was taken back by the donor. Other local names are chosen from a stock of already used names, sometimes after a particular person, such as one child named Ambrose Kiapseni after the Lihirian Bishop of that name.[17] This practice of reusing names means that there are often people on Mahur with the same local name.

While names in Lihir are not unique to each person, they do carry a connection with the person, such that when it came to choosing pseudonyms for my doctoral thesis due to ethical requirements, people could not simply pick a name at random. Instead, most names used here are alternative names held by the people, which are almost unknown to other Lihirians. In some cases these were names given at birth but never used, or are a name the person was only called by someone who has since died. Lihirians found it impossible to suggest a name for me to use in this book that had no tie or identification with themselves.

Despite the fact that Lihirians have many names, they are generally known by only one of these, which may be either their local or their Christian name. For some families, most are known by Christian names, while other families use all local names or a mixture of local and Christian names. Often the Christian name is used where the local name is long, such as a woman called Bertha, whose local name was Bosimsenie.[18]

The relationship between persons and names cannot be characterised in the way that Iteanu describes for the Orokaiva:

[17] Occasionally this includes the Christian name as well, as occurred in this case.

[18] Most local names that are commonly used are one to three syllables in length. Christian names or occasionally diminutives of local names are used in preference for names that are four or more syllables long.

> a person's most individualised name is never simply his own, since it has been passed on to him through a chain of namesakes (*saso*). 'Personal' names like kinship terms thus form a system of relations and the persons who momentarily bear them are simply caught up in it. (Iteanu 1990:38)

Despite similarities in naming practices, people in Lihir are never just caught up in any 'system'. Lihirians make names their own, and it is up to them, and their *trongbar*, to make something of a name, to 'strengthen it'. As will be seen in later chapters, people are remembered through their names, and part of the process of 'forgetting' a person (finishing grieving) is to detach a particular person's identity from the name they carried.

## Friendship

One day I questioned my close friend and informant Kupulie about grief, particularly severe long-term grief, and she offered the following story that highlights the nature and importance of friendship in Lihir:

> Tienmua [Kupulie's brother] was really good friends with a man who worked for the gold mine. Tongop was his name, and he came from Masahet Island. They were good friends and shared their food. On the afternoon before the death, Tienmua had a pineapple and shared it out. He left a piece aside, and when his friend Tongop came, he halved this piece for him and his friend. Another man in the group said this wasn't good behaviour. However, Tienmua said it was a good behaviour because you never know the hour or day of a person's death.
>
> After this Tongop got in the car. Tienmua got in too, but another man called him back. So then Tongop went by himself. He crashed the car at Londolovit beach [on the main island], and it rolled on top of him. Word came to Tienmua and the other men, and they rushed down to the beach. Tienmua ran all the way down the hill. They got there and they were all lost for what to do. They just held him and cried. He was under the car—it was on his head. So they just held the back of him.

> Eventually they got organised and went to the hospital at Palie [on the other side of the main island]. As they arrived there he stopped breathing.
>
> They were to bury him at Masahet. Four helicopters were used to fly him from Niolam to Masahet. A red one held the body, with a blue one beside it. Then there was one at the front and one behind. Tienmua stopped the helicopters from leaving: he just stayed and cried. They knew he was really upset and they just let him be. They eventually took off, leaving Tienmua behind.
>
> A contract boat brought Tienmua to Masahet, but by this time Tongop was already buried and they were eating. Tienmua 'cried like a woman' and went into the men's house. He did not eat on that day.
>
> The mining company gave Tienmua three years off work to recover. However, he has never gone back to work. It is only now that he has recovered [about five to six years after the death], and his family can joke about him going back to work.

I was somewhat surprised at this story at first. Given the emphasis on kin relationships in most work on Melanesia, here was Kupulie telling me that the most severe grief she remembered was of her brother at the death of his friend. Tienmua and this man lived on different islands, and had formed a friendship in the course of working together at the gold mine. While the story seems a little far-fetched in places (the four helicopters, and being granted three years off work), these elements in the story serve to portray the severity of her brother's grief at the death of his friend.

There is no abstract noun for 'friendship' in the Lihirian language. Terms are applied to people rather than the relationship between them: a friend *a truan*, my friend *a trong*, your friend *a tro*, two friends *lo truan*, a group of friends *bertruan*. Discussions about the topic, then, centred less on abstract understandings of a relationship and more on characteristics of persons.

Friends generally appear to be of the same age, and often are parallel cousins of the same sex (i.e. *ksien* or *kesnalik*, classificatory sisters or brothers respectively). In addition, other types of kin, if of the same sex and age, could be friends. For example, two girls were friends even though one was classificatory mother to the other. While same sex friends seemed to be most common, one man explained to me that people of the opposite sex could be friends. These were people who would eventually be married, or people who were already married. However, mostly I observed that friends were of the same sex.

Friends walk around together and go to the gardens together. In the case of Zilio and her classificatory sister Bertha, they would fish on the reef at night using coconut frond torches. They often went to the gardens together as their gardens were in the same area (they gardened on their fathers' land which was contiguous as their fathers were brothers). Sharing food was also critical to friendship; it was something that was always mentioned when I asked people about what friends do or about what makes a good friend.

On a number of occasions people referred to older, important men having friends. On all occasions these were mentioned, it was observed that these men were of different clans. One time I was in Li village and there was a hamlet with two men's houses. I was told that this was so because two 'big men' were very good friends and chose to jointly own the hamlet area. This meant that there were two men's houses (one for each clan).

Children are considered to be capable of having friends. An example is that of Zkol and Holol, who were girls both about six years old. Zkol was temporarily staying on Mahur with her mother, and she and Holol lived next to one another and spent each day playing together. When it came time for Zkol to go back to her home on Niolam, people did not tell Holol—they said she had already been crying to go with her friend Zkol. Hence, while friends were often described in terms of practical aspects of sharing time, food and activities, there was also an assumed emotional dimension to being friends.

Joe told me that the relationship between friends must be based on trust. This is termed *nornor* in Mahur, best translated as 'to believe in (someone)'. For friends who are married, this means belief that the other person will be faithful. In addition to *nornor* is respect (*sio*), which means that friends respect each other and treat each other accordingly (see discussion in Chapter 5).

The concept of a group of friends is expressed in the term *bertruan*, and such groups often comprised boys or young men. Boys would walk around together after school, attempting to shoot birds in the trees or collecting shellfish on the reef. Young men would gather to learn new tunes on their guitars. For women, occasions for such larger gatherings were rare, given their heavy workload, and even young schoolgirls are busy looking after siblings and sweeping the household area. Women on Mahur tend to be friends with those people who are in the immediate areas doing the same tasks. Larger gatherings of women were often restricted to the hours after dark, and on the pretext of other activities such as attending church services.

In the context of the development of the goldmine, new contexts for friendship are emerging, particularly for women. The existence of workplaces such as the various departments of the mining company, the hospital, contractor companies and the Tutorme Sewing Centre when it was open during the early 2000s have provided new opportunities for men and women to gather as workmates. People from different areas of Lihir, Papua New Guinea or even from elsewhere on the globe are able to meet, get to know one another and spend large amounts of time together. Generally these friendships still remain gender specific, and retain the features of spending time together, talking, joking and sharing food.

It was in the context of friendships that I saw the only public physical displays of affection while I was in the field. Friends would often walk with a finger or two entwined; either two male or two female friends would do this. Friends could also scratch each other's palms in the course of shaking hands, this being a sign of '*laikim*' (T.P. like or love). Occasionally people other than friends could make this very intimate gesture—as my *papa wein* ('FZ') Pule did to me a number of times during church services.

I made a number of friends in the field, the most important being Kupulie, my classificatory sister. She was about ten years older than me, unmarried, with four children. I spent a little time with her early in my fieldwork, but then she became very ill for about two months. During this time I developed my relationships with other people, especially my *puelkan* (cross-cousin) Zilio, with whom I had a joking relationship. We would go to the gardens together, and chat before and after church services. She would come to my house and talk, and collect me to go and eat with her household. Occasionally she would link fingers with me as we were walking.

When Kupulie recovered from her illness I had to carefully balance my time and relationship with her and Zilio. Kupulie was older than Zilio and more knowledgeable, and thus a better informant, yet with Zilio I had a good time and through her I met Thomas (my *yamung* or classificatory nephew, yet about my age). He was from Malie Island and was knowledgeable about events happening there (such as a mortuary ritual that occurred late in the year), as well as being a very obliging boat captain. It was not appropriate for me to simply be friends with Thomas, and besides that, I enjoyed my time with Zilio. She was someone with whom I could have fun and very occasionally try to forget I was doing fieldwork.

In the last five months of my fieldwork I spent much of my time with Kupulie, who was identified as my *truan* by other people in the village. When I was walking alone through the village, people would ask where she was. For females it was rarely appropriate to walk through the village alone, especially at night as it suggested to others that the person was on her way to meet a lover (something very frowned upon). When we were together, people would greet us '*a uwa lo truan*' ('good morning two friends'). Kupulie and I often ate together and she became my translator of everyday conversations. Kupulie came to know my project, and said she knew I was not Pulerau. With Kupulie I was 'Susan' and friend, rather than Pulerau or Butbut.

Unlike Hendry (1992:172), I did not feel that 'one can only pretend to be a friend' while in the field. Hendry states that 'during fieldwork, it might be thought better to avoid expressing negative matters close to the hearts of informants' (ibid.). I would agree with this, but argue that this does not simply apply to relationships in the field: in Australia I do not insult my friends by criticising what they value dearly. My relationship with Kupulie was complex, but I was not pretending to be a friend.

Friendship in Lihir entailed trust (*nornor*), respect (*sio*), sharing food and sharing time together. Kupulie and I were friends in Lihirian terms. She stayed on Mahur longer than she intended so as to be with me (before moving to mainland Lihir). She farewelled me at the airport, rising at 4 a.m. to walk up a steep hill with her youngest child to do so. I shared my food and gave her sons clothes, and she reciprocated.

The topic of my fieldwork was dependent upon such close trusting relationships as the ones I had with Kupulie and Zilio. This did not mean I shared all my thoughts, emotions and dreams with them, but to do so would not have been appropriate in the context. Lihirians are not 'open' with each other in the way that is idealised in Western notions of friendship. In Lihirian terms, being a friend does not imply sharing all one's thoughts and dreams: they do not place importance on communicating introspection to others. Those Lihirians that have been exposed to Western influences through schooling and work appear to increasingly share their contemplations with others. Christina was one of these people, having worked with expatriates (Australians, New Zealanders, etc.) over a number of years. She took the opportunity of her friendship with me to discuss her problems and worries, explicitly stating that Lihirians do not talk about such things.

While most of my relationships were shaped by the expectations of Lihirians about friendship, a few of my relationships were somewhat out of character with Mahurian standards. My language teacher, Isidore, and I were friends—in my sense of the term rather than the Lihirian sense. Isidore was the teacher of the Elementary School at Kuelam. He conducted classes in the local dialect and was one of the few people on Mahur who knew how to write the local language. I would see him for lessons in the classroom when he finished teaching the preschool children at noon on weekdays. It was these factors that made our relationship acceptable to others in Kuelam: that we met for a defined purpose in a public place. Isidore and I never identified a kin relationship between us, and nor were we ever identified as *lo truan* (two friends) by others in the village. We did not walk around together, and I did not go and see him at his men's house, although he would occasionally visit me at my house. However, Isidore did share some food with me, giving me bananas from the school's palms. At my farewell day, Isidore said that I had given him and his school children a lot of help (*erim*: an ABC poster I had made in the local language). I considered him a friend. However, we were not friends in terms of Mahurian conceptions.

My other relationships with males were characterised in terms of kinship rather than friendship. My good informant Joe was my classificatory nephew (*yamung*), as was Thomas. I learned a lot about esoteric matters from my grandfather Ngalparok (*pupu*). Three other male informants were in the position of father (*papa*).

In addition, then, to navigating *within* Lihirian ideas of relationship in terms of clans, kinship and friends I was also negotiating between my assumptions and theirs about the nature of relationships. Sometimes, as in the case of Kupulie, our ideas corresponded—both I and they thought us to be friends. On other occasions I had to couch my ideas of friendship in terms of kin terminology.

## Marriage in Lihir

On my return to Lihir in December 1999, people on Mahur became aware that I had found a partner who worked for one of the companies contracted by the gold mine on Niolam. At the time I was spending a much greater proportion of my time on Niolam doing research on issues surrounding the gold mine, yet Mahurians were not satisfied with this explanation of my absence from

Mahur. Instead, they suggested this was due to my relationship: not because I couldn't bear to be away from my partner but because they assumed my choices were much more limited now that I was paired with someone. When one person heard that I was in a relationship, she exclaimed 'Ah, that explains why you haven't been over to Mahur. You'd better not come around too much to see us or he will beat you.' When I tried to clarify that my partner was not restraining my movements, and that he would never beat me, this woman responded with the disbelieving comment: 'Oh sure, he hasn't beaten you yet.'

Mahurians hearing of my partnership assumed that my choices would now be limited by my partner's desires. They also expected that I would soon become pregnant, which would further restrict my autonomy, and possibly mean I would be unable to finish my doctorate. In this way, the time before marriage or partnership is portrayed as one of relative freedom in Lihir, particularly in my case where Lihirians came to know me as a person separated from my kin and friends. It was apparent that I had a great deal of freedom of movement and choice, and the addition of an important relationship was seen only as restricting my choices.

Most of the navigations concerning marriage in Lihir are spoken about by Lihirians themselves in terms of choices. Marriage in Lihir is intimately bound with issues of choice and autonomy, for both men and women. Exactly who has the ability to choose, what choices are available to them in terms of marriage partners, and choices about whether to partner at all were the topic of many conversations, the most scandalous of which were about people who had tried and sometimes succeeded to force the hand of others. Being a locus for issues of autonomy, choices related to marriage can often be sites of conflict.

## *Making choices*

Marriage in Lihir typically occurs when people are between the ages of 20 and 30. Since men are quite often five or even 10 years older than their wives, women tend to marry while in their early twenties, while men are in their late twenties or early thirties before they are paired. While marriage must occur outside of the clan, there is no rule or practice of moiety exogamy on Mahur—unlike some areas in New Ireland. Marriage is generally no longer arranged, but parents of prospective spouses always have some say in whether a couple will be married. Marriage is explicitly expected to be lifelong in Catholic areas of Lihir: there is no divorce allowed.

The issue of choice of partner was one that was constantly raised in my presence, and mature and elderly people raised this as their major area of concern. All said to me that in the past they had married their spouses on the basis of the spouse's behaviour, whereas in the present people got married based on physical desire of another person's body. In the past, a number of people said, they made careful examination of whether the person was a hard worker: whether a woman knew how to look after pigs and grow gardens well. One man remarked '*sapos man i maritim meri i no save gut long lukautim pik, em bai dispela man i wari bihain*' (T.P. 'If a man marries a woman who doesn't know how to raise pigs, then he will be worried later'). This man, a retired catechist, explained that nowadays people did not make choices based on knowledge (*nanse*) but simply on their desires (*leimulien*), and that this was the source of broken marriages and spousal abuse.

Younger people with whom I talked expressed that they felt that being able to make their own choices was a positive thing, and didn't seem to think that they made poor choices in finding a spouse. For them, they made choices based on love and desire (*leimulien*). This emotional basis for decision-making seemed far more important to young people than a systematic examination of another's behaviour, or the wishes of their elders. Mostly, however, young people talked little about differences in the choices they made in comparison with those of their forebears. Instead, their concern was more about what they saw as the undue influence that their parents and older relations had upon their choices, as well as on specific examples of choices that their contemporaries were making.

It was never apparent to me how relationships started on Mahur. Relationships between young men and women were heavily proscribed, and quite often the first sign to me of the existence of a relationship was a young woman's pregnancy. Relationships before marriage certainly were not encouraged, and were never particularly obvious, unlike the case of the Vanatinai in Milne Bay, for example, where relationships between young people are expected and even encouraged (Lepowsky 1993:102–5).

It is expected on Mahur that once a relationship is known about through gossip and speculation (and perhaps pregnancy) that the couple will get married, assuming their parents are willing. This is not always the case, and in the next section I discuss situations where either parents or children aim to force the decisions of others not satisfied with a particular marriage choice.

Marriage in Lihir occurs both in church and through the payment of bride price by a man and his family. Both the woman and man donate a pig towards the feast accompanying the bride price payment or church ceremony. Payment of bride price is made in *le* (shell money; T.P. *mis*) and Kina just before the feast, and this is followed by payments to particular in-laws by both the man and woman called '*baim sem*' (T.P. to buy the shame). People I talked to on Mahur were in dispute about whether this payment was 'Lihir *kastam*', some saying it was the *kastam* of New Ireland and Tabar but not Lihir, while a few men said this was called *arapar*. The actual bride payment was called *arapar* by some (those who said *baim sem* was not Lihir *kastam*) and *puolpuol* by others. The one thing that people consistently commented on was the practice of payment of *ipiz*, a promissory payment of one *le* (*mis*) by a man and his family for a young woman. Following the payment (which rarely occurs now), the woman would then spend time with the man and his family in the gardens and they would look after her, but the couple would not live together until later.

A number of women on Mahur chose not to marry at all. While a few of these women dedicated themselves to the service of God by becoming lay nuns, others simply never found a man that they wanted as a life partner. All of these women on Mahur, like my good informant Kupulie, were actually single mothers, despite the disapproval of the community about such choices. Women who became pregnant while unmarried were not allowed by the priest to take communion when the priest came to the island, and it was sometimes said that the children should not be baptised or even given a Christian name.[19] Despite these sanctions, quite a number of women were single mothers, and remained that way throughout their life. Some women had one or more children before being married, and in these cases the stigma of being a single mother gradually faded, especially if the woman was able to marry the father of the child or children. Other women, like Kupulie, decide never to marry, and often have a number of children by different fathers.

In the pre-colonial past, divorce was permitted and the casting off of a wife or husband who was adulterous was accepted, as was the return of an infertile wife to her natal family. Such flexible rules relating to divorce still prevail somewhat, despite the fact that the Catholic Church disallows divorce. For those people that do decide to marry, there are choices available to them if the marriage does not appear to prosper. A number of couples were formally divorced or separated, and had found new partners. This sometimes occurred in cases of severe abuse. Other couples appeared to me to be informally separated—they were said to be married, but each had their own house and they lived discrete lives. These arrangements occur with a frequency above what is acceptable to the Church.

### *Forcing choices*

Quite often in navigations about marriage relationships, Mahurians employ methods to force the choice of reluctant others. Either a potential spouse or a relative is opposed to the union, and others aim to reverse this by influence of some sort. Both sexes are able to employ love magic (*pupulu*) to induce another's desires. This leads to a state called *sa ba*, which corresponds to

[19] This is in addition to their local name.

Western notions of being in love. The person thinks of the one who performed the magic all the time, follows the person around, and cannot resist sleeping with them. Kupulie told me that the person affected appears to be slightly mad to others.

Very occasionally a person threatens suicide to convince either the potential spouse or a parent of themselves or the spouse to agree to the union. This was the case with a couple who had two children by the time I arrived on Mahur: the wife had threatened suicide in a successful attempt to convince her husband's mother to allow the marriage to take place.

Perhaps the most common method used to force other's choices about marriage is for a woman to get pregnant. This was generally not to trap the man into marriage but to obtain his or her parents' agreement to the marriage. Most of the marriages that occurred on Mahur during 1998 involved couples that already had a child together, and a number of these were conceived in an attempt to secure the blessing of the parents. In one extreme case (described above in the section on clan) this strategy failed. A couple that had had three children together (one a still-birth) had been prevented (as of 2002) from marrying by the community as they were of the same clan and subclan. While most Lihirians would see this relationship as incestuous, there are several cases in other villages where similar marriages have occurred. Some of these marriages are still viewed as incestuous, but I was told they were allowed because the two parties were fixated upon each other and they had a number of children.

Certainly, marriage choices on Mahur could not be adequately described through concepts of prescribed or proscribed marriage, preferential clan marriage, marriage alliances or some other system that is seen as determinative of marriage partners. As discussed in references to kinship, the rules that exist simply delimit the choices available. Mahurians then make their choices, which often involve contestation and attempts to force other's decisions. Lihirians are not just passively 'caught up' in a system that exists prior to themselves, but actively negotiate their relationships.

## Navigations

Marriage is one realm where choices and navigations are expected and fairly obvious: young people negotiate to make or force their choices while parents attempt to make the best marriage possible for their children. However, other types of relationships often seem more fixed, particularly those of clan and kinship, where individuals are born into already existing systems that appear to lock them into place.

Do Lihirians really navigate through their relationships in day-to-day life? It was a question that perplexed me somewhat. I certainly spent much time navigating between my work, being a good friend the Lihirian way, and my various ties to a number of lineages. When was I a guest and when was I a member of the community? At times I was treated like a visitor, and at other times I felt bound by duty to sweep around my house and collect dry coconuts for the evening meal. I suppose that, in part, is the meaning of 'participant observation'.

In comparison to my navigations, it sometimes appeared to me that Lihirians were doing nothing of the sort. With clan, lineage and much kin terminology set at birth, it appeared that there was little flexibility for renegotiation. There was also little need for it on first sight: Lihirians do not need to gather information for research and balance this with daily chores and socialising. Nor do they have to navigate between two very different sets of cultural assumptions about personal relationships.

However, as argued above, Lihirians too spent time negotiating and navigating their relationships with one another. The kinship categorisations that are given at birth do not determine the relationships that arise from them, but rather delimit possible choices of action. Relationships instead are formed from daily interactions, of food exchanges, time spent together and help given to another. Relationships are not given at birth and either affirmed or denied. This will become quite apparent in the next two chapters, which deal with the household and the Lihirian concept of the person and '*piot*'. In relation to the household, Lihirians make demands on one another in terms of duty; they affirm connections to places and to each other. They migrate between places to renew ties, protest against poor treatment or move away from strained relationships. In terms of *piot*, people complain and comment on other people's migrations.

Clan, lineage and kin terms shape the social universe. It is in terms of these that Lihirians navigate. As I have shown, even within the range of a particular kin term there is a great deal of variation in actual relationships. Having someone as a 'sister' does not mean that no negotiation or creation of the relationship is needed. Relationships in Lihir cannot be viewed as given or taken for granted.

Friends are extraordinary instances of particular kin relationships. They are a renegotiation of what may be a sister relationship, or a cross-cousin, or even a mother-daughter relationship (where ages are similar). Friends are one particular form of navigation of interpersonal relationships in Lihir.

'Navigating the seas of relationship' seems to be an appropriate metaphor for Lihirians' renegotiations of their ties to others, especially given the sometimes-treacherous waters that divided people from one another. While, as I discuss below, they are gardeners at heart, and are bound to place through lineages, relationships with others in the Lihir group and on other islands in the region compelled Mahurians to navigate those seas.

# 2

# NURTURING CHILDREN, VISITORS, PIGS AND YAMS: HOUSEHOLD RELATIONSHIPS

Located toward the back of Lalakam hamlet was Zilio's household. Headed by her father Rau and mother Aniodun, Zilio lived there with her sister Elizabeth and classificatory daughter Darmas. During most of 1998, Zilio's brother Peter and her sister Mangris, Darmas's mother, were living elsewhere in Lihir. For much of that year Zilio's *yamung*, Thomas, came and went from the household to his home on Malie island. He and Zilio married some years later, but in 1998 a relationship between the two was not apparent.

Of the two houses belonging to this household, one was located at ground level with split bamboo walls and sago leaf roofing, understood to be traditional in design, and was the sleeping quarters for Aniodun and Rau. The other was more haphazard in construction, with a corrugated iron roof, and was the sleeping quarters for the young people of the household. Located outside the second house was a bamboo sitting bench, often piled high with newly washed saucepans, and the site of many late night conversations, laughter and the consumption of food by household members and visitors (*wasir*), including myself.

Rau was a senior member of Nawus clan, while Aniodun and her children were Njol. Their household was located on Nawus land of the Masnahuo lineage, and their carefully tended gardens were located atop the plateau mostly on Nawus land, neighbouring those of Rau's brother Taruh and of the children of his deceased sister Lomuet. All members of the household nurtured these gardens, using them for family consumption as well as for contributions to feasts. They allowed the adult members of the household to provide nurturance for Darmas (*ertnin*) and for visitors (termed *pniari wasir*). On the way to the gardens young members of the household such as Zilio and Elizabeth would stop on the lower levels of the plateau on Mahur to call their household pigs in to feed them (*tnanie bol*), the pigs recognising the particular voices of their carers. It was these forms of nurturance—of children, visitors, pigs and gardens—that stood out as core practices of the household, and that are the subject of this chapter.

## Households in New Ireland

In his ethnography of Tanga, the island group neighbouring Lihir, Foster employs an explicit conjunction of household and *bisnis* (T.P. capitalist ventures; cash cropping) in everyday life to contrast with the association of lineage and *kastam* (T.P. customary practice, in this case mostly mortuary ritual). In doing so, he argues that the household and the lineage are diametrically opposed, this separation having developed because of the growing importance of cash cropping to the Tangans:

> circumstances ... precipitated a local copra economy in which individual households replaced cooperative societies as the significant units of production. This development signalled the retreat of big men from the copra industry and the establishment in practice of the discrete domains of *kastam* and *bisnis*. (Foster 1995:57)

Foster states that the household on Tanga, and not the lineage, was the unit responsible for producing and marketing copra and then using the profits, and, further, that the lineage had no role in the redistribution of cash income.

He argues that *kastam* opposes *bisnis* as non-consumption to consumption. Moreover, Foster contends that *bisnis* produces inequalities between households, while ritual produces the lineages as an 'enduring, self-replacing solidary group of enates' (ibid.:67).

Foster provides little analysis of the meaning of household in Tanga; instead, he appears to conflate it with 'family'. There are a number of instances where the two are confused: 'the household or "family" (*fumbarat*) is potentially …' (ibid.:88), 'the household or family becomes …' (ibid.:91), 'The household or family is …' (ibid.:92). The form of 'family' that Foster discusses as constituting a household appears based on a married couple, and is possibly nuclear:

> The household and not the lineage is the unit responsible for marketing copra. Usually a man, his wife, and their children collect the nuts... (ibid.:88)

> Because *bisnis* is a household or family concern, both *bisnis* and family become conceptually assimilated to patrilineality and opposed to the matrilineage (ibid.:91).

This assumption, of the household as a family and also as a stable unit, allows Foster's analysis that '[c]onsumption through feasting sustains or extends relations; household consumption contracts or involutes relations' (ibid.:91).

In his ethnography of Sursurunga on the New Ireland mainland directly south of Lihir, Bolyanatz explicitly questions the composition of households (2000). Like Lihir and much of New Ireland, Sursurunga has hamlet areas (*kuranu*) that are constituted, in general, by a men's house (*bang*) and one or more women's houses (*rum*). He states that the *rum* is 'the symbolic representation of each household', and normally houses a marriage (2000:52). He goes on to state that by 'household',

> I mean an English gloss of the Neo-Melanesian term *wanpela sospan*, literally 'one saucepan,' or 'one kettle.' In other words, these are units that provide, prepare, and consume food together. (2000:53)

He also notes that this sometimes equates to a nuclear family, and sometimes with more than one nuclear family unit. Hence, a household can be defined in terms of residence (the *rum*), shared food production and consumption, and often marriage or a nuclear family.

For much of the rest of ethnography in New Ireland, households are not seen as particularly relevant. Instead, the central concepts are those of lineage, clan and moiety, and how these are organising principles for relations of nurturance (cf. Clay 1977; Wagner 1986).

Despite the New Ireland location of Lihir, the household in Lihir appears more fluid than the way it is characterised by Foster for Tanga, or Bolyanatz for Sursurunga. In Lihir the household is not aligned with *bisnis* and opposed to *kastam* and the lineage. Rather it is a pivotal unit in the organisation of gardening, consumption, and socialisation of children, in short, for the practice of nurturance. The household on Mahur is the site for the extension of relations rather than their involution, and only occasionally corresponds to a nuclear family. As a pivotal unit, the household in Lihir is worthy of critical appraisal.

## The organisation of social space on Mahur

The population of Mahur is divided into three villages: Kuelam on the west coast, Lakamelen on the south coast, and Li atop the plateau on the eastern side. Kuelam and Lakamelen both have populations of over 300, while Li is a smaller village of less than 200. Land on Mahur is roughly divided into three portions corresponding to the three villages, the division taken from the centre of the plateau almost like a pie diagram. This is then further divided between clans and lineages, as discussed in Chapter 2.

Each village is divided into a number of hamlets (*a den anio*), these being contiguous in Kuelam and most of Lakamelen village. A number of hamlets in Lakamelen village, and all those in Li, are atop the plateau, scattered through the forest and gardens. Each hamlet comprises at least one men's house enclosure (*a rih*) where men and older boys most often sleep, and a number of houses (*liom*) that are the abode primarily of women and young children. Houses often surround and face an open central area used for feasting and children's games. Within a hamlet may be cooking houses (*polpol*) or at least a number of areas dedicated to fires and cooking, one for each household.

Hamlets in Kuelam village comprised between one and about 10 households. Each household had at least one house, but more than one was common. Households within a hamlet often were related by close kinship ties, such as households of siblings, of parents and children, or of cousins. Where a household had a number of houses, these were often angled at about 90 degrees so as to face each other. Houses were bush material (bamboo with sago palm or pandanus thatching) or permanent (wood planks and a corrugated iron roof), or a mixture of both. Some were on the ground while others were on pillars, the mixture of house types giving the village a heterogenous look. All houses inside men's house enclosures were on the ground on Mahur. The building of a two-storey men's house on Malie Island in 2000 sparked criticism and debate, which indicates both some innovation and considerable conservatism in this domain.

*A rih* (men's house) refers to both the men's house enclosure as well as the buildings it contains, and together these constitute one aspect of the somewhat dual nature of hamlets in Lihir. Unlike other places in New Ireland, I would not declare that the men's house is the locus of social activity (for example, Wagner 1986; 1987), for this would ignore the contribution of women and everyday activities to sociality in Lihir. The men's house by itself rarely encompasses the sociality of the hamlet, even in the context of fairly rare 'men-only' feasts, as outside of its boundaries the women of the hamlet cook and eat their own meal.

There were two types of men's house enclosures on Mahur, the 'clan men's house' and the 'family men's house', both known as *a rih* in the local language. Men's houses belonging to the clan had a low stone wall and a 'Y'-shaped stile (*mdelaklak*). It was in these men's houses that major feasts were conducted, and there were eight such houses in Kuelam village. Family men's houses, on the other hand, were enclosed either by a stone wall or a fence of picket stakes, with a flat-topped stile or none at all. These type of men's houses were quite common in Kuelam village, which had seven of them (of 15 hamlets with *a rih*), in comparison with many other villages that had only a few. In Kuelam these men's houses were in the southern half of the village, in hamlets that have been cleared and occupied well after World War II, Lalakam hamlet having been cleared most recently in about 1990 (see Figure 4). These family men's houses can evolve into clan men's houses over time through many small feasts, including those for the building of the low stone wall and the crafting and placing of the 'Y'-shaped stile.

Men's houses in Lihir are seen as male space, yet this does not mean that women are not allowed to enter. Women who are of the clan of the men's house can enter to clean the area, pick fruit from trees or talk with men who are in the enclosure, and it is these women who do most of the cooking and cleaning in the enclosure during major feasts. Women of other clans can enter the men's house enclosure if they are not married to a man who is of the clan of the men's house. These last women are effectively 'in-laws' (T.P. *tambu*) to the men's house, and cannot enter it even for their husband's funeral.[1]

The rest of the hamlet space is devoted to households, and are not simply a female domain. It is unrestricted space, with the main path through Kuelam going through the middle of many hamlets. Each household has a loosely defined area of space, and boundaries in space between households

[1] Rules relating to this last point are relaxing somewhat, and at some funerals a small part of the wall of the enclosure was removed to allow these women to enter, as they are not allowed to climb over the 'Y'-shaped stile. However, in most cases these women still stayed outside the enclosure, watching the funeral over the stone wall.

could often be seen when people swept around their houses: they would sweep to the edge of their household area. In this household area the tasks of daily life were carried out: cooking and eating, laundry, visiting and talking, basket-making, child rearing, and sleeping.[2]

Lalakam was a somewhat unusual hamlet in that it was fenced into two separate areas, one at the front where I had my 'permanent house' occupied by the Sion lineage, and one at the back with Tandum lineage. Zilio's household occupied this space at the back. This division meant that the front part of the hamlet, with its men's house enclosure was occupied by only one household as well as myself, and yet appeared as a discrete hamlet in itself. The area was clean white sand, with a number of coconut and smaller shade trees, as well as a few fruiting trees around the border. It was fenced on the front and one side with a stone wall, while the sides of the men's house and the fence along the back (really the middle of the hamlet) were of *bumbrier* picket stakes. Only a few metres from the reef and water, the breezes in the afternoon cooled the hamlet. The sun rose late in the day at about 8.30 a.m. over the cliff at the back of the hamlet, and then set at about 6 p.m. over the Tabar Islands on the horizon directly in front of Lalakam.

## Defining household relationships

What exactly constituted a household in Lihir? The household was a somewhat elusive entity and, in many respects, drawing boundaries around them on the basis of some sort of objective criteria was problematic. Other researchers have spent time trying to define household in such a way that the concept will be universally applicable in social analysis (for example, Hammel 1984). Much of the theoretical work in anthropology on the household was inspired by Bender (1967), when he argued for a clear separation between concepts of family and household, the latter being based on co-residence and domestic functions

[2] By this I do not mean to imply that these activities are restricted to this household area of the hamlet, but these are the activities that happen in this area. Naturally, these activities occur in other areas as well, including the beach, church and school and their grounds, in gardens and in the coconut plantation areas.

rather than kin relations. Co-residence by itself has been seen as insufficient criteria for definition:

> In a great many ethnographic settings it cannot be assumed ... that each residential unit corresponds to an independent household or that a household contains only those persons resident in its principle domicile at any particular moment. (Carter 1984:53–4)

Many anthropologists thus take into account other factors when defining the boundaries of a household, such as food sharing and common cooking, the degree of cooperation in production, and sharing of the tasks of child rearing (for example, Wilk and Netting 1984; Yanagisako 1979).

I could define the boundaries of households in Lihir on this basis: shared location, tasks and consumption. However, to draw rigid boundaries around households would misrepresent their nature in Lihir. Rather than being entities, households in Lihir are constellations of relationships between particular persons. I came to know households as identities: they were definite groups of people who often did reside in a location, who shared many tasks, and ate together, yet who did so in a way that implies neither rigidity (that the household was always to be that way) nor chaos or complete fluidity (that households have no stability or permanence).

While it is possible to refer to a household as a nuclear family with either a male (*bertman*) or female (*bertnian*) head, most often the group was not referred to by any term at all, this implying that Lihirians too saw households not as entities but as constellations of relationships. Given this fluidity it becomes impossible to classify an individual's relationship to particular households on a simple membership/non-membership basis. Instead I argue that households were constituted by three types of relationship: kinship and marriage relationships, relationships to place, and relationships of nurturance.

On their own, none of these three types of relationship implied a household. Rather, the combination of these relationships composed a household. Marriage was not a necessary condition for a household, and for the nine households I watched consistently for nine months, three did not involve a current marriage relationship.[3] Nor did marriage imply a household, as a number of couples lived separately from each other. Being kin did not imply being members of the same household as most people were related by kinship in some way; however, households most often implied kinship.

Households involved shared relationships to place: both to residential areas and to gardening land. Yet there were people not involved in a household who shared these relationships; often members of the same lineage had a relationship of ownership to a hamlet area despite not having an active relationship of residence in the area, and often they gardened in the same area. These people were regular visitors, and occasionally slept in a household, due to these close relationships.

Relationships of nurturance are those including the giving and receiving of food (*ertnin* for members of households; *pniari* for visitors), socialisation of children (*owo zik*), and the work of a household such as laundry and sweeping. Such relationships are not restricted to the household, but are given different significance by Lihirians themselves. Within the household, this nurturance is naturalised, whereas such relationships outside the household are understood as help or support (*erim*).

In a particular constellation, these three types of relationships—of kinship and marriage, of ties to place, and of nurturance—constituted a household. Given that households are constituted by persons connected by particular assemblages of relationships, then what is normally discussed as links between households (for example, Segalen 1984) can be seen as relationships between persons; relationships that have similarities to those that constitute households. Rather than seeing reified households interacting with other such entities, ties between households can be seen in terms of relationships between persons. Thus a person may visit a household because of kinship ties, or persons in one household may help those in another due to contiguity (ties

[3] One household had a man separated from his wife with his grandchild, one a widow and children, and one was a number of single women and their children.

of place). In this perspective, households become known collections of persons bound by particular relationships (of kinship and marriage, of place and of nurturance), who have relationships with other persons.

Members of the household of which I was a part in Lalakam hamlet had their closest relationship of cooperation with Ngalparok, their *mduan* (MB), and head of a household in Liematon hamlet at the far end of the village. There was frequent visiting between members of these households, food sharing, gardens were made in the same area, and members of the households cooperated in hosting feasts for the men's house in Lalakam.

Viewing households as constellations of relationships rather than as reified entities allows an alternative view of relationships between households and lineages on neighbouring Tanga. Rather than household and lineage being opposed, as Foster argues is the case, kinship ties in Lihir, and particularly those of lineage, are constitutive of relationships both within and between households. Given this, Lihirians view lineage and household not in opposition but rather as intertwined.

While relationships between persons of kinship and marriage, place, and nurturance constitute households, the significance of households is perceived primarily in terms of the third: relationships of nurturance (*owo*, *ertnin* or *pniari*), of children, visitors, pigs and gardens.

## Nurturing yams: gardening on Mahur

Until very recently, Lihirians relied upon subsistence agriculture for most of their food requirements, supplemented by some fishing, pig raising for feast contexts, and a small amount of copra production to gain money for additional items such as clothing, lamps and kerosene, and rice. While the existence of a gold mine has changed this somewhat, with many people wage employed or running a small business (such as trade stores or construction groups), on Mahur subsistence gardening remains the most highly valued activity. Mahurians pride themselves on their superior gardening skills, their fertile land and their large yams.

Mahurians employ quite considerable skill and effort in gardening in an effort to increase the yield of plants. These techniques are labour intensive, and are generally not carried out on Niolam (those few people on Niolam who use these techniques are often originally from Mahur). Mahurians have a special relationship to their gardens—one of intense nurturance.

Households clear gardens each year from virgin or secondary forest on land atop the plateau. Each adult member of a household, and sometimes children as well, has a piece of garden named as his or hers in a garden belonging to the household. A household's gardens may be spread over two or three different sites, and are often contiguous with gardens belonging to other members of the lineage. Work in the gardens is done by household members, and garden produce is stored in garden houses or carried down to the village for household (or occasionally feast) consumption.

Teams of men and women clear gardens, often with helpers from other households who are repaid at the end of the day with a meal for their labour, and sometimes assistance in their own gardens. Underbrush and small trees are cut and piled at the base of large trees, left to dry in the sun and finally burned, occasionally killing the large trees which may be cut but are more often left standing. The ash is then swept out of the garden area, leaving it clean.

In the first year, such gardens are planted with yams (*a wih*; *Dioscorea* sp.) and *mami* (T.P. another form of *Dioscorea* sp; *a ko*), sometimes with pineapples to mark the borders between individual gardens within the household plot. In the second year, or in areas where stone is too close to the surface, other crops are planted, primarily sweet potato (*a kosniel*) but also manioc (*miaka*), pumpkin (T.P. *pangen*), and greens (for example, T.P. *aibika*; and snake gourd).

Gardens dedicated to yams and mami have the ground 'broken' in about October or November (holes dug with a digging stick) by men, and a tall bamboo pole (up to about 4 m in height; sometimes wood is used if there is a bamboo shortage in the area) is planted next to each hole. The women of the household then collect the seed yams, cutting some in two or three to match the number of holes, as well as mami and take these to the gardens. During the night or early morning a member of the household or lineage who knows the procedures of garden magic prepares the tubers for planting by rubbing their skin with particular leaves, and bespelling them in some cases.

In the morning the women go to the garden and plant the tubers, this being done with care. The women check each hole by digging into it, removing any roots, loosening the soil, and checking if limestone is close to the surface. Some holes are judged inferior, and it is in these that mami are planted. Each yam is planted by facing its 'head' (the end which sends out leaf shoots) towards the central mountain of Mahur, Toyen, or uphill if on a slope. Those sections from the lower part of yams that have been cut are planted accompanied by a noise made pursing the lips and sucking in air ('*miz*') to make them shoot quickly. Holes that have yams in them are marked by a small stick, and later a cordyline (*a zir*) will be planted next to each yam to facilitate its growth.

The garden is then closed to most people until the shoots of the yams and mami are long enough to tie to the poles. A person knowledgeable about garden spells carries this out, and he (for it is men who learn this knowledge) ties the first few yam and mami shoots to poles with bespelled cordyline leaves. The members of the household are then free to enter the garden and continue the work of tying the shoots to poles as they grow.

After a month or two the seed yams and mami are carefully removed from the growing plants. The garden is kept clean and weeded for the growing season as the yams and mami climb the tall poles and set tubers. In March or April men of each household carry out a procedure called *yientnes* (see Figure 6). They dig underneath each yam to loosen the soil to facilitate even longer growth, and resettle yams that may not be growing straight into the earth. They carry out a similar procedure with mami, though this also requires the removal of many small mami to make the others grow larger. The household eat those removed and those accidentally scraped during this delicate procedure.

The harvest proper occurs between about May and July. In the year I spent on Mahur the harvest was carried out through July to early September due to the drought the previous year that had delayed planting. All adults in the household, as well as some of the older children, participate in harvesting. Women then carry most of the produce to the garden house, where it is placed in piles based on whose garden it grew in: each yam and mami can be traced to the garden in which it grew, this being necessary because the men who perform garden magic are unable to eat from any garden that they bespell.

Often people from outside the household help in this process of harvesting, and are given a basket full of yams and mami in return for their work. Kupulie and I helped to dig and carry yams and mami from Kupulie's sister's garden, and we were both given a basket of yams and mami for our work. We also ate some small yams and mami baked on the fire while we were in the garden. While Wilk and Netting say differences in exchange within and between households mark their boundaries (1984), the boundary of the household was also highlighted by the fact that our work was seen as 'help' (*erim*) rather than as our nurturance of gardens of the household.

Mahurian gardening differs from that practiced on Niolam and in other areas of New Ireland such as Tanga, in terms of the effort expended on the nurturance of yams. Most gardeners on Niolam and Tanga do not *yientnes* (dig under yams to loosen the soil; Holding 2000:124–34; pers. comm), and many on Niolam do not practice garden magic. Yams on Niolam are often co-planted with sweet potatoes, and seem to be planted closer together, with shorter poles up which to climb. Quite often gardens do not have the neat, cleanly swept appearance of most Mahurian gardens (see Figure 7). Not only do these differences equate to smaller yams but also to a difference in relationship between people and their gardens on Mahur and Niolam. Mahurians view themselves as gardeners *par excellence*, with members of each household carefully nurturing the growth of their yams.

## Nurturing pigs

As with other places in Papua New Guinea, pigs in Lihir are crucial as a feasting food, most being bred and raised on the group of islands, but with some being bought from the neighbouring island groups of Tabar and Tanga, from the New Ireland mainland, and, in some cases, from as far away as Rabaul.

Pigs (*a bol*) raised in Lihir are generally the property of individuals, and are raised together with pigs belonging to other members of the household. They are kept both at the beach in the coconut plantations and at various levels atop the plateau.[4] Fed a diet mostly consisting of coconut flesh, with some tuber peelings and waste food, they are expected to forage (but not in other people's gardens) for the rest of their food. To feed a pig is called *tnanie bol*, the same term used for nurturing humans (particularly with food), and thus implying nurturance of the pigs.[5] Often it was a particular person's responsibility in the household to feed the pigs of the entire household, though if they were kept on the second level of Mahur's plateau they were fed simply when someone of the household was passing through that area on the way to or from the gardens.

While some people developed close relationships with their pigs, and were upset when they were killed for feasting, this was quite rare. In general, people seemed to have an ambiguous relationship with their pigs, finding them crucial for feasting, to maintain their relations of exchange and fulfil their responsibilities to others, yet at the same time they found pigs annoying: trespassing into people's gardens and eating crops, having to be fed, breaking stone fences. One pig in the neighbouring hamlet to Lalakam developed a technique of breaking into locked houses to eat stores of tubers while everyone

[4] Mahur has a number of levels, connected by a few paths and slopes in some areas, and sheer cliffs in others. The beach level I mentally called level one, and then there were another three levels including *aniozep* (big bush). Pigs tended to be kept on the slopes between the first and second levels, as well as on the second level itself. Most gardens were on levels three and four, with only a few on level two.

[5] *Tnanie* is another form of the verb for nurturance that has other forms such as *ertnin* (to look after someone) and *tnindan* (to completely look after someone).

was at church, inciting much anger. Pigs were nurtured, and provided the means for nurturing others through feasting, yet were often the source of annoyance and complaint.

## Nurturing children: reproduction and socialisation

Almost without exception, households on Mahur comprised children as well as adults. Lihirians see a child as the product of the relationship between its mother and father, and this is one instance of the person being clearly construed in Strathern's terms, as the objectification of relations (1988:313 *et passim*; see next chapter for details and conception ideas). Often on Mahur, pregnancy or birth is the first indication of relations between a particular man and woman, and marriage commonly follows after this event.

Most pregnancies in Lihir are unplanned, and children are generally seen more as the inevitable product of sexual relations. The average number of children per woman on Mahur is four to five, with extremes of none and 13. Most couples on Mahur attempt to space their children at least two years apart, but often the time between births is shorter, leading to rapid population growth. Lihirians see it as harmful to the infant for its mother to be pregnant while still breastfeeding,[6] saying that the breast milk becomes thin and greasy. In a survey of over 150 mothers around Lihir, over a third of mothers reported that their last child weaned themselves at about 18 months to two years of age, though if the mother becomes pregnant she will forcibly wean the child earlier (Hemer 2002b). Women often exclaimed '*laik bilong en*' (T.P. 'his/her choice'), highlighting both a child's autonomy in this and mothers' inability or unwillingness to force a child to continue to breastfeed. In the past, birth spacing was maintained by the practice of husbands sleeping in the *rih* (men's house), though often now men share the family house in the main part of the hamlet.

[6] Breast-feeding is on demand for children, except when mothers are in the gardens for the day and children are left in the care of siblings or grandparents.

In recent years the concept of birth spacing has been emphasised by health workers as being beneficial to the child and mother. Those couples that do not practice birth spacing are said to be '*wokim lata*' (T.P. creating a ladder of children with heights like the steps of a ladder; see Kowal 1999), this behaviour viewed as being opposed to ideas of proper nurturance of children. Approximately 85 per cent of the population is Catholic, and almost none of these see contraceptives as an option, leaving the ovulation method as the only way to space children. Husbands who insist on having sexual intercourse with their wives when they are fertile, and thus limit the woman's choice not to have children, are seen as having a lack of *sio* (respect) for their partner. However, Kowal reports that this was quite common.

While still breastfeeding, and up to about the age of three or four years, life for Lihirian children is simple and unstructured. Towards the end of this time they begin to be disciplined by adults or other children, with the aim of teaching (*erzer*) the children about proper behaviour. At the age of about six years the children start Elementary school, and by this age are also expected to begin helping with the household chores, such as sweeping and picking up rubbish. From this age until about 15 years of age, the workload of children gradually increases until it is equal to that of an adult. Young girls, in imitation of Lihirian women, do more of the tasks of the household, including food preparation, cooking and serving, sweeping, laundry, childminding, and gardening (planting, weeding, harvesting) in addition to attending school. Boys have a lighter workload, with some food preparation (mostly scraping coconuts), childminding, and gardening (breaking the ground), with other activities, such as fishing, carried out by choice.

Children are taught (*erzer*) through three main pathways, verbal, physical learning and physical punishment. People said that children should be gathered together from an early age and spoken to quietly about proper behaviour, and the appropriate person for this task was the *mduan* (MB). I saw this occur on a number of occasions, once by the *pupu* (MF) as he claimed the *mduan* was unreliable. The *mduan* lectured even adults on proper customary behaviour in relation to a planned major feast.

Children learn how to carry out tasks primarily by watching and imitating the behaviour of their parents, siblings and others in the household and hamlet. By the age of about seven or eight, each child is able to husk a coconut, break the shell and eat or scrape the flesh to make coconut milk. They are also able to cut firewood, start and maintain a fire, prepare and cook food, do the laundry and so on. There appeared to be no explicit schooling for these tasks and, for example, I never saw a parent show a child how to properly hold a bush knife.

When children overstep the constraints imposed upon them they are physically punished, this occurring quite regularly. Physical punishment seems the only method of control used, rather than removal of privileges or rewards for good behaviour. Often punishment occurs when children are classified as being *bikhet* (T.P.), or arrogant and not listening to parents.[7] The characteristics valued in children on Mahur are compliance and a hard working nature, the ability to listen to adults and learn from them, and a good temper and the ability to have fun. Children who sulk or anger easily are deemed to be annoying, as are those who do not contribute to household tasks and those who do as they please.

Non-compliance with the wishes of adults is primarily dealt with by physical punishment, so children learn to respond to the will of others in order to avoid it. This does not imply, however, that children lack personal agency or lose their own will. Nor is socialisation concerned with learning to act entirely in terms of others (Strathern 1988:272–4). Rather they learn to submit their will to others higher in a hierarchy. Amongst their age mates the same children who submit more or less meekly to the wishes of their elders, argue and sometimes physically fight over just whose will shall triumph in that particular context. As both children and adults, Lihirians may follow the will of others, especially if the relationship is one of hierarchy, just as anyone in the

[7] The Tok Pisin term is generally used rather than a Lihirian one.

West may do if confronted with the threat of violence or the wishes of their boss. At the same time, even while they are children many Lihirians are known as being strong-willed, and no amount of physical punishment is believed to be able to change this. Lihirians cannot be seen only as persons who 'from [their] own vantage point act with another's in mind' (Strathern 1988:272, italics removed).

In many ways, children seemed to receive less nurturance than did the gardens of yams on Mahur. Measured against ideology in the West, Lihirian children were shown little affection, were not expected to spend 'quality time' with their parents, were punished regularly and quite harshly, and did a great deal of work of the household. Yet one of the tasks of the household is to raise children (*owo zik*) and occasionally to adopt completely unrelated children and raise them (*sorkinia*: adoption of unrelated children). Children are valued, and infertile couples are pitied and often adopt children to remedy this. Raising children is seen as relatively uncomplicated much of the time, nurturance being provided in the form of food, shelter, clothing and education. These practical aspects are emphasised, and the psychological needs of being loved, cherished and valued are rarely discussed or problematised. While children were seen to acquire bad habits from their parents, they were rarely seen to suffer from poor parenting, except in extreme cases such as malnutrition.[8] Hence, concepts of nurturance or caring highlight physical aspects, of provision of food and shelter, rather than emotional ones.

Anthropologists working in other parts of New Ireland Province have generally explored nurture in the form of paternal nurture: nurture given by fathers to their children. It has been argued by Battaglia that such nurture in matrilineal systems is repaid by the children through feasting later in their lives (Battaglia 1985; 1990), because the father in these systems is conceptualised as

[8] In the few cases where people complained about other's poor parenting it was in terms of a lack of food. One was a case where twins were malnourished and nearly died, people complaining about the father not buying milk powder to supplement breast milk. The other case was a woman whose children were fed by her mother and sister as she had too many church commitments. It was remarked that she didn't have time to go to the gardens. These instances of a lack of provision of food were understood as a failure of nurturance.

being 'outside' the lineage and his contributions are therefore gifts that carry an obligation to reciprocate. Paternal nurture thus appears as a problem in contrast with maternal nurture, which is naturalised and unreciprocated (Clay 1977; Wagner 1986; Foster 1995). This separation of parental obligations is not elaborated in Lihirian constructions of responsibility for children.

In Lihir, nurture was seen as the responsibility of both parents as well as that of the classificatory *mama* (MZ) and *papa* (FB), *mduan* (MB), *papa wein* (FZ) and *pupu* (any grandparents). None of this nurture was naturalised, with all nurture expected to be reciprocated later in some form through feasting, night vigil at the burial site, or through the nurturance of feeding later in life. Lihirians did not accord any special place to the nurturance given by fathers. This at least partially reflects and constitutes the bilateral tendencies in Lihir, where land quite often (for an explicitly matrilineal system) is inherited through paternal ties and residential patterns are not prescribed in terms of matrilineal rights.

## Nurturing *wasir* (visitors)

*Pniari wasir*, 'to give (food, betelnut etc) to visitors', is one of the most important moral responsibilities of the household. All who come to visit a household should have their needs satisfied: be given betelnut to chew, tobacco to smoke, food to eat, and coconuts or water to drink. *Pniari*, then, is a form of nurturance, and extends relations of sharing of the household to all who enter the area. It was not the case in Lihir, as described by Foster for Tanga, that people know they will be given food and are embarrassed then to go into houses until they can no longer hear the clinking of plates, meaning the evening meal is finished (Foster 1995; pers comm). Rather, in Lihir people generally ate outside, in full view of those passing along the road, and would call out for them to come inside the hamlet and eat. People did not hesitate to visit others at night even though they may be eating. There was no shame in being fed by others, everyone aware that they in turn would feed visitors.

When I first arrived on Mahur it was at the end of the severe drought that occurred throughout Papua New Guinea in 1997. Many people on Mahur were embarrassed as they were unable to *pniari wasir*, to give me food in a way that was appropriate. Mahurians apologised for their lack of food, saying it would have been better if I had arrived a while later when the gardens had had time to recover. Unlike Tangans, who are embarrassed to be fed, Lihirians were embarrassed not to be able to feed visitors. The ideal in Lihir is to nurture through the giving of food.

*Pniari wasir* was also a form of food distribution at major feasts, where food was given to groups of two to four people directly from a main pile rather than being split into clan groups first. There is no opposition of household and lineage/clan in Lihir as Foster documents for Tanga, arguing that 'feasting sustains or extends relations; household consumption contracts or involutes relations' (Foster 1992:91). In Lihir in both contexts relationships of cooperation and exchange may be expanded, and the household certainly does not imply the involution of relations.

The ability of a household to *pniari wasir* is dependent upon the household's nurturance of its gardens. It is a demonstration of the productivity of the relationship between members of a household and the land, as well as the household's ability to marshal its other resources (for example, money to buy tea and sugar). Being unplanned, in contrast to feasts, it is crucial to the presentation of the household as productive and nurturant on a daily basis.

## *Ertnin*, social relationships and bodies

Feeding and fatness were the primary metaphors and indicators for social relations in Lihir. After about six months of fieldwork on Mahur people began to comment that I was fat (*sa hon*), and being a self-conscious Western female I was quite horrified: I did put on a little weight during fieldwork but it seemed not enough to spark these comments, let alone the more extreme ones that I was *hon muet*, or 'completely fat'.

Over the time of my fieldwork I came to understand that this comment was about social relations and nurturance (*ertnin*) as well as about body size. *Hon* actually means full rather than fat, and also refers to a boat that is full of people or cargo (*a bot sa hon*), as opposed to empty (*sa mas*). People were implying that my social relations were in a good state, that I was 'full' of relationships. In a sense they were being self-congratulatory in suggesting that they were nurturing me in an appropriate way.

Holding described a similar experience during his fieldwork: Tangans said he was getting fat, despite his losing weight due to the serious drought in the region as mentioned above. Holding reported that when people made these comments they were 'reminding me that I was standing on the shoulders of others' (2000:4).

Using the same concept, when wanting to comment on what are perceived to be poor social relationships, people on Mahur would note that a person was thin, or had been asking them for food (instead of other kin who should have been more directly responsible for them). This bodily state was seen as an indicator of the failure of social relationships, a failure of nurturance (*ertnin*), and was a moral comment on the actions of others. Social relations and the body are clearly interlinked and mutually constitutive.

*Ertnin* is intimately bound to food and the feeding of others. Refusal of food can be seen as a refusal of social relationship. In expressing that I was *hon muet*, people were commenting not only that I was well nurtured by themselves but that I had accepted this from them (c.f. Kahn 1986 on food and social relationships).

On my return to the field in June 1999, I was interested to note that some people said that I was *hon muet*, while others said I was *trar* (thin). Those people who had quite distant relationships from me said I was fat, indicating that I had gone home to my kin in Australia who had nurtured me. Those who had nurtured me and given me food while I was on Mahur alleged that I was thin, referring to the distance that had existed between me and them, and their inability to nurture me from afar. These people were making note of the capacities of themselves and others to carry out the moral work of nurturance.

## Moral household relationships

The household is primarily concerned with the nurturance of its members, gardens, animals and visitors: this is the work (*pniez*) of the household. While it may be translated simply as work or labour, this term signifies duty in the sense of tasks or labour that are obligatory. It is seen as the moral responsibility for those key members of a household to carry out the work of nurturance discussed above. Members who leave and return at regular intervals are also expected to devote some of their labours to the household, and part of their wage if it is that which keeps them from being present. For those with more irregular movements, on the other hand, work for the household is seen more as a choice than duty-bound, while *wasir* (visitors) are expected to be the recipients of the work of the household rather than its authors.

It was sometimes the case that key members or regular floaters of a household did not fulfil their moral duty, and I discuss the consequences of this, particularly in relation to conflict, in Chapter 5. Unless key members are ill they have little excuse for shirking their responsibilities. Occasionally it appeared to me that people overstated the seriousness of their illness in order to exempt themselves from work, particularly in cases where there was conflict within a household and they had been doing more than their 'fair share' until the point when they became ill.

There is also a moral duty for members of a household earning money to contribute at least some of this income to the household for consumption and savings. While men on Mahur spend some money on beer, people do object to this use of money for individual consumption. I witnessed an incident late in my fieldwork where the female head of my household, Lolot, became extremely angry and publicly upbraided her husband for spending much of his wage on beer and not coming home to Mahur while he was on break from work. Lolot said she was angry as she was on Mahur alone with the children, her baby was extremely ill and so she could not go to the gardens, and she had no money to buy food. She was aggrieved because her husband was part of the household and so had a responsibility to the other members that he was not fulfilling.

Money is not only used for food items, but also for church offerings, schooling costs, clothing, soap, kerosene and so on. Occasionally members of a lineage are called upon to contribute money for the lineage to buy a pig for an upcoming feast. This money comes from the reserves of households, meaning that funds are not kept for household consumption alone, but instead are used in cooperative activities with other lineage members.

Women in employment are often expected to give a significant proportion of wages or savings to senior men when a feast is planned. While young men are also expected to do this, their contribution is individualised, so they gain some prestige as transactors. Money contributed by women is absorbed by the senior male and prestige accrues to him as lineage leader. Yet if women do not give money this becomes known, and she is harshly judged by others as selfish, more so than a man if he spends his money on alcohol rather than feasting.

It is through this *pniez*, this moral work, that emotional bonds of the household are practised. Lihirians appear not to separate emotion and practical action, as is the case in Western ideas of human interaction. Relationships that we might consider emotional, such as ties of love and caring between people, are always required to be evidenced in action, such as the giving of food. The emphasis in Lihir was on the practice of emotion, and Lihirians read emotions in others through their actions.

Thus, while nurturance of children in Lihir is in practical terms, this does not imply that the bonds entailed are not emotional ones: the two are certainly not mutually exclusive and emotional bonds are always practised. In Lihir a lack of nurturance implies a lack of care and love, and no one would say in Lihir that they love someone despite their failure to nurture them. As

I show throughout this book, while analysing verbalisations of emotion and the emotion lexicon can illuminate the ways that emotion is conceptualised, studies of emotion need to go beyond lexical and discourse analysis to the everyday contexts and practice of emotion. Emotion needs to be studied with respect to other key concepts such as of the person and relationships.

In Lihir the household is the site for some of the closest of what could be considered purely emotional ties between people. While the household on Mahur did not necessarily imply a marriage or couple, where the household did include a couple their relationship was crucial to the household. Marriage is said to be based in *leimulien* (love, sexual desire), *nornor* (trust, belief in someone) and *sio* (respect). Where these ideals of marriage were met, the household often seemed more harmonious, the food more plentiful and the children better behaved than in households with a couple in conflict. In one case, a man and his wife seemed in conflict about the work to be done each day. People said she did not follow his wishes (a lack of *sio* [respect] for him) and that he beat her when she was pregnant (a lack of *sio* for her). This household was known for children who often went hungry and who were badly behaved. The lack of *leimulien* in the household was inferred from the bodies of the children. Lihirians saw practical consequences for the lack of ideal emotional ties.

Where *nornor* (trust) was lacking between a couple, the relationship was characterised by incidents of *eremsu*, or jealousy, reflected in arguments and violence, generally on the part of the man. While jealousy can hardly be seen as a positive emotional bond, it is still viewed in Lihir as a relationship, this evidenced in the linguistic form *er-*, denoting joint action. Hence, jealousy evidences a continuing emotional relationship, even if it has negative consequences.

The household has a hierarchical structure, and certain members had more authority than others, particularly in their ability to enforce the moral responsibilities entailed in being a member of the household. Adult men were generally the 'heads' of the household, though Lihirians never described them in these terms. Children were at the bottom of the hierarchy, and could be coerced by shouting and physical punishment into performing work. Women were higher in the hierarchy than children, and in some households were considered the 'head,' generally in cases where there was an absence of men (through employment or death, or in the case of single mothers). The head of the household had the final say in decisions about what work was to be done that day, and how to use the resources of the household.

Discussing the authority of the head of the household on Mahur is somewhat misleading, in that the authority and even the idea of a singular 'head' was continually open to change and renegotiation. Given that the membership of households was fluid, changes in the constitution of the household continually affected the hierarchy and authority structure. In Lalakam, for two weeks in three the head of the household was Lolot, a woman in her thirties with two children (as of 1998). She made the decisions about the children's schooling and activities, her own daily routine, and the use of the finances of the household. Yet in the third week, her husband Iruo would return from work at the mine site to Mahur, and he and Lolot negotiated decisions, with Iruo often having the final say.

It was also the case that a member of one household occasionally had authority over another household. This was the case in Lalakam where Ngalparok, *mduan* (MB) to Lolot and from a household at the other end of the village, had some authority over where Lolot made her gardens for the year, and occasionally over the use of household funds and produce. Given his kinship relationship to Lolot and his place in their lineage on Mahur, he had the authority to direct some of Lolot's household resources to lineage concerns.

## Conclusion

The work (*pniez*) of members of a household is that of nurturance (*owo*, *ertnin* and *pniari*), particularly of children, visitors, pigs and gardens. Households are primarily the sites for action (often nurture) in Lihir, and do not act in their own right. Action remains the province of persons in Lihir, and while children learn in the household to respond to the will of others, their own will does not become that of the household. Households cannot be reified as entities capable of action, instead being the site of action of a group of persons. In this way, I am able to talk about the moral responsibilities that being a member of a household entails, but to discuss this as 'household function' would misconstrue the situation in Lihir.

Perhaps most importantly, the household and the lineage are not binary opposites, but rather have a complex and intertwined relationship. The lineage may act as an organising force for some of the household activities, such as members of separate households but the same lineage gardening side by side, or members of a lineage having some authority over the actions of members of a household. At the same time, the members of a household contribute to the lineage in terms of giving resources for feasts, such as pigs, money and tubers. It is not the case in Lihir that the household relates only to the sphere of bisnis, while the lineage is concerned with *kastam* (Foster 1995). Nor is it true that paternal nurturance takes precedence over nurturance by others.

Relationships are continually renegotiated rather than households being static entities. This fluidity of households brought about by the ongoing movements of people to and from households gives rise to the Lihirian condition of *piot*, the subject of the next chapter.

# 3

# *Piot*, PERSONHOOD AND PLACE

'*Piot, piot, piot.* Everyday *piot.* I'm so sick and tired of *piot.*'
— Isidore, 12 June 1998, in English

*Piot* was one of the great puzzlements of my fieldwork in Lihir. It was a concept I heard used continuously throughout my time in Lihir once it came to my attention about six weeks after my arrival. In this chapter I employ the concept of *piot* as a window onto Lihirian notions of personhood, as well as the importance and high frequency of mobility between households, villages and islands. *Piot* highlights one aspect of the nature of the relationship between people and place.

## The nature of *piot*

In general, *piot* is a condition with a number of bodily symptoms that arises when people either leave the house to sleep elsewhere or people come from elsewhere and sleep in the hamlet. While the person who moves feels nothing, those who were occupying the house/hamlet prior to the arrival/departure develop a range of symptoms including headache, bodily pain, tiredness, and if already ill they feel worse generally for one day after the arrival/departure. *Piot* makes people sleep late. I once had my sore throat ascribed to *piot* by a neighbour, as a number of people had returned to the hamlet after a few days absence.

If a person moves between houses within a household, other members of the household will feel *piot* but other people in the hamlet will not. If someone moves to sleep in the men's house, or leaves it to sleep elsewhere, the entire hamlet will feel *piot* and sometimes those in neighbouring hamlets will as well. If people arrive from a long distance, or depart to go far away (another island, distant village), everyone in the hamlet and sometimes people in neighbouring ones will feel *piot*. Thus, the distance of movement often correlates with the extent of impact of *piot*.

*Piot* is experienced by all those in the affected area (household or hamlet) regardless of whether they normally occupy the area, or whether they arrived only a day before the arrival/departure that caused the instance of *piot*. Likewise, *piot* is caused by anybody's arrival or departure, be they visitors or owners of the hamlet.

*Piot* varies in severity: some people are known to cause more intense *piot*. The subclan Alonsiat on Mahur was renowned for its ability to inflict severe *piot*, and people in my hamlet would complain when a number of people of that subclan had arrived or left the previous day. The *piot* I caused was said to be not too bad, but when a friend from Australia visited me, I was told that his *piot* was severe.

There are a number of ways that *piot* can be avoided. Bespelled ashes can be sprinkled around the house, which sends the *piot* away. One informant, Ngalparok, said that *piot* leaves to return to the person who caused it but gets lost on the road. Another method is to place a bucket of water by the door of the house to capture the *piot*. Ngalparok said the *piot* would put its foot in the water and, feeling the cold, would not want to stay and affect people in the house. Both these methods prevent *piot* but there appears to be no cure for *piot* once it has affected people: they must just wait until it has past.

While Lihirians characterised *piot* above as having legs, feeling the cold or getting lost, in general people do not personify *piot* or even have much idea of what it might be. One woman stated that you cannot see *piot* but can feel it, like wind. Ngalparok said it is a heaviness that people leave behind when they go, or bring with them from other places when they arrive. Most people, when asked what *piot* was, or how to characterise it, simply described the symptoms and what causes them.

Above I have been using '*piot*' as a noun. People can say '*A piot e se yo lamuel*' (literally: a *piot* hit/attacked me today). While it is sometimes used in this way in Lihir, more often it takes the form of a verb. People say '*Blewa na piotpiot*' (literally: Don't *piot*). They also say '*O piot eh*?' to mean 'Where did you sleep last night?' (literally: where did you *piot*?).

There are similar conditions to *piot* described in the literature for Papua New Guinea. Andrew Holding (pers. comm.) says that there is a similar condition called *fitum* on the neighbouring Tanga Islands. Fajans, in her ethnography about the Baining of East New Britain, describes *awumbuk* as a sentiment. It is a lassitude that occurs when people leave the hamlet or die. It lasts for three days, leaving people tired, lazy, having a lack of success in activities, and is due to a 'heaviness' that the departing people leave behind. She argues that with the departure the 'socially extended persona is ruptured and individuals must reconstitute their boundaries' (Fajans 1997:120) and that this is even more pronounced at death (Fajans 1985:380–1; 1997:120–1).

Kuehling, in explicating the nature of the person in Dobu, Milne Bay, describes a 'social syndrome' called *gwasa* or *nadiwala*. This too is caused when someone leaves the hamlet, and is experienced through headaches, tiredness and a general feeling of being unwell. Kuehling analyses *gwasa* in light of personhood, relating that it is something left behind when the person goes away, and its strength depends on the strength of personality. She argues that it is a sanction discouraging people from staying away overnight without good reason (Kuehling 1998:64).

The two syndromes or sentiments described above, *awumbuk* and *gwasa*, lend themselves to explanations in terms of the problems of separation of the single person from the group. In an ASAO-net[1] discussion of *gwasa* in 1997, correspondents raised the issue of loneliness in Melanesia, where persons are often described as relational or as dividuals (for example, Strathern 1988). However, in the case of *piot*, explanations in terms of loneliness or separation from the group are not sufficient. *Piot* can occur when people arrive as well as when they go. Nor is it dependent upon close social relations between the person moving and those in the hamlet. For example, when my friend from Australia left, he had been on Mahur for less than two weeks, he spoke no Tok Pisin and the inhabitants of the hamlet spoke no English. He was a fairly quiet person, not forceful in personality, and yet the *piot* he caused was severe. When I asked why some people have more intense *piot* than others, I was told '*i olsem yet*' (T.P. 'its just like that'). Given that *piot* appears to be an attribute of the person, to better understand *piot* it is instructive to examine the nature of persons in Lihir.

## Personhood in Melanesia

Attention to the nature of the person is quite a recent development in the anthropology of Melanesia, most studies occurring since the 1980s. Early works such as Read's seminal paper on the person for the Gahuku-Gama (1955), has found fertile ground mostly since the 1980s. Likewise, the full impact of Leenhardt's *Do Kamo* (1979 [1947]) was not felt until it was available in English: it took up the issue of the nature of the person for the first time in Melanesia, arguing that Melanesians were personages:

---

[1] ASAO (the Association for Social Anthropology in Oceania) has a listserv through which there are often ongoing discussions of ideas and concepts central to the region.

> He is unaware of his body, which is only his support. He knows himself only by the relationships he maintains with others. He exists only insofar as he acts his role in the course of his relationships. He is situated only with respect to them. If we try to draw this, we cannot use a dot marked 'self' (*ego*), but must make a number of lines to mark relationships … The empty space is him, and this is what is named. (Leenhardt 1979:153)

Leenhardt went on to say that the Melanesian could become a person, primarily in the context of colonialism, by escaping the socio-mythic domain (ibid.:161–4). The person for Leenhardt is the union of two elements, individuation centred on the body and communal rapport ('a personal rapport maintaining person-to-person participation') (Leenhardt 1979:168–9). For Leenhardt, then, both personages and persons inhabited the Melanesian world at the time of early colonisation.

More recently, Marilyn Strathern has argued that the Melanesian person and Melanesian sociality is diametrically opposed to that in the West, where the person as unique individual is opposed to society (1988:12–13). It is important to note that Strathern is not concerned with 'specific local contexts for events and behavior' but instead with the symbolism or root metaphor of 'the distinctive nature of Melanesian sociality' (ibid.:10). The 'root metaphor' of the Melanesian person is the 'multiple person produced as the object of multiple relationships' (ibid.:185). This person is dividual or composite: 'the plural and composite site of the relations that produced' him or her. The person is an objectification of these relations (ibid.:13, 272). Strathern separates the concept of person and agent, the agent being the one who acts with another's vantage point in mind (ibid.:272). Agency and cause in her analysis are split, agents not being the authors of their own actions (ibid.:273). In her analysis, relationships are taken for granted, being prior to the persons that are their objectification (ibid.:274). Persons do not act to create or maintain relationships, rather relationships 'are merely the condition for action, not themselves acts' (ibid.:305). Being multiple and composite means that the person is also partible, 'an entity that can dispose of parts in relation to others' (ibid.:185). These parts are not alienated, but 'circulate as parts of persons' (ibid.:192).

When closely read, Strathern's analysis does allow space for non-relational aspects of Melanesian personhood. She argues that 'Melanesian persons are *as dividually as they are individually conceived*' (ibid.:13, added emphasis), indicating that Melanesians still conceive of persons individually at least partially. Persons are products of relations and so are internally differentiated, but this differentiation is eliminated to produce the 'unitary individual' (ibid.:14). In the case of action, Strathern contends,

> The separation between agent and the person who is the cause of his or her acts is systematic, and governs the Melanesian perception of action. *To act as one's own cause becomes an innovation on this convention.* (Strathern 1988:273, added emphasis)

That Melanesians can act as their own cause suggests possibilities for selfishness and individualism that are not elaborated in the rest of Strathern's text, but which resonate well with Lihirian perceptions of action that I detail below.

Strathern criticises Leenhardt's portrayal of the Melanesian 'person' (she appears to be referring to the concept of personage) in that he attempted to find even a blank centre of the relationships that constitute the personage (Strathern 1988:268–70). She makes no comment on his attempt to chart the change in the concept of person in Melanesia with colonialism and Christianisation, her account being deliberately ahistorical.

Other anthropologists have followed Strathern's lead, particularly Battaglia (1990) but also Iteanu (1990), who seems never to credit any of his ideas about the Orokaivan person to her. His position is somewhat more extreme, in that he argues that only relations made in the context of ritual contribute to the social person:

> During his life, a social person continues to 'grow' by accumulating relations each time he participates in a ritual. (Iteanu 1990:40)

> [An Orokaiva child's] parents, his family, and the other villagers, by performing numerous childhood rituals … gradually construct his social person. (ibid.)
>
> … a 'big-man' or a 'big-woman' is someone who has a 'big' social person, that is, who has many social relations which he or she has acquired by taking part in numerous rituals. (ibid.)

Robert Foster, in his study of the sociality and mortuary ritual of the Tanga Islands, uses Strathern's definition of the Melanesian person as composed of relations:

> My interpretation of the two glosses 'finishing' (*farop*) and 'replacing' (*pilis*) the dead draws on the model of personhood, agency and exchange informing the New Melanesian Ethnography. For my analysis works within a set of propositions that do not take for granted autonomous individuals (or groups of individuals) acting as their own cause. I treat Tangan mortuary practices as a form of collective action that constructs collective individuals—matrilineages, in this case—out of composite persons. (Foster 1995:11)

While Foster does not take autonomous individuals for granted, he does assume that Tangan persons are 'composite' (composed of relations): there is no discussion of Tangan notions of the person beyond this statement of his assumptions.

Many of these more recent studies of personhood move beyond Strathern's position of relational personhood as a root metaphor to conceive of concrete elements of personhood as radically different in Melanesia. Patterson and Macintyre note that this 'radical alterity between Western and Melanesian notions of the person and sociality—has been developed into a rigid social fact' (2011:16; see also Smith 2012). This is particularly the case for Mosko's work on the partibility of the Melanesian person, where he argues that the dividual character of Melanesian personhood can be seen even in examples of the assimilation of Christianity (for example, 2010).

Other studies dealing with personhood in Melanesia have argued that personhood in Melanesia encompasses both relational and individual aspects (Clay 1986; Harrison 1985; Maschio 1994; Strathern & Stewart 1998). Recent discussions of the rise of possessive individualism in Melanesia provide interesting insights into the character of personhood in Melanesia (Martin 2007; Robbins 2007; Sykes 2007). Billings in particular provides highly nuanced ethnographic analyses of two cultures of Northern New Ireland, arguing that the Lavongai people are individualised while the Tikana are 'group-oriented' (Billings 1987; 1991). Billings draws upon divergent aspects of life in these cultures, such as their solutions to conflict, their speech patterns, performance forms and so on to construct her comparison. While not couching her discussions in terms of 'Melanesian personhood', it is clear that this is what she is addressing.

LiPuma argues that the idea that personhood in Melanesia and the West are diametrically opposed is false:

> I would … like to take issue with the view that Western and Melanesian images of personhood are fully incommensurable because the West constructs individuals while the societies of Melanesia construct dividuals or relational persons. Though this theory is politically appealing to an anthropology that fetishizes difference, it is ethnographically, theoretically, and in the context of the emerging nation-state also politically troubled. (LiPuma 1998:56)

LiPuma argues instead that in all cultures there are individual and relational aspects to personhood, and cultures differ in the status and force granted to these aspects. He, like Leenhardt, sees that individual aspects of personhood gain ground in Melanesia in the context of modernity (LiPuma 1998:74).

It is this second view of personhood in Melanesia that most closely characterises the case in Lihir, where both individual and relational qualities of personhood are apparent. While Clay argues that the Mandak person is better conceived of 'as "relational" than as "individual"'(Clay 1992:722), and that persons are composed of relations rather than 'have' them, she concedes that they have 'a relational aspect and a sense of productive agency' (ibid.). Her position on Mandak personhood appears consistent with the situation I found in Lihir:

> Mandak persons are conceptualized through both relational and autonomous images. A person is thus defined within relationships yet is also perceived as an independent source of thought and action. (Clay 1986:31)

Epstein (1999) argues that a failure to draw a distinction between individuality and individualism lies at the heart of much of the discussion about the nature of persons in Melanesia. For the Tolai, individuality is valued and can be seen in their 'entrepreneurial ethos and emphasis on individual achievement' (Epstein 1999:7). However individualism, in the sense of indifference to the reactions of others, and a lack of moral connectedness to others is recognised but not esteemed (ibid.:24).

Cohen contends that individuality is 'a property of selfhood: the perception of an individual's distinctiveness' (Cohen 1994:14). While Lihirians see persons as composed of relations, a person's individuality or distinctiveness is also recognised, as is their ability to act in ways that privilege themselves over others. Below I detail notions of personhood in Lihir, both its relational and individual aspects that are crucial to an understanding of concepts such as *piot*, only partially comprehensible in terms of relationality. In later chapters, I also analyse the shifts in the ways particular aspects of personhood are emphasised across the life course and through changes brought by Christianity and mining. In doing so I am arguing both here and throughout this book that when 'Melanesian personhood' is defined as solely relational there is little space for the perception and comprehension of the complex relationships that are created and maintained between Lihirians, and that are rarely taken for granted.

## The nature of the person in Lihir

### *The physical person*

Human beings in Lihir are designated by form, being either *ziktun* (if recognisable) or *zikzin* (if unrecognisable due to distance or darkness). As in many Papua New Guinea languages, corporeality is denoted by the skin, termed *a kuil*. The skin is critical for determining the health of a person, both physically and in terms of social relations. Various illnesses are qualified by fever ('*a kuil sa dodo*' literally: skin is hot), the colour of skin (*barus* is a condition where the skin is seen as blue, with red around the eyes and white cheeks) or the skin/body being tired (*a kuil sa pong*) or painful (*a kuil sa kengen*), as in *piot*.

Social relations are inscribed on the skin or body: many people in Lihir can tell when women are first pregnant by the appearance of their necks, and the condition of their skin, indicating both a new life starting and the sometimes-illicit relationship that started it. As described in the last chapter, Lihirians gauge and comment on the state of relations in terms of fatness (*sa hon*). Quite strangely, the status of my relations was also characterised through my skin colour. When I first arrived in Lihir, and for quite a while after that (about three months), I was described as being 'white-skinned' (*kuil kapuiz*), yet later I was called red-skinned (*kuil bliablia*). When I returned in June 1999 I was again termed *kuil bliablia* (although they commented that my skin had lost its tan—it being winter in Australia), while Emma Kowal, a fellow researcher and new to Lihir, was termed white-skinned (*kuil kapuiz*). It appeared to be inappropriate to label me either white-skinned or black-skinned (*kuil maket*) due to my ambiguous position in the community, as one with close social relations, with a house and knowing the language yet still an outsider.

The body is said to comprise of various organs,[2] bones (*a tio*), meat (*a pniz*) and fat (*a mniok*). The brain is seen as the receptacle for thought (*nanse*),

[2] Such as *a pol* (brain), *a yate* (liver), *a buzo* (heart/lungs), *a tien* (intestines).

and it is for this reason that people should not refer to the head of a big man, and women should not refer to the head of their brother or cross-cousin. One man also commented that it was the reason that men did not carry baskets suspended from their heads: the weight might ruin their ability to think. The body is also the site for experiencing emotions, and I deal with this below.

While social relations can be inscribed on the skin, Lihirians also often mark themselves as individuals via the body. People are known by unusual physical characteristics, such as being an amputee (T.P. '*Wanlek*') or having only one eye (T.P. '*Wanai*'). One child was known by her extremely long naturally blond hair, and would not allow it to be cut. People also tattoo the skin of their faces and arms: these are often individual designs or depict the person's name.[3] There is a concerted effort to be noticed by others and to appear individualistic, especially by men in their early twenties, who carry extremely large baskets and put leaves and flowers in their hair. While this leaves them open to the socially sanctioning label of *mdengniat* (see below), it does not curb such individuality.

### *The metaphysical person*

People are said to have a spirit (*tombuer*), which can move in dreams. Mostly the spirit is mentioned in the context of Catholicism: *Tombuer Ros* is the term for the Holy Spirit (literally: spirit true/straight) and *tombuer* refers to the human soul. It is only in the context of Christianity that '*tombuer*' is used to refer to the spirit of a person after decease. In that context, *tombuer* are discussed as the bearer of traits such as sin and virtue beyond death: the redeemed person as a soul in Heaven is referred to as *tombuer*.

Life is equated with breath (*molmol*), and it is in the absence of this that one is declared dead (*a molmol sa wet* literally: 'breath is finished'). Consciousness is termed *tolam*, and it is this term that has been used in translations for the

[3] Many Lihirian women have a diagonal line tattooed on their cheek. Some said that this was done during the women's ritual Tolup and was a mark of adulthood, while others said it was a sign of 'Lihirianness'. This is not, then, a mark of individualism.

Catholic Church to mean life. People gain *tuatua* (energy, strength) from their food. Unconsciousness is termed *muetlih* and death *muet*, the close etymological connection reflecting Lihirian belief that unconsciousness is one step away from death.[4]

After death, both the body and spirit are referred to as *kanut*. In the past there was great reverence for skulls, and burial practices involved temporary burial followed by mortuary ceremonies where skulls were unearthed and decorated (*mormor*) before secondary burial, often in caves. There appears, then, to have been much greater emphasis on the bones as still being 'the person'. It appears that with the acceptance of Christianity there has been a greater split between body and soul, with focus after death shifting away from the fate of the body (*kanut*) to the spirit (*tombuer/kanut*).

While the corpse is always referred to as *kanut*, after death people become either a *kanut* or *ihlio*. The spirit of a person who dies a sudden or violent death or is killed by sorcery (this includes car accidents, murder, drownings, falls from trees and so on) becomes an *ihlio* rather than *kanut*. *Ihlio* can appear as lights at night near the place where they died, and can appear to people in disturbing ways. On one particular occasion when a boat was lost from Mahur, the *ihlio* of the deceased appeared to people about a week after their deaths. A number of people were awoken from sleep at night, one with images of blood in a pool of water, and others with visions of the final demise of the deceased and the *ihlio* speaking to them about their deaths.

*Kanut* also have the ability to appear to people and are able to impact on the physical world, yet do so in a much less disturbing way. One day Lolot said that '*a kanut*' had taken her pipe while she was in the bush. She had been given the pipe by a man called Azroh many years earlier. He had died several days before the disappearance of the pipe, and this was the '*kanut*' to whom she was referring. Thus *kanut* and *ihlio* retain their individuality, and when they appear to people they look like the physical person they once were rather

[4] Lihirians do know that people awake from states of unconsciousness, as several incidences during my fieldwork attest.

than becoming faceless and nameless (but see Chapter 8 on the relational status of *kanut*).

There is another class of the spirits of the deceased that is known as *tumbuna* in Tok Pisin, and as *tumngiet* in Lihir. These are the long deceased, and do not have individual identities, except for a few unusual named ones, such as Lemesa, Mirkou, Romgou, Tamangerepe, Tgorous and Tumngiet, who were said to look after things such as wind, rain, and various activities such as building stone walls. Tumngiet was said to have made laws for people to follow (see Chapter 4 for the story of Tgorous). These named ancestors as well as the unnamed *tumngiet* are associated with particular places in the forest on Mahur and elsewhere in Lihir. At these places the *tumngiet* have an impact on the living—they can harm those people who enter areas without appropriate respect, or can affect the fertility of gardens.

There are, therefore, a number of different metaphysical states of the person in Lihir, from the *tombuer*, with its soul-like nature, to the recently deceased *kanut* and *ihlio*, which both retain individuating characteristics but have very different dispositions, to the generally nameless and faceless *tumngiet*. Thus, *tombuer*, *kanut* and *ihlio* retain their characteristics and individuality, and certainly *kanut* and *ihlio* have social responses to living persons: elements of the person are inscribed on the spirit/soul.

### *Ontogeny*

Theories of conception in Lihir are mostly based on the Western model of sexual relations between a man and woman leading to an egg being fertilised by sperm. On Mahur all couples undergo relationship counselling prior to marriage, and this includes information on conception and prevention of pregnancy via the ovulation or rhythm method. In addition, while I was in the field, members of the Catholic Church conducted a Family Life course for youth, part of which was information on conception and pregnancy. When asked about the past, one man said that before they believed that the bone came from the mother and the blood from the father, but then the church had come and 'straightened them all out' and so now they know that God made them from the ground, with a bone from Adam for Eve. Despite their supposedly wholesale acceptance of Western ideas of conception, people sometimes expressed doubt that conception could ever take place from a single act of sexual intercourse and also expressed total horror at the idea of continuing sexual relations after a woman knew she was pregnant: they said it would break the head of the child.

Newly born children, until they are considered to have conscious thought (*nanse*), are known as *zik mandion*, or simply *zik*.[5] *Zik mandion* is also the term for an old senile person, the commonality being the lack of understanding and intelligence (*nanse*). Until they are married, boys (*zik*) and girls (*zken*) are expected to learn from their elders and at school, and to work for their parents and other kin. Puberty is marked by physical growth of the body, particularly the growth of breasts for girls. With puberty, children become ashamed to go naked or remove their clothes in public, particularly boys of their trousers. At this time adolescent boys (*zik or*) and males in their twenties become the workforce for older men, building houses and clearing new gardens. Girls at this age (*zken or*) are highly restrained in their movements beyond the hamlet. It is their task to mind their siblings, cook and garden for the household.

In general, growth is seen as a simple process but in certain cases the growth of children is highlighted as being abnormal. In Kuelam village there was a teenage boy aged 15, who was thin and quite small: more like a 10- or 11-year-old child. His grandparent explained that when he was younger his mother kept beating him, especially on his head, and this had significantly retarded his growth. Growth is also thought to depend on proper feeding: a larger amount of food consumed did not lead to more growth. Instead, the stomach or buttocks were said to grow while the child would actually be short for its age. The issue of feeding and growth relates to Lihirian ideas of fatness and nurturance that I discussed in Chapter 2.

[5] This term is either gender neutral or refers to male children when contrasted with *zken*, girl. *Mandion* means unripe.

Maturation is marked in a variety of ways, and these indicate social distinctions based on ideas of the physical changes to the body and changes in behaviour. After the physical changes in the body of puberty, the most significant transformation is seen to come with the production of children. Women (*wok*) and men (*tkian*) are expected to be in prime physical condition, and this is marked by the conception of many children as well as by the physical labour involved with the nurturance of large gardens. *Wok* are considerably constrained in their movements by their husbands and sometimes by *mduan* (MB), as well as by the work required to sustain large numbers of children. For *tkian*, this is a time of freedom from being the workforce for older males.

Older men (*tkianlik*) and women (*woklik*) (in their fifties and older) are often the leaders of the community. They are expected to be knowledgeable and to impart this knowledge to their juniors, particularly their grandchildren. As *tkianlik* and *woklik* are in physical decline and many cannot manage the climb to the gardens, they rely more on their children and grandchildren for food. In the past when people became unable to carry out physical work, I was told that a person could elect to finish their life by having a large feast (*niazroh*) and then arranging to be drowned in the sea. For *woklik*, however, freed of the responsibilities and most of the hard work of caring for large families, this can be a time of the greatest freedom in their lives. In addition to these terms describing people at various times in the life cycle, there are also terms for male and female: *tomat* and *wein* respectively.

Pivotal points in the life course are marked by rites of passage (cf. Van Gennep 1960). In Chapter 4 I discuss one ritual, confirmation in the Catholic Church, which has taken the place of ceremonies that occurred at puberty. In addition, baptism, marriage and funerals are critical life cycle events dealt with through Catholic rituals. In the past there were a number of rituals at and around birth (first pregnancy ceremony—*tektipsasie*; a ceremony at birth; and the hair cutting ceremony—*kuirkoh*—held some time after the birth of the first child) that are not very commonly held now.

## *Gender*

There is a strong sexual division of labour in Lihirian society. Men, in general, are the ones who do all the talking: in village courts, for church announcements, to plan feasts, after feasts inside the men's house, and in political roles (for example, local government). In addition, it is men's job to build houses, break the ground for planting, dig under yams to encourage their growth (*yientnes*), to captain boats travelling between islands and to fish using canoes on the high seas or with spear guns. Women, on the other hand, are more often the ones who do things rather than talk: they garden (planting, weeding, most harvesting), cut firewood, cook, sew, do laundry, weave, and care for children.

This summary does give a somewhat distorted picture. There are many tasks that either sex can do, such as clearing gardens, childminding (more often it is done, however, by women and children), climbing coconut trees, feeding pigs and sweeping around houses. It is my impression, however, that women do a much greater share of the manual labour, and are more restricted in their movements by the responsibilities of nurturance and children.

The ideal female is one who is a hard worker, for through her work her husband has access to sources of shell money (*a le*: that is, by raising pigs to trade or use in feasts). A woman of this calibre can incite jealousy in other males. In one case the mental illness of a woman was explained as the result of sorcery because she had been such a capable woman that her husband had grown in renown through the shell money he had acquired through her labours.

Males and females are also distinguished in ways other than labour. Women are said to gossip more and be more prone to sulk (*mus*; see section on emotion and Chapter 5); they are also the ones to cry at funerals (see Chapter 7). Despite this, women do not appear to be seen as more emotional, or to be less able to control their emotions, than their male companions. The distinction is not seen in terms of quantity of emotion and its control as it often is in the West. Instead, emotional differences between men and women are viewed qualitatively.

Men and women differ in terms of self-presentation. In the later teenage years and throughout their twenties, males try to be quite conspicuous in their dress and decoration. Males in their early teens until a peak sometime in their twenties, carry small baskets that grow in size up to about a metre square, from which time they shrink to a small shoulder or hand-carried basket that remains that size (about A4 size) until their death. Young men put decorative leaves in their hair and frequently smear lime or red colour (*tol*; from ochre or a plant) on their faces. Clothes are dark or drab colours (khaki, black and so on), which serve to heighten the small amounts of colour on their faces or ribbons tied to their baskets. Males thus bedecked are said to be trying to attract females, and much derision is accorded older males who dress likewise.

Young women, on the other hand, dress in bright colours, with little decoration except when going to church on Fridays and Sundays. They carry small baskets or none at all, and in general their appearance is more modest, highlighted by their shyness at passing by groups of young men. Young women normally move around in groups of two to four, with lone women seen to be attempting or organising a rendezvous with a man. Older women are freer to move around by themselves, their virtue somewhat assumed by their position as wives and mothers. However, those older women who are single and walk around by themselves are watched and gossiped about.

Unlike some places in Papua New Guinea (see Clay 1986; Harrison 1985), Lihirian women are not viewed as embodying the more relational aspects of personhood, and men the more individualist tendencies. For the Mandak, men are the initiators and women the nurturers (Clay 1986:25), yet in Lihir it is the duty of both genders to nurture (*ertnin*; *pniari*) children, pigs and visitors, as well as to plant and harvest: individual and relational aspects of personhood are not separated by gender.

## *Thought and will*

Thought (*nanse*) is located in the brain. The words for remembering (*nanse mle*; literally: 'thought back') and forgetting (*nanse baliye*; literally: 'thought lost') share the base root of 'thought'. However, apart from these two forms *nanse* is not a commonly used term on Mahur: people do not express opinions by saying 'I think that you should …' or 'I think it is best that you …'. Instead, they simply say 'You should …' or 'It is best that you …'. Rather than offering opinions or advice, Lihirians issue directives to one another that do not really allow the right of refusal. It was rare under such direct ordering that Lihirians did refuse one another. I found it difficult to do so, and had to make excuses when people said to me, for example, 'When you leave that camera is mine.' This is an instance of one person's desire (*le*) directing the actions of another.

Will or desire (*le*), in contrast to thought (*nanse*), is a very commonly used concept. *Le* covers the ideas of will, desire, and to like or want, and is the base of the term *leimulien* (love, desire) that I discuss in Chapter 4. *Le* is similar in meaning to *mukat* (sexual desire, lust) and *ermden* (to want/covet what belongs rightfully to another), though these forms of desire are often seen as destructive and also overpowering in the case of *mukat* (inability to resist). In addition, there is the idea that sometimes the will of others can lead a person astray. One man said to me '*Die sa i num yo*', literally translating as 'they drank me' but meaning 'they made me drink' (alcohol). Phrased in this form, there is no sense that the man could resist his fellows and choose not to drink.[6] The concept of will, then, relates both to individual desire and will, as well as the ability to influence the actions of others.

[6] This is one of the factors contributing to the high levels of binge alcohol drinking occurring in Lihir since the advent of the gold mine. Men finish work, and rather than go home to their families they stay on the main island and drink as a group (in the case of workers from Mahur). People on Mahur said that only one wanted to drink, and they were all keeping him company, or that they had been 'forced' to drink (generally by people simply offering them a drink or suggesting that they should).

## *Emotion*

In Lihir there is no overall term to mean 'emotion' and there is no singular way of referring to emotion. Instead there are a number of linguistic forms of expressing what we call emotion. The first refers to a person's 'inside' in general (*a ling sa* ...; 'my inside is ...')[7] rather than specifying any particular organ or area in the body (for example, heart, liver or intestines). This is echoed in other Austronesian languages and in particular in Tok Pisin, where '*bel*' similarly refers to general internal organs and is the site of many emotional states. Many emotions are characterised in this way: anger '*a ling sa tua*' (literally: my inside is hard or energised), sadness or worry '*a ling sa wir*' (literally: my inside is turning/churning), or happiness '*a ling sa ngat*' (see Table 3.1 for a list of emotion-related expressions).

Kidd, writing on the Enxet of Paraguay, describes a similar way of expressing emotion:

> affects are often expressed by reference to physical states of the *wáxok* ['physical and metaphysical organ of the body in the region of the stomach' (Kidd 2000:115)] such as: the *wáxok* spreads out' and 'the *wáxok* is sweet', which suggest happiness and contentment; ... 'the *wáxok* shivers', which is one way to describe fear. (ibid.)

However, thought is also expressed through the idiom of the *wáxok*, and in this context agency is ascribed to the *wáxok*, such as 'the *wáxok* says' or 'the *wáxok* despises'. The *wáxok* is also viewed in a developmental way, and people are expected to develop a good or beautiful *wáxok* (Kidd 2000:115–6). In this, the concept of *wáxok* is very different from that of the *ling*, which is not associated with cognition nor viewed in a developmental sense at all.

The second way of expressing emotions in Lihir is in the form *Yo sa* ... ('I am ...'), such as *Yo sa mus* 'I am sulking'. Most emotions can be expressed in both forms, such as happiness, which can be said as *a ling sa ngat* or *Yo*

---

[7] This term *ling* 'my inside' or *lien* 'his/her inside' is related to the general term for inside '*lia*', for example, *lia liom* 'inside the house' or *lia pulo* 'inside the forest'.

| | *a ling sa ...* | my inside is ... | *Yo sa ...* | I am ... |
|---|---|---|---|---|
| Contented,<br>Calm | *puet*<br>*malum*<br>*prar* | good<br>cool<br>clear | *puet* | good, well |
| Happiness | *ngat*<br>*gas* | happy<br>happy | *gas*<br>*ngat*<br>*non*<br>*eretek* | happy<br>happy<br>laughing<br>joking |
| Love | *ktetan* | | *lemuli*<br>*ba*<br>*mdenie*<br>*tnanie* | loving (you)<br>in love<br>coveting<br>(someone/thing)<br>caring, nurturing |
| Fear | *kum*<br>*nder* | trembling | *ẓkol* | fearful/shy |
| | *ẓket* | bad | *ẓket* | bad |
| Worry,<br>Sadness | *tenden*<br>*wirwir* | crying<br>churning | *tenden*<br>*tandanis*<br>*madanis* | crying<br>regretful<br>compassionate |
| Shame | | | *mdo* | ashamed |
| Surprise<br>Startle | | | *rbet* | startled |
| Anger | *tua*<br>*soso*<br>*dodo* | hard<br>hot<br>hot | *mus*<br>*kaserpit*<br>*ẓmuarie* | sulking<br>crying/angry<br>arguing/<br>haranguing |
| Metaphors | | | | |
| Fear | *a yateng sa niong.*<br>*a kakeng sa ndender.* | my liver is in my throat.<br>my legs are trembling. | | |
| Sentiments | | | | |
| | *akne*<br>*nornor*<br>*sio* | praise<br>trust/belief<br>respect | | |

**Table 3.1: List of emotion and related expressions.**

*sa ngat*. Only shame (*Yo sa mdo*) and surprise/startlement (*Yo sa rbet*) can be expressed solely in the form *Yo sa ...* . While I asked informants the difference between the forms *a ling sa ...* and *Yo sa ...*, I was unable to receive any answer. Often people said that the various forms were the same, thus *a ling sa ngat* and *Yo sa ngat* were the same thing.

The form *a ling sa ...* is almost exclusively used to express emotional states, except in the case *a ling sa buerbuer* 'I feel nauseous'. In this case, informants somewhat reluctantly agreed that this could be due to being very scared or upset. However, the form *Yo sa* … is commonly used for states of hunger and thirst (*Yo sa itol, Yo sa malo* respectively) and for various actions (for example, *Yo sa tutun rais* 'I am cooking rice'; *Yo sa zieng to anio* 'I am going to the bush'), as well as for expressing what may be termed emotion.

In his book on the Rauto of southwest New Britain, Papua New Guinea (1994), Maschio describes two different ways of referring to emotions: via idioms implicating the heart (*momso*) or the skin (*tandra*). Maschio explains:

> Idioms that refer to the heart are metaphors for the inner being and for the strength of persons. In a way they convey a sense of people as individuals who posses varying degrees of power, capability and sentience. These idioms stress the differences between and the separateness of persons. Another type of idiom stresses the way in which the person is influenced or affected by the actions of others. This altogether different emphasis is conveyed by idioms that refer to the skin (*tandra*). (1994:53)

Idioms of the heart are used for emotions such as sorrow, anger and love, while fear, shame and contentment (feeling threatened, embarrassed or at ease) are referred to via the skin.

While Maschio argues this case convincingly for the organisation of emotion among the Rauto, the situation in Lihir is not so easily resolved. Particular emotions cannot be categorised into two forms, even if we take 'heart' as an analogue of 'insides', with, for example, sorrow and anger expressed via the 'heart' idiom, and shame and fear on the 'skin'. In Lihir, as said above, most emotions are described either by referring to one's 'inside' (*a ling sa* …) or making a general statement of being (*Yo sa* … 'I am …'). There is not a dichotomy of emotions based on whether they implicate social relationships or assert features of the individual.

I received a number of clues as to the nature of these different forms of expressing emotion in Lihir. Lolot once said to me that first a person feels anger in their inside (*a lien sa tua*), then s/he sulks (*ye sa mus*), and later will exchange angry words with the implicated person, or argue (*Die sa erzmuer*). In her account, the various forms of expressing emotions appear sequentially.

The second clue came when I returned to the field in June 1999. Kupulie and I were discussing emotions, and how they are expressed and felt. Only some had an impact on the body: worry (*a ling sa wir*) made the head painful and the skin feel tired; anger was felt in the stomach being hot (*a ling sa tua*); fear was felt in the stomach like a heavy stone, or the stomach or sides of the abdomen could hurt—this was fear in the form *a ling sa kum* (my inside is gripped). I found confirmation of this relationship between the body and emotion from an incident in June 1999. A fellow researcher was climbing on a wet and slippery rock and was perched somewhat precariously over a long drop. I was terrified she would slip to her death, and unthinkingly drew in my breath and clutched my stomach. My other companions, two young Mahurian women, understood that I was afraid: the relationship between my fear and clutching my stomach was meaningful for them.

Together these clues indicate that at least sometimes people in Lihir construe emotions as developing sequentially, and that what is felt in the body may then transform or lead to a state of being. If, as an example, I take the case of the missing boat described in the Prologue, once the boat was believed missing, first Kwildun was worried (*a lien sa wir*) and later she felt regret for not spending much time saying goodbye to them (*ye sa tandanis*) and she also cried (*ye sa tenden*). Others in the village were also worried (*a lien sa wir*), had compassion for them (*die sa madanis*), and expressed the desire that God would care (*sa ertnin*) for them, particularly to send coconuts towards the boat for the youngest boy to drink.

The example of emotions associated with the missing boat shows that in addition to these two forms (*a ling sa* … and *Yo sa* …) of expressing emotions, there are a number of actions associated with particular emotions. If someone is angry (*a ling sa tua*) and sulks (*sa mus*), that person can go on to act in a number of ways such as arguing (*erzmuer*) or fighting (*ersas*).[8] With happiness,

[8] The linguistic form *er-* denotes action involving more than one person.

the associated action may be laughter (*sa non*). If sad (*a lien sa wir*), a person may cry (*sa tenden*).

Regardless of whether an emotion is embodied or not, observers are able to attribute and comment on the emotional states of others. Thus, people will comment on the emotional states of infants, saying they are shy (*sa zkol*), laughing (*sa non*) or angry (*a lien sa tua*). While people will not comment on the emotional states of adults within their hearing (generally), they did comment on my emotional states in my hearing: they would say 'she's laughing' (*sa non*) or 'she's shy' (*sa zkol*). Unlike the discussion on the ways that Melanesians often see minds as opaque (Keane 2008; Robbins 2008; Schieffelin 2008; and see also Fajans 1997 and Iteanu 1990), there was a fairly high level of speculation in Lihir of other people's motivations and emotions. However, Lihirians did not value introspection in the way that Westerners do with their industries of psychiatry and psychology. There was nothing explicit about emotion work—controlling emotions, working through emotions and so on. While I could elicit some information on this subject when I asked, there was certainly a lack of interest and engagement with processes of introspection.

### *Personality*

While they have no term for personality, in addition to ideas of transient emotional states Lihirians do have a notion of enduring and distinguishing characteristics of persons. In contrast, Fajans reports that for the Baining of New Britain,

> most personal descriptions reflect judgements not on the 'personality' of the subject, but on his or her social, relational, and productive characteristics. (Fajans 1997:114)

Lihirians also comment of the social, relational or productive characteristics of persons, but see these as inherent to the person and as enduring. Hence, I would suggest that these are personality characterisations. Lihirians will characterise other people as being a hard worker (*ai pniez*), an angry person (*a wein/tomat wan a lil tua*), a person who is lazy (*pkapuez*) or greedy (*a*

| Lihir Personality Term | Translation | English Equivalent |
|---|---|---|
| *zikzin potpot* | person who gives | generous |
| *zikzin gasgas* | happy person | |
| *zikzin ngatngat* | happy person | |
| *zikzin puet* | good person | |
| *ai pniez* | a worker | hardworking |
| *zikzin sa wengweng tun* | person who talks true | honest |
| *ai tunu* | | knowledgeable |
| *ai erzmuer* | an angry person | short-tempered |
| *wein/tomat wan a lil tua* | woman/man of anger | short-tempered |
| *wein/tomat wan a mus* | person who sulks | sulky, bad-tempered |
| *a sialien* | | hypocrite, all talk and no action |
| *ai krim* | a liar | dishonest |
| *a ba* | silly, stupid | |
| *ai nglo* | mentally ill, silly, stupid | |
| *a pro* | | selfish |
| *yienkeh* | | greedy |
| *tbusor* | doesn't help others in work | selfish, ungenerous |
| *pkapuiz* | lazy | |
| *ai pniel* | person who steals | thief |
| *mdengniat* | show-off, attract other's attention | |
| *zngar* | female show-off | |
| *kasi lolon* | doesn't listen | arrogant, badly behaved |

**Table 3.2: Partial list of trait characterisations in Lihir.**

*yienkeh*—particularly about food, that is, not sharing), and so on (see Table 3.2 for a partial listing of personality characterisations). The two most common characterisations of people is as *mdengniat* or *zngar* ('show off'; T.P. *hambak*) or as a person who *kasi lolon* (literally: doesn't listen: 'badly behaved,' 'arrogant'; T.P. *bikhet*). The first two terms describe people who do things to attract others' attention, particularly the attention of the opposite sex: these people dress and act to attract attention (show off). Most men in their early twenties can be considered to be *mdengniat*, but this is quite normal. Small children who show off are also considered *mdengniat*. Females who display this behaviour are more often termed *zngar*, though *mdengniat* may also be applied to them. There was one man living in my hamlet who was in his late fifties. His wife was dead, and his many children were scattered, living all over Lihir with various relatives. He did no work in the garden, and dressed like a young man, in bright clothes, with a large basket, his hair bleached and decorations on his face. People called him *mdengniat* and said he was aiming to attract young girls' attentions. He was often the focus of derision and the butt of jokes while not present, but was still fed and generally treated kindly.

The other very common characterisation of people was that they *kasi lolon* (literally: 'don't listen') or, in the commonly applied Tok Pisin word, are *bikhet*.[9] This was most commonly applied to children of both sexes, who did not do what they were told. However, people would refer to themselves as *bikhet* in church if they felt they were not following Christian teachings properly, and women could be characterised as *bikhet* if they did not care for their husband properly or follow his instructions. The characterisation '*bikhet*' occurs in situations of a power differential, where one party is seen to know better or be able to direct the other, who then ignores advice or orders.

Both of these two characterisations, *mdengniat/zngar* and *kasi lolon*, are applied to people who act in ways that is individuating: as attracting attention primarily through the physical body or as flouting the expectations or orders of those (generally) in a superior position. That these are recognised behavioural types implies an awareness of individualism, while their sanction expresses preference for a more relational mode of behaviour. The existence of behaviours such as these and the criticism of them is thus an expression of the tension in Lihir between ideals of relational conduct and the everyday practice of individuality.

When I asked why people had certain characteristics, I received one of two answers: that the behaviour was learned or that the person I had asked did not know. When I noted to Kupulie that my neighbour Soklas was an incredibly hard worker, she agreed, and added that he was never angry with other people. I asked why, and her explanation was that Soklas and his older sister Martha were adopted by Kupulie's mother when they had just been weaned. While their mother, Woklik, was a woman known to sulk (*a wein wan a mus*), Kupulie and Woklik's mother was much more even-tempered.

[9] The Tok Pisin term '*bikhet*' was used even while speaking Lihirian, and by people who spoke very little Tok Pisin.

This, Kupulie stated, explained the similarity in temperament of Martha and Soklas, and the difference between them and their two sisters, Niezkuenkuen and Aniodun, who both sulked like their mother.

In another situation, two brothers were not considered very good people: one drank all the time and the other excessively beat his long-suffering wife. A number of people said they did not know why these two men were like that. People said that their parents were 'good' people. Thus, personality characteristics are either attributed to learned behaviour from primary caregivers or are seen as being incomprehensible. Some of those characteristics that are viewed as incomprehensible are said to have been present since birth, which indicates the possibility of a belief in innateness of dispositions, though not necessarily their inheritance, in certain cases.

### *Mental illness*

Mental illness (*nglo*) is quite common on Mahur, and there are a number of types subsumed under the term *nglo*. In Kuelam village there was a group of women who would have episodes of what is considered to be strange behaviour: stealing others' garden produce, being violent, saying or doing things that made no sense, or lying. While these individually are not seen as indicators of a state of *nglo*, taken together and lasting for a period of time they do constitute *nglo*. Two of these women were sisters, and the other was their father's sister. While the illness of the father's sister was often explained by sorcery motivated by jealousy, the mental illness of the sisters was explained as being in the family (which included the father's sister): '*samting bilong dispela famili*' 'its something of this family' or '*dispela famili i olsem tasol*' 'this family is just like that' (T.P.). Sometimes this explanation also suggested that the women in the whole family had been ensorcelled. Alternatively, it was explained by a few as being due to the level of education the two oldest sisters attained. Both had gone to Year 10 and one had gone to teachers college, and then had been struck with *nglo*. It was not explained exactly what about education had made them *nglo*, but it seemed that the strain of being away from home for long periods of time and the advanced learning of teacher's college were viewed as the causative factors. The third sister in the family stopped her education at the end of Year 9 expressively in fear of being effected in the same way as her elder sisters.

Another case that was also classified as *nglo* was that of a teenage boy who had palsy on one side of his body, and was unable to speak or comprehend speech. People said that he was fine until about one year of age when his mother went to the place of a *tndol* (spirit, T.P. *masalai*; in this case Yisyis) and left him unguarded on the beach while she went fishing. The *tndol* caused him to be *nglo*. People said that he did not have thought (*nanse*) nor most emotions (such as anger, love or sulking), however he could recognise his family and was happy (*sa ngat*) when they would arrive from the gardens.

The term *nglo* is also used to tell someone they are silly or stupid (often in a well-meaning but exasperated way). Thus if someone forgets their bush knife when going to the gardens to clear the bush, a person will comment '*wa nglo*' (You are silly/stupid).

People with mental illness are treated quite well in Lihir. They remain in the community and do what work they are able to. One of the three sisters mentioned above has married and had two children, though she is still commonly prone to episodes of *nglo* behaviour. In the case of such episodes, people gently humour her but also laugh at some of her comments.

In other contexts, most behaviours classified as *nglo* are simply seen as bad behaviour or bad personality characteristics (if more than transient behavioural occurrences). Often these behaviours could be classified as going against relationality: behaviours such as stealing, lying, violence, and staying inside a men's house are all instances of asocial behaviour, that is, behaviour that ignores the ties and relationships between people. When a person continually exhibits such behaviours they are classified as *nglo*, a large part of this classification implying that the person appears to be outside of the realm of sociality (for a similar analysis of madness among the Kakoli of the Papua New Guinea Highlands, see Goddard 2011).

### *Leadership*

During the 1970s Ambrose Kiapseni of Masahet island, who was later to become Bishop of New Ireland Province, wrote a detailed treatise on leadership in Lihir as part of his seminary training, both in 'traditional' society and within the church. His writings are revealing for what they say about Lihirian understandings of personality or character, willpower and the rights and responsibilities of individuals.

Kiapseni is scathing of the colonial administration's appointment of Luluais and their successors in the independent Papua New Guinea, the councillors. These people, he argues, have no skills or appropriate personality, and are 'ego centric' (Kiapseni 1976 Part B:5): 'They got involved in matters only if the result would enhance their name and position' (ibid.).

Kiapseni clearly describes the qualities required of a good leader or big man. He must have shell money and pigs; he must be a man of principle, be wise, admired, ruthless with enemies and stern with black sheep; and he must prove his strength, wealth, power, kindness and so on. The big man will 'create the general atmosphere be it that of fear or joy' in the community (Kiapseni 1976 Part A:5).

In choosing appropriate church leaders or catechists, Kiapseni argues that they must be much more like the big man than the Luluai or councillor.[10] They must be someone

> who is a man of strong character … who does not allow others to push him around. One whom the community trusts and recognises as a possible leader with a will that does not easily bend. (Kiapseni 1976 Part C:14)

[10] Luluais and Tultuls were leaders appointed by the German and later Australian administrations, and acted as links between their village and the government administrators.

Note here that valued leadership qualities are those that in other people may be considered *bikhet* or potentially selfish. However, they are acceptable in a leader because they team with other qualities such as kindness and wisdom.

Kiapseni goes on to describe from where such qualities arise: 'People are either born leaders or they are not' (1976 Part C:14). Here again we have a clearly documented instance of a Lihirian arguing that certain qualities are inherent in the person from birth. People can be trained to have knowledge of certain ritual practices, magic or even Christian teachings, but the essentials of leadership cannot be taught or learned. This is reiterated by Bainton (2008a:200), who argues that the 'qualities of traditional big men are not inherent to all Lihirian males'.[11]

### *Personhood in Lihir and* piot

There are both individual and relational aspects to persons in Lihir, both in the physical body, where relations may be seen on the skin but where people mark themselves as unique beings, and in the metaphysical aspects of the person, such as in the case of the will of persons do to what they wish and their ability to direct the actions of others.

What are the implications of the nature of personhood in Lihir for an understanding of *piot*? There are a number of factors that stand out. One of the most crucial is that *piot* is not an emotion: it is not expressed linguistically as emotions are. People do not express it in the forms '*a ling sa* …' or '*Yo sa* …'. Instead, *piot* is expressed in a similar way to illness. People will say '*a piot e se yo*' (literally: *piot* attacked me) in the same way they say '*a mniat e se yo*' (literally: an illness attacked me). *Piot* is thus something that comes from outside the person, in the same way that illness does.

Second, *piot* encompasses both individual aspects of the person as well as relational aspects. There is something about the nature of the person in Lihir that allows someone to have an affect on others via the medium of space.

[11] He analyses the shifts in leadership that have occurred with modernity that I explore in Chapter 7.

People leave a trace in places when they go, and bring something to a place when they arrive: this something is like a heaviness that is felt in the bodies of those others present. Thus, the movement of people in space implicates others. However, despite their impacts on others, and people's complaints about these impacts, people still choose to move between places, indicating individualist aspects of the person. To understand *piot* further it is necessary to analyse these movements in space.

## Place and mobility

One feature of Lihirian life surprised me more than any other when I began my fieldwork: the incredible amount of personal mobility. Having read so many ethnographies of Papua New Guinea that portray the population as stable or static, I had not expected the continual flux of people to and from households and hamlets. Given the concept of *piot*, which makes movements somewhat debilitating to others, I found such mobility even more perplexing.

The literature on population movement in Papua New Guinea was not illuminating of most of the mobility that occurs in Lihir. Studies based on census data only deal with migration across district or provincial boundaries that occurs between censuses. Thus if someone moves and then returns, this is not recorded. Nor is the complexity of movement captured: if people move between a number of places, only the start point and the end point will be noted in the census (May & Skeldon 1977; Skeldon 1977).

Much of the literature on internal migration in Papua New Guinea deals with instrumental migration, that is, for labour or economic purposes, or for education, and generally involves movement from rural to urban areas or across provincial boundaries (Dundon 2005; Koczberski et al. 2009; Skeldon 1977; Young 1977). This has some relevance to Lihir, as with the advent of the gold mine there has been migration to Lihir in an attempt to gain work. In addition, some Lihirians work a 'two week on, one week off roster', which means they move to the mining camp for two weeks and then return to their home village for a week's rest. However, this accounts for only some of the mobility of people in Lihir.

Other studies deal with the factor of circulation in migration: the return of those who move away (Chapman 1979; Ross 1984) or of rural-urban drift (Baxter 1977; Ross 1984). The basic assumption of this literature is that mobility occurs for economic reasons, and that circulation (return mobility) is based upon the security of home.[12] Very little in this material helps illuminate the nature of population mobility in Lihir (but see Curry and Koczberski 1998 for the unpredictable nature of Wosera—West New Britain migration). One of the key authors of this literature states:

> Metaphors such as 'rural-urban drift' and 'circulation,' or technical terms like 'emigration' and 'depopulation' that evoke powerful images, do not ipso facto convey the contemporary ebb and flow of Pacific Island movement, nor its inherently volatile and ambiguous character. (Chapman 1991:265)

It was this floating nature of people, the ebb and flow of mobility at the local level, that caught my attention in Lihir, and required a nuanced understanding of household membership. People in Lihir move for a number of reasons. Children move to gain an education above primary school level. People move to get medical care for illnesses that are too serious to be dealt with in the context of a local aidpost. In addition, most babies are born either at the Londolovit hospital or Palie mission hospital, both on the main island of Lihir. As noted, some people do move to go to work, their moves regulated by the shifts and work cycles of the mine. Catechists, church leaders, local government representatives and others on Mahur regularly go to meetings on the main island. People move for *kastam wok*, the various feasts that occur between July and November when the gardens have been harvested, either to buy pigs from other islands for such feasts or to participate in the actual feasting and dance performances. Women move when they feel their husbands

[12] But see Chapman (1979:111), who mentions movements for meetings, *kastam wok*, exchange, marriage, education and so on.

have unfairly treated or beaten them: they go home to their mother for a while. People move to escape other forms of conflict such as arguments with fellow household members (see Chapter 5). Finally, people move just to visit friends and relatives, or because they are bored or need a break from work in their own gardens. In summary, people in Lihir need very little reason to move, it is just part of life.

In recent years, such mobility has become increasingly simplified by the proliferation of motorised 'banana' boats and, on Niolam, by cars. With the advent of the gold mine, more people have had the money to buy such boats, and they are in ready supply on the main island of the group (rather than having to travel to the New Ireland mainland to purchase them as they did in the past). Boats are owned by individuals, clans or by the community as a whole on Mahur, and each boat is named, decorated often by flags, and is known by all. During my time on Mahur there were seven or eight boats just for Kuelam village, having increased from just one boat and five motorised canoes for the whole of Mahur in 1985 (Filer & Jackson 1986). The 23-foot boats take up to 14 people plus goods, while the 19-foot boats take a few less people. Boats were available for hire for about K70 (approximately US$35 in 1998) for travel to the main island of Lihir. Once the boat has been hired, other people can ask to jump aboard for free. In addition, there is a 'contract' boat, contracted by the mining company to travel each day between Kuelam village and the main island to carry workers to the mine. Most days there is a maximum of two to three workers, and the rest of the boat can be filled with whomever wishes to travel. While it can take some negotiation, travel has become an option available to all.

Mobility was important before the advent of motorised banana boats. Before the 1960s, large canoes (*takop*) were paddled between the islands groups of Tabar, Tanga and the New Ireland mainland for trading of pigs and shell money. Later, boat engines were added to these *takop* to make the trip easier and quicker. Such motorised canoes were still being used in 1986, when one from Mahur ran out of petrol on the way back from Tabar and drifted all the way to Tench Island.

There is very little restraint on most people's movements in Lihir, except perhaps for young or newly married women. People make individual choices to move, and are not generally hindered in such movements. While I was in Lihir, even young children could make the choice to board a boat and go to visit their relatives, as three young boys did one day arriving from Samo village (on south-west Niolam) to visit their *mama* (MZ) and her children in Kuelam village. My neighbour Zilio, aged about 20 and unmarried, was able to visit Malie Island whenever she wanted to help in her cross-cousin's garden or simply visit people there. Mobility is one of the major areas where Lihirians exercised a great deal of autonomy.

## *Piot* and place

*Piot* is predicated on the autonomy of people, but at the same time subverts it. While people are free to move, and do so often, such movements have impacts on others who then complain via the medium of *piot*. *Piot* is a legitimate reason for complaint. I realised this when I had my neighbour, Martha, sleep on my verandah one night, then somewhere else another night, then back on my verandah again, and so on. I was finding it stressful as she would have visitors until all hours of the night talking. I needed to sleep at night so I could work during the day, but this reasoning made little sense to Lihirians who will sleep during the day if they wish, and stay up much of the night. One night I confronted her and explained that she was causing me to suffer *piot* each day as she came and went, and thus I was unable to work. The next day I was *mus* (sulking, not speaking to her) and my other neighbours supported my stand against Martha on the basis of *piot*. My complaint was culturally meaningful, and Martha stopped sleeping on my verandah.

In the case of mourning (*mbie*) for the death of a person (see Chapter 7), the creation of *piot* is seen as a serious infraction. For *mbie*, various people sleep close to the site of burial for a number of weeks. Should one of those persons leave before the final feast is given (*mbiektip*) then that person is liable to a fine of a pig for creating *piot* to afflict the other mourners. One man explained that they use *piot* as a medium to complain about a person's lack of respect for the custom of mourning (*mbie*) and for the dead person.

Kuehling argues that *gwasa* is a legitimate cause for complaint on Dobu:

> To my understanding, *gwasa* is a way of reinforcing the ethic of *miabaula* (the injunction to stay at home and mind one's own business); it is an embodied sanction because it discourages people from staying away overnight without good reason, as they are scolded about *gwasa* when they return home. (Kuehling 1998:64)

Like *gwasa*, *piot* suggests an ideal of sociality that is fixed, for if no one leaves then *piot* is never experienced by those who are left behind or by those to whom the person goes. Yet if this were the extent of the explanation of *piot*, it would make more sense that the person who was moving should experience the *piot*: then they would be more likely to remain stationary. As it stands, the person who moves feels no sanction other than the disapproval of those people inflicted with *piot*. *Piot* is made real through the experience of others.

The final key to an understanding of *piot* lies in the relationship between people and place, and the role *piot* plays in that relationship. There are a number of factors that suggest that *piot* is crucially tied to notions of place. The first and most simple is that *piot* arises due to movements between places. When Ngalparok was describing the nature of *piot* he said 'when you come from another place, you bring heaviness' (T.P. '*sapos yu kam long narapela ples, yu kam wantaim hevi*'). The second factor is that both ways of avoiding *piot* are predicated on sending the *piot* away to another place: either by sending it via bespelled ashes along the road in search of its creator or via a bucket of water that makes the *piot* not wish to stay around. *Piot* is conceptualised as leaving, rather than, for example, as losing its potency or turning into something else.

In Chapters 1 and 2 I discussed various ties that Lihirians have to places, such as through the lineage and clan, through their nurturance of gardens, through hamlet areas, and through origin stories. The Lihirian world, like most places in Papua New Guinea, is composed of named and meaningful places, some of which are sites for *a tndol* (*masalai*) while others are sites connected to the memory and history of particular events, as well as social and emotional relationships (cf. Kahn 1996; Neumann 1992). Places can be considered dangerous, not simply as abodes of *a tndol* but in themselves. This became clear after I went to Tgietgien. This was the site where a men's house had stood in the past, and it was being reclaimed for that purpose and as a garden. The area was fenced off to exclude pigs, and I went inside to plant a mango tree with my companion Weinrau. Later that day when I had returned to the beach, Ngalparok chastised me, saying it was okay to look over the fence but why had I gone inside? He put bespelled lime on my joints to prevent any illnesses or injuries arising from my visit to that place.

The importance of place for Lihirians can also be seen in that they have a concept of homesickness called '*mniat en a anio*' (literally: illness for place). They also say people can have a sadness and wish for a place, '*a ling sa wir*'. Such terms are not homesickness due to missing particular people but to missing the place itself. Thus people said that when I left I would feel that '*a ling sa wirwir ne Mahur*' (literally: my inside churns for Mahur; see Chapter 7 for more on '*a ling sa wir*').

*Piot* is crucially tied to place in that people do not directly inflict *piot* on others, but it must be mediated by place. If everyone leaves an area, no one feels *piot*: the *piot* is not inflicted on people who then carry it with them but rather the *piot* is tied to that particular place. People leave echoes or traces in space, which only those people remaining in that place then experience.

Seen in this way, *piot* is only one (very particular) instance of people's impact upon place. People leave traces in the form of memory that others recall once they return there. Even more powerful than this are the impacts on places such as Tgietgien described above. There are a number of sites scattered across the plateau on Mahur that are said to be where a men's house had stood in the past, and where people displayed *mormor* (like *malangan*) in the past.

These places retain the traces of these events and people that were there, and remain dangerous to visitors.

## Conclusion

I began this chapter by using the concept of *piot* as a window into Lihirian notions of personhood, and in doing so I have reflected back to illuminate the nature of *piot* itself. *Piot* is a trace, an aspect of the person in Lihir that is mediated by place in its impacts on others. *Piot* is made real only through the experience of its embodiment by others. Through the experience of *piot*, people comment on the autonomy of mobility of other people in Lihir, and yet do little to curb such autonomy. In this way, the tension between the ideal of relational behaviour and the individuality that Lihirians practice is expressed in the context of *piot*.

Were Lihirian personhood just relational, if Lihirian persons were the objectification of their relations and acted only in terms of others, then Lihirians would never be so mobile in the face of the complaints and discomfort of their fellows. In being mobile, Lihirians create and maintain some relations at the expense of others. It appears to me that rather than simply a composite of relations with not even an empty space at the centre, the Lihirian person is composed of relations yet is recognised for its distinctiveness, is an active agent, and while not valued, egocentric or selfish behaviour is conceivable and recognised. *Piot* is predicated on the aspects of agency and individuality of the person in Lihir. At the same time, *piot* highlights an ideal of sociality that is fixed, both the relationships between people and people in space. Lihirians continue to exercise their autonomy of mobility, and others continue to experience *piot* and complain about it, the two aspects of personhood in Lihir endlessly in tension and negotiation.

# MAPS AND FIGURES

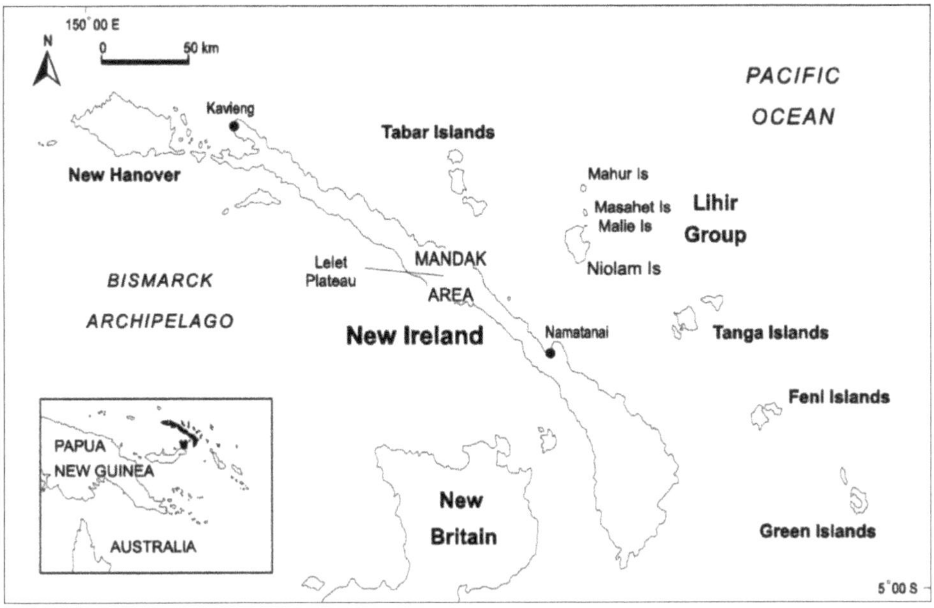


**Map 1: Map of Papua New Guinea and New Ireland Province.**

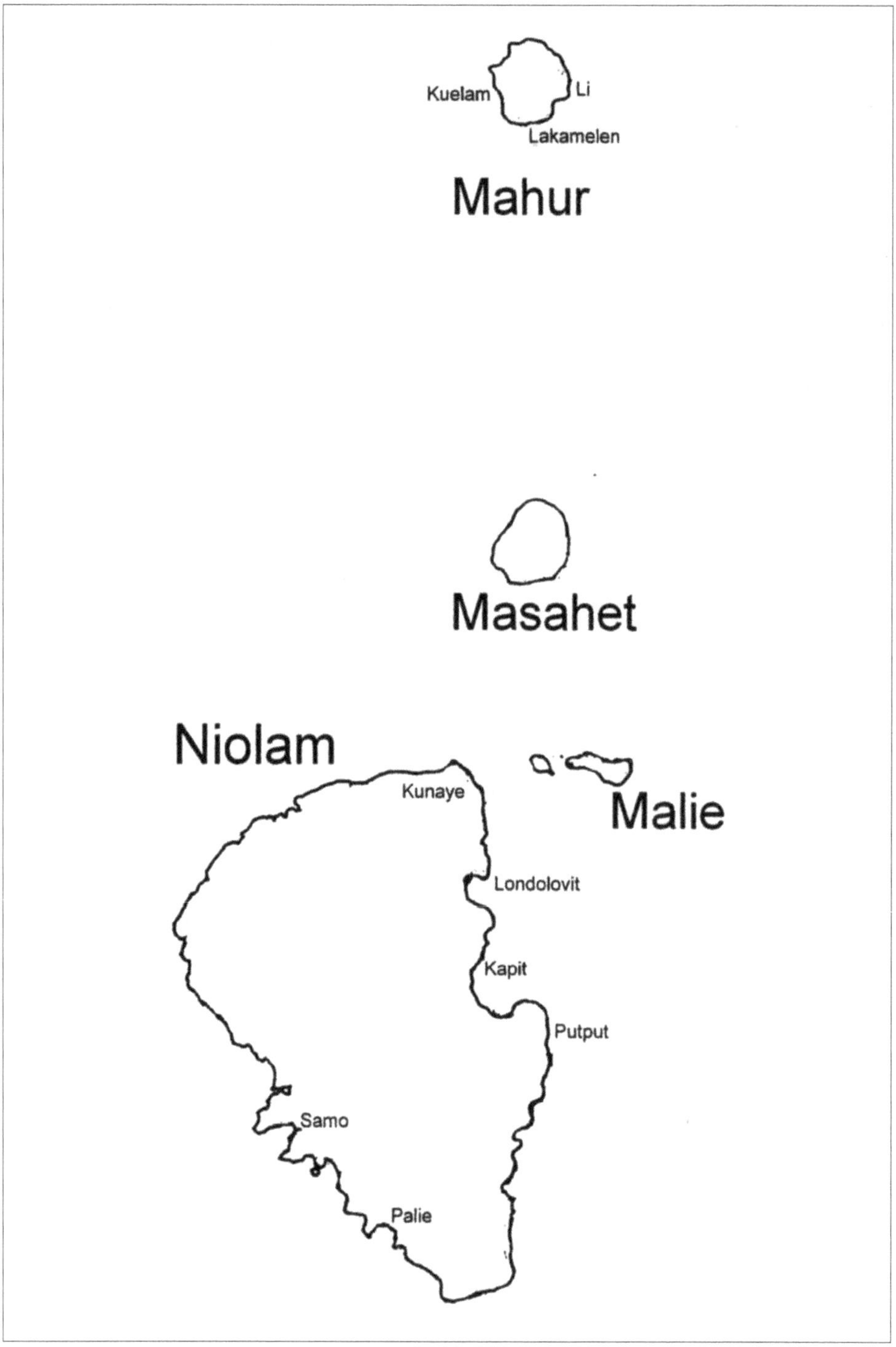


**Map 2: The Lihir Islands, New Ireland Province.**

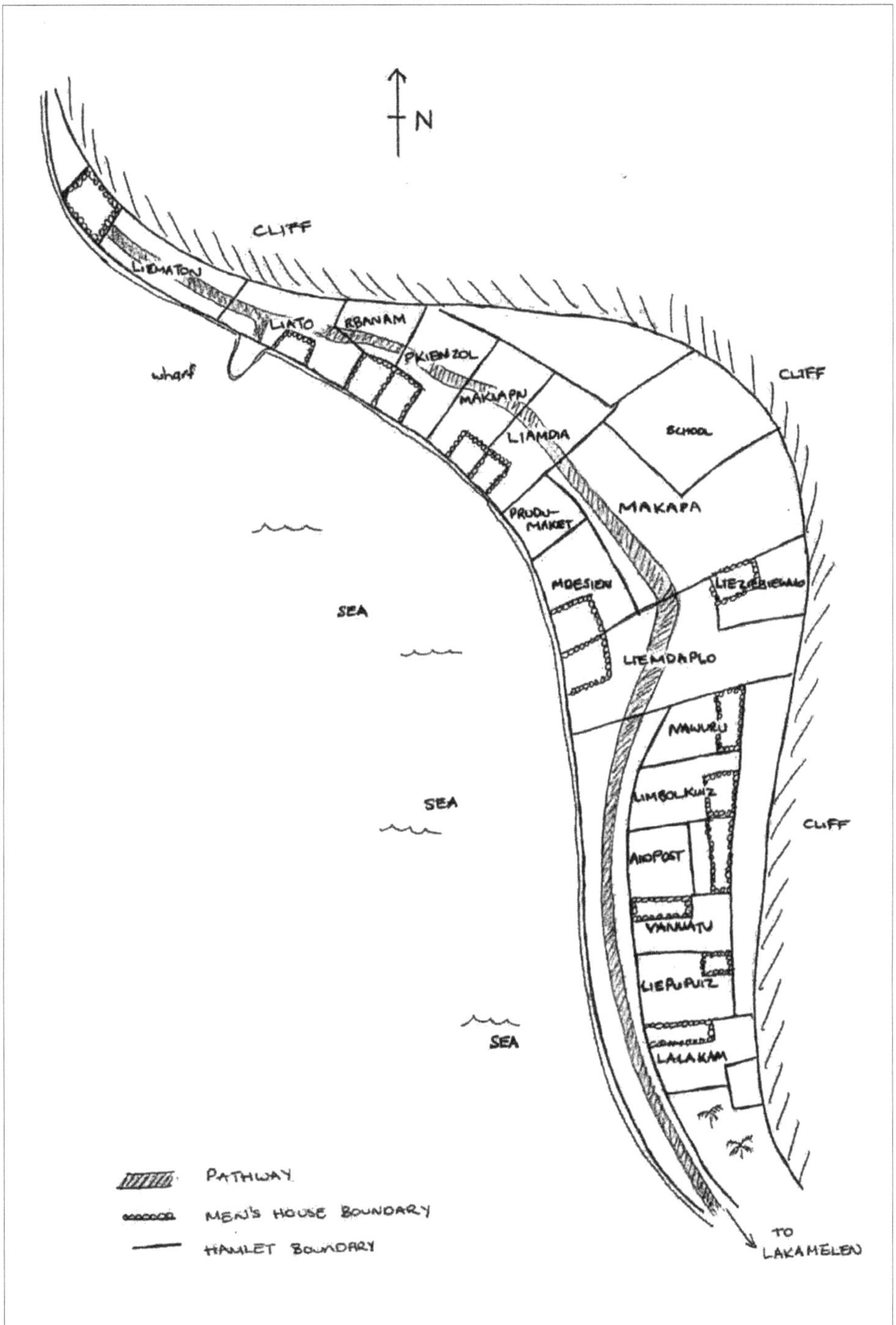


**Map 3: Kuelam Village, Mahur Island.**

**Figure 1: Aerial view of Masahet (foreground) and Mahur Islands.**

**Figure 2: View from Niolam of Masahet (left) and Malie (right).**

**Figure 3: The author doing fieldwork in Kuelam village.**

**Figure 4: Lalakam *a rih* (men's house) in 1998. This is a 'family' men's house and so has no 'Y' shaped stile.**

**Figure 5: Linge and Kso clearing a garden atop Mahur. Note the rockiness of the terrain.**

**Figure 6: Toetna practising *yientnes*: digging under a yam to loosen the soil to encourage further growth.**

**Figure 7: A carefully weeded mature yam garden with long poles on Mahur.**

**Figure 8: The large yams produced by intensive gardening.**

**Figure 9: Wengbeh descends one of the difficult and steep paths from the gardens to the beach on Mahur with a basket of tubers suspended from her head.**

**Figure 10: Boats such as these provide an easy source of mobility for most Lihirians. Photo taken of Londolovit boat harbour 1999.**

**Figure 11: Kuelam's new church built in late 1998.**

**Figure 12: Celebrations for Confirmation/*pindik*.**

**Figure 13: One of the altars present in each hamlet with a statue of Mary.**

**Figure 14: Preparation of the *pako* (canoe) for Sion's burial.**

**Figure 15: Painting the *pako*.**

**Figure 16: Sion's burial.**

**Figure 17a: Heating stones atop a *lon* (ground oven).**

Figure 17b: Constructing the *lon*: spreading out the hot stones.

Figure 18: Constructing the *lon*: placing leaf parcel of pork and vegetables on top of the hot stones.

**Figure 19: Food distribution within the *rih* (men's house). Note the Y-shaped stile.**

**Figure 20: Pigs lined up at Malie feast 1999.**

**Figure 21: Lawrence Klamga calling out the person each pig is dedicated to.**

**Figure 22:** ***Zna bol*****: to bring pigs to the feast. Malie Island.**

**Figure 23: Sham fighting between *bukarot* (hosts) and *wasir* (pig donors).**

**Figure 24: *Zna bol* with sham fighting.**

**Figure 25: Making relations visible in the dance. Nalo and Kolie approach their cross-cousin Niez to put lime on him.**

# PART II

# MORAL CONDUCT AND CONFLICT

# 4

# Christianity and the moral universe

In Chapter 3 I argued that there is tension between relational ideals of conduct and the everyday practice of individuality in Lihirian personhood. When Lihirians complain about the mobility of others, they are making a comment on the morality of others' behaviour. Barker notes that Melanesians continue to grapple with 'the tensions between, broadly speaking, communitarian values founded on reciprocal exchange and individualism' (2007:10). This chapter is an exploration of the moral universe of Lihirians, particularly in terms of their commitment to Christianity, and its impact on personhood, emotion and relationships.

Of particular concern for this book is the impact of Christianity on the ideals of moral conduct. Perceptions of moral conduct are appreciations of the appropriateness of relations between persons, and so are commentaries on the exemplary forms of personhood and relationships. Moral conduct is quite often based on ideas of moral *emotional* conduct—the emphasis of certain emotions and sentiments, and the construction of others as immoral. Also crucial here is the impact of Christianity on ideals of moral conduct in relation to gender relations, sexuality and the family.

Lihirians have embraced the relatively recent introduction of Christianity enthusiastically, and do not view it as an alien institution imposed upon them. It is not a simple shift between two types of society (Barker 2007). Their commitment has not been at the expense of the practice of *kastam*, such as mortuary rituals and other feasts. Rather, Christianity is now an integral and integrated part of life in Lihir. This is very different to the situation for the Urapmin of the Highlands as explored by Robbins (2004), where he argues that social change in the form of adoption of new values and ways of life has occurred, leaving much of the 'traditional' system intact but now valued differently. In this chapter I explore how, in their acceptance of Christianity, Lihirians have not passively assumed Christian moral virtues. Instead, specific moral principles have been inflected with Lihirian values and understandings: there has been a transformation of Christian morality rather than a simple overlaying of foreign concepts, and Christianity has become local (Hemer 2011a).

## Catholicism, commitment and *kastam*

On my return to Mahur in June 1999, I found that a new church had been built in Kuelam village (see Figure 11). This had been planned while I lived on Mahur during 1997–98, however the planks and corrugated iron had lain idle, used only as a shelter against the rain during meetings. I was surprised to hear that the church had been built before Christmas 1998, within two months of my departure from Lihir.

Despite few people being in paid employment, each family had contributed two bags of cement for the floor and bricks. Women used baskets to carry coronous[1] from the beach, and money had been pooled to hire a barge to bring gravel to the island. The church was built within a few short weeks during the season for planting gardens. Most of the work was carried out

[1] A gravel-like substance consisting of coral pieces.

during the evenings: people would return from the gardens, wash and then go to work on the church. Each hamlet was rostered to cook on successive nights for those working. Even Anos, an elderly man with one leg, was said to have worked hard pulling nails from old pieces of timber. The retired catechist for Kuelam said to me '*Mipela wok olsem ol Israel*' (T.P. We worked like the Israelites).

The story of this church building captures the commitment of Mahurians to Catholicism. The retired catechist for Kuelam, Poz, commented that when the priest for Lihir, Father Steve Boland, visited Mahur after the church was built he was astonished as he had not realised that they were ready to build. Obviously there was no directive from him to build the church, or to get it built by a certain time. Mahurians themselves made the decision. Nor was this simply the case for Mahur; one of the changes that has accompanied the development of a gold mine in Lihir has been a rush to build new churches in each village, be they United or Catholic, using funds from wage employment, compensation and royalties. There is an element of competition in church building regarding which village has the largest church, the best decorations, the most lavish opening ceremony.

However, the commitment of funds and time to Christianity was not at the expense, or exclusion, of Lihirians' dedication to what is known as *kastam*. The first major ceremony I witnessed on Mahur was that of *pindik*/confirmation, and this was classified as a *karot*, a feast involving pigs and the gathering of many people, and a term reserved in the past for feasts in the mortuary sequence (Ramstad n.d.a:8). On 8 May 1998, a ceremony of confirmation in the Catholic Church was held at Kuelam village on Mahur. All the grade five and some grade six school students were confirmed, with the Bishop of New Ireland Diocese, Ambrose Kiapseni, and the parish priest, Father Steve Boland, present. The confirmation ceremony was merged with the *pindik* (puberty/initiation) ceremonies, indicating the apparent congenial relationship between *lotu* (T.P. religion, worship) and *kastam* in the Catholic areas of Lihir (see Figure 12).

As I said in the Prologue, in the past *pindik* was the context for the teaching of specific skills needed for adulthood. In many respects, *pindik* is spoken of as an 'entity,' personified and present in a specific place. *Pindik* has a spirit, which is awoken or 'stood upright' (*tu*: stand up) for the ceremonies and then put back to sleep or sat down (*kez*: sit). The spirit of *pindik* is considered dangerous, being able to walk the village and harm people.

The ceremony of *pindik*/confirmation was a joint ceremony encompassing both *kastam* and *lotu*. The initiates were decorated, the girls in a grass skirt (*muel*) and decoration over their chests (*sasie*) and the boys with leaves. They were led into the *wel* (boat structure), which was enclosed in a coconut leaf fence (*benben*) directly in front of the church early in the morning on the day of the ceremony. At the other end of the village, men painted in red and black emerged from a men's house, lined up and began to sing and play the music of *pindik*, while walking and dancing from the north end of the village. The walls of the *benben* were then broken to expose the initiates to all those watching, including Bishop Ambrose and Father Steve. The 'door' of the boat was opened and one by one the initiates emerged after Ngalparok placed *knus*[2] on their heads. When this was done the master of ceremonies,[3] Peter Marwan, said:

> *Nau lotu kastam i pinis. Nau yumi go long sait bilong lotu confirmatio.* (T.P. Now customary worship is finished. Now we will do the confirmation worship)

We then all moved into the church and the children received the sacrament of confirmation. There was singing (mostly in Tok Pisin) with music played on *kundu* drums (T.P. hourglass drums) by those who played for *pindik*. Later I wrote:

---

[2] *Knus* is a substance made of crushed plant leaves, lime and water, the mixture varying according to its purpose, which may be to ward off illness or a *tndol* (bush spirits). It is generally dotted onto the head and joints, but in this case was put only on the head.

[3] They use the term 'MC'.

> What struck me later as I listened to the tape [cassette tape of the music] was that the tune for giving sacrament was the same as that when Ngalparok put *knus* [on the children]. And when we sang 'Kam God Spirit Takodor' in the *Haus Lotu* [church], it was the tune they used for breaking [the] *benben*. Thus the *lotu* and *kastam* sides were like interlocked mirror images. (Fieldnote book 9:82)

Christianity thus appeared to be highly integrated into Lihir life, including having a congenial relationship to *kastam*. However, was that all there was to it or was Christianity simply a veneer (cf. Kahn 1983)?

## Christianity in Lihir: skin deep or more than that?

The question I was asked when I first arrived in Lihir was not whether I believed in God, or was religious, but simply what religion I was (T.P. '*yu bilong wanem lotu*').[4] People assumed I followed one religion or another. At the time this seemed incongruous to me. While the ethnographies I had read at the time about New Ireland mentioned Christianity, it was generally dismissed in a few lines or less (for example, Foster 1995; Wagner 1986; but see more recent work by Eves 2000; 2010; 2011a; 2011b). It had never occurred to me prior to going to the field that Christianity would be a major part of life in Lihir and therefore of my studies there. As Barker argued,

> few anthropologists incorporate the Christian presence into studies of village societies. Christianity is the perennial outside force—threatening, corrupting, or merely dusting the surface of the authentic focus of anthropological concerns. (Barker 1992:165)

While many anthropologists had studied aspects of Christianity in Papua New Guinea, this had generally been in terms of missions and missionisation, as well as cargo cults' relationship to Christianity (Barker 1992:148). Often such studies opposed the incoming 'foreign' Christianity to traditional customs or practice (*kastam*). Early anthropologists predicted the imminent

[4] *Lotu* is the term used in Tok Pisin to refer to religion and religious worship. The church is called *sios*.

death of *kastam* at the hands of missionaries (for example, Groves 1934–35; Malinowski 1961:464–6), while F.E. Williams suggested that Christianity incorporate more feasting and excitement so that it be accepted more quickly than it was (1928:84–6). Many anthropologists later argued that people had rejected Christianity in preference for *kastam* (for example, Keesing 1982). Others said Christianity had been accepted but not totally, and remained only skin-deep or a veneer (for example, Kahn 1983). A number of anthropologists have documented a lack of understanding on the part of those missionised, such as the Baruya, who don't understand the concept of sin, or people of Lobada village in Milne Bay Province who are confused about sheep, rabbis and Hebrews (Godelier 1991:397; Thune 1990:118).

It seems that the necessity to define Christianity as foreign, incomprehensible and in conflict with other 'traditional' modes of being or knowledge is an effort to preserve difference. Just as LiPuma argued was the case with anthropologists who proposed a Melanesian relational personhood in complete opposition to a Western one (1998:56), proposals that Christianity for Melanesians is a foreign veneer oppose Melanesians to Westerners as fully incommensurable, rendering the anthropological project impossible.

Since my doctoral fieldwork, there has been an efflorescence of studies on Melanesian Christianity. While some still appear to oppose Christianity to 'traditional' ways of life (for example, Robbins on the coming of Christianity to the Urapmin that overlays the pre-existing structures so that they remain intact, 2004), many provide accounts of the ongoing messy negotiations surrounding the coming of Christianity (for example, Dundon 2011; Hermkens 2007b; McDougall 2009; Were 2007).

In the past, the relationship between Christianity and *kastam* in Lihir was not so congenial as that which I witnessed in 1998. Members of the Catholic Church banned the ceremonies of women's seclusion, *tolup*, sometime early in the Mission period after realising they involved women remaining naked and dirty in huts for some time, and one *tolup* house was burned to the ground. Practices and attitudes of members of the Catholic Church changed considerably following Vatican II in 1962–65, a document that stated that traditional customs not in explicit contrast with the view of the church should be encouraged and that missionaries should be trained in appropriate social sciences (Arbuckle 1978:281).

Despite the reluctance of members of the Catholic Church to accept certain traditional customs, the relationship between Christianity and *kastam* in Lihir is not one of an either/or opposition with one or the other destined to 'win' the battle. This approach ignores the dynamism of Melanesian cultures. In the case of Lihir, borrowing from neighbouring cultures was common before the arrival of Europeans, and continues to this day. While Lihirians themselves like to propose *pindik* as indigenous to Lihir, in fact *pindik* groups are common throughout New Ireland as secret organisations involved with magic, fishing and hunting techniques, the attainment of warrior status in the past, and the teaching of initiates (for example, Wagner 1986; Eves 1998). Whether *pindik* was imported from or to Lihir, innovation and borrowing between groups is common in the New Ireland area.

Another example of this can be seen in regards to the case of the TFA (Tutorme Farmers Association), a cargo cult-like association mainly active during the late 1960s and early 1970s. This began as the Johnson cult in New Hanover, where they voted for President Johnson of the USA in the elections (Bainton 2006:67–85; Billings 1969; 2002; Ramstad n.d.b). After opposition from the Australian Administration, this cult changed into the TIA (Tutukuvul Isakul Association), an association in New Hanover concerned with cooperative farming and expectations of the arrival of wealth. This spread throughout New Ireland under the new title TKA (Tuk Kuvul Aisok), and was enthusiastically taken up by many Lihirians who refused to pay council tax, took children out of schools, and in some instances voted for Jesus Christ in the elections. It was officially registered as a business group called TFA on Lihir in 1973, and while as an organisation it died out eventually, some of the ideas it represented continue to find expression in Lihir (see Bainton 2008b; 2010:54–72).

As they have with *pindik* and the TFA, Lihirians have claimed Christianity and its values as their own. Histories on Mahur tell of Tgorous, the man who took up a *golgol* plant (used to taboo areas and trees) and travelled throughout Mahur and then the rest of Lihir declaring '*a maniel; a maniel*' (peace; peace). It is said that he brought the time of warfare and cannibalism to an end before the arrival of either the church or German administration. This history declares in retrospect that Mahurians began to value peace and cooperation before the coming of the church. Whether this is 'true' or not is beside the point. Mahurians have declared the values of Catholicism to be their own. A picture of Tgorous, in fact, was painted on the front of the old church in Kuelam village.[5]

## Christianity in Lihir

There are a number of Christian religions in Lihir. The outer three islands of the group, including Mahur, are completely Catholic. Niolam has many villages that are solely Catholic, but also has a number of villages (seven of about 20) that are United (formerly Methodist), four villages that have Pentecostal churches and one with Seventh Day Adventists. Some villages have two denominations, and two villages support three. Missionaries of the Sacred Heart arrived first in Lihir, with Trompf stating that there 'was … expansion of Sacred Heart work from Rabaul to New Ireland, especially through Lihir and the outlying islands (from 1902)' (Trompf 1991:169). Despite the Methodists being permanently stationed in Lihir prior to the 1933 establishment of the Catholic mission station at Palie in South Niolam (Filer and Jackson 1986:107), a much greater proportion of the Lihir population are Catholic than are Methodist (85 per cent in 1986 according to Filer and Jackson). The Pentecostal churches are newcomers to Lihir, arriving in about 1993.

As in other parts of Papua New Guinea, the churches provided schooling and medical services in Lihir until relatively recently. Palie is the site for the

[5] The story of Tgorous was known elsewhere in Lihir, and on the front post of the church in Lakaziz on Masahet Island there was a carving of Tgorous.

Sacred Heart Hospital, which was the major health care provider apart from a number of small aidposts scattered across Lihir, which are government funded. The developers of the gold mine built a hospital in 1997 at Londolovit (north-east Niolam), and it now serves much of the population. Palie is also the site for a school and vocational centre, and thus was the centre of medical and educational services in Lihir until the 1990s.

There is little sectarian tension between the various Christian denominations in Lihir, and they do not attempt to win converts from each other. People from Mahur will go to United services when they are staying in a village on the main island that has only a United church. The services of the two denominations are certainly different, and people will often compare the denominations unfavourably with each other, yet they also add that it is the same God that they are worshipping.

In recent years various charismatic movements have taken hold in Lihir, in particular the Catholic Charismatic Renewal (Hemer 2011a). Some friction has arisen between Lihirians who choose to follow these new movements and other Lihirians. On Mahur some Catholics see these movements as unnecessary given people's level of commitment to Catholicism, while others view these as an opportunity to make a personal choice to renew one's commitment to God. This tension was expressed in criticism by Kuelam and Lakamelen villagers of charismatic worship by people of Li village in the latter months of 1998. However, by the time of my return visit to Lihir in June/July 1999, some Lakamelen people were involved in charismatic worship. Such charismatic movements are also occurring in villages that are United, such as Samo on the main island of Lihir, and represent the continuing importance of innovation in Lihir.

### *Catholicism on Mahur*

Only one priest, Father Steve Boland, an American based at Palie, served Lihir parish when I arrived. In February 1998, Father Dominic Maka of Manus Province joined Father Steve to lighten his workload, as during 1998 the Anir parish (a group of islands to the south-east of Lihir) was without a priest and was being served by priests stationed in Lihir. By the time of my return in mid-1999, Anir had its own priest, and Father Vincent Takin of Namatanai had replaced Father Steve and Father Dominic. It was reported to me that Bishop Ambrose had stated that Father Steve would be the last 'foreign' (i.e. non-Papua New Guinean) priest stationed in Lihir.

Mahur has a Catholic church for each of its three villages. The main church on the island is located in Kuelam village, which is also the site for the school, aidpost and wharf. The church in Kuelam village is located in Makapa, land that was bought by the Catholic mission as a site for the church and school.

A priest made the journey to Mahur about once every two months, staying for three or four days to give services at the local churches, to hear confessions[6] and to give Holy Communion. At other times services were run by catechists, who were Mahurians trained by the Catholic Church at Fissoa in New Ireland (generally). While Barker (1992:155) states that at the time he published, the Roman Catholic Church in Papua New Guinea had not localised its staff and become a national church, by 1999 in relation to Lihir this no longer applied. The Catholic Church in Lihir retains its hierarchical structure and its links to other areas of Papua New Guinea and the world, but has a Lihirian Bishop, a Papua New Guinean priest, and Lihirian catechists. People on Mahur do not relate to the church as an alien institution, however they do understand that its centre is in Rome.

In a 1992 report written on attitudes of Lihirians to Western forms of contraception, Kowal comments on the impact of the Catholic Church:

> Women's relationship with the church is an allegiance that … limits women's capacity to express a western type of bodily autonomy. (Kowal 1999:42)

[6] This was mainly in Kuelam only: people would walk there from other villages to confess.

> Women are willing to accept the moral authority of the church where it conflicts with their own choices. (ibid.:43)

These two quotations raise the issue of the relationships between people and 'the church', and moral authority and autonomy in Lihir. Having argued in Chapter 3 that personhood in Lihir encompasses tensions between ideals of relational conduct and practices that often foreground the individual, what has been the impact of Christianity upon Lihirian personhood? The statements above suggest that Lihirians' relationship to the church limits their ability to exercise their own will, or individuality, yet Christianity is part of a corpus of Western institutions that comprises notions of individuality.

For most Lihirians it is not appropriate to speak of their relationship to 'the church' as an external body that has moral authority over them or as something to which they have 'allegiance'. Instead, the church is a building in the village where they go and worship. Lihirians do accept that Catholicism in the form particularly of the Pope, but also the bishop and priests, has some sort of moral authority over Lihirians. They expect these members of the elite of Catholicism to set the tenor for moral conduct in Lihir.[7]

## Christianity and a changing moral universe

Lihirians view their history in terms of changes in the moral nature of their relations with others, particularly as the expansion and contraction of the moral universe. They divide history into three phases: pre-Europeans, post-gold mine, and the intervening period. In the time before the arrival of Europeans, Lihirians explicitly state that they were amoral, engaging in warfare with clans from other areas in Lihir and the neighbouring island groups of Tabar and Tanga, as well as the New Ireland mainland. They describe it as a time of fear, when they could not go to areas belonging to other clans, and had to show respect for leaders or be killed and cannibalised at their behest. It is also seen as the heyday of magic, when people listened to their elders and learned the

[7] This is not always the case, and Mahurians recognise and criticise the hypocrisy of those people such as catechists who preach one thing but act in another manner.

skills and words to be able to fish and garden with great success (cf. Neumann 1992 on the Tolai view of history).

In the distant past, the local clan, and possibly some allied clans, represented the extent of those to whom a person was morally responsible and from those one could expect moral conduct. Kiapseni states that there were no 'human rights, only clan rights' (Kiapseni 1976 Part C:4). This moral responsibility was highlighted but also withdrawn in situations such as disrespect shown to a leader, which is said to have lead to the death and consumption of the offender by members of a neighbouring group. Whether this accurately reflects former practices is not significant. Lihirians view this time as one when moral ties were somewhat tenuous, and narrowly defined. Lihirian perspectives on this section of their history generally ignore aspects such as innovation and borrowing between areas, as well as trading of pigs, shell money and malagan carvings that imply relationships of cooperation. It is possible that this negative view of their distant past is an artefact of the ways that Lihirians have incorporated missionaries' views of themselves as moving from 'darkness to light' (cf. Neumann 1992).

The second phase of history begins with Tgorous declaring peace, and the arrival of the church and administration. This time is seen as peaceful, when the boundaries of the moral universe expanded to encompass those who had been enemies. It is characterised most succinctly in the custom of *pniari wasir*, to give food to visitors, described in Chapter 2.

The final phase of the history is the present, a time when Lihirians see themselves as in moral decline. The arrival of the gold mine is seen as the arrival of money and all it entails: greed, jealousy, inequality (see Chapter 6). Often people bemoan the loss of the custom of *pniari wasir*, particularly on Niolam, where the affects of the mine are more acute. Ignored in the view of this phase of history is the wave of new church building occurring all over Lihir, and the flourishing of new charismatic movements in both the Catholic and United churches.

In the second phase of history, the moral universe expanded. Christianity preached 'love thy neighbour' and Lihirians responded. On Mahur, least affected by the mine, and often seen to be still in this second phase of history, the explicit value on this expanded moral universe has remained. For me, one of the most salient aspects of life on Mahur was the overarching sense of community. Partly this is created by the fact of living in a small-scale society, where you are known to everyone and most activity occurs in public with the knowledge of everyone. However, Mahurians also use the Tok Pisin term '*komuniti*' to refer to the people of the village (for example, *komuniti long* Kuelam) or the people of Mahur or even Lihir as a whole. Christianity promotes this emphasis on community: each *lokal sios* (T.P. local church) is a unit that meets to share in church services every week. After the service, most people sit outside and have an informal meeting about community issues (such as planning church activities for festival days).

People worked with the assumption that they should live in harmony (*lil malum*; T.P. *bel isi*). Court cases, gossip and the like were viewed as deviations from this. They were negatively valued and if they arose, it was believed that harmony should be restored as soon as possible. A sign of this harmony was handshaking (*ersek*; T.P. *sekan*). This formed a part of all church services, and also was an important part in one village court case that I witnessed, where everyone present shook hands with everyone else, including me. One woman said that this was a sign of the restoration of harmony (*lil malum*).

Besides the values of community associated with a village or island, *lotu* promotes the importance of the family. In particular, I remember one sermon in Kuelam in which the catechist talked at length about the (nuclear) family: how children should obey or respect their parents but also how parents should love their children as Mary had loved Jesus. He said that love (*laikim*, the sermon was in Tok Pisin) was the basis of the family, and that the family should not be in conflict (T.P. *bel hat*). Here the family is constructed as a microcosm of the wider community, and for the community to be in harmony (*lil malum*), the family needs also to be.

In addition to emphasising connections and *komuniti* on the scale of the family and village, the Catholic Church in Lihir has also promoted connections between islands and, on an even wider scale, within the Diocese of Kavieng. For Pentecost in 1998 there were two massed services: one at Palie on Niolam and one on Masahet island for the three smaller islands of the Lihir group. Both services were held on Sunday morning the 31 May, and the one on Masahet was attended by hundreds of people.

Pentecost was one context where the Catholic Church promoted links between the islands of the Lihir group. These three smaller islands do have a sense of identity as a group, in contrast to the rest of Lihir. This sense of group identity has been highlighted with the advent of the gold mine in the late 1990s and 2000s, as people on the outer islands (especially Mahur, which is the furthest from the main island) have to grapple with problems of transport to Niolam to shop, sell food at the market, or to go to work. They see themselves as excluded from benefits, especially compensation monies that groups on the main island have received.[8] Catholicism does provide some links between people on the outer islands and on Niolam as Lihir is one parish; kinship ties are another source of connection, and people frequently move between villages in Lihir. However, ideologically there is a separation between the outer islands and Niolam. Catholicism fosters the group identity of the outer islands but seems unable to overcome the separation between these outer islands and Niolam. It appears that this separation has become more entrenched since the arrival of the mine and the unequal distribution of benefits, and perhaps represents another change in the moral universe of Lihirians (see Chapter 6).

### *Limits of morality*

Christianity has not made the moral universe of Lihirians infinite, though it may have expanded it beyond the immediate clan and ally boundaries. Unlike

[8] Specifically the villages of Putput (which was relocated for the plant site of the mine) and Kunaye, which received much money from the building of the airport.

in the West, the majority of Lihirians do not concern themselves with the situation of people beyond their immediate world or judge others in terms of universal human rights. Most Lihirians have not been able to easily obtain information on these others. This is changing with the presence of the gold mine, which has brought televisions, mobile phones and travel to people who had no chance to experience such things in the past.

Lihirians also do not extend their moral universe to animals, which they say have no soul. There is no concept of animal cruelty in Lihir, and animals are often treated quite harshly by Western standards. Pet dogs are generally unfed and beaten into submission; crabs and insects mercilessly squashed. One of the things that provided the most mirth at a couple of feasts was the pain and actions of supposedly-dead pigs that awoke atop the *lon* (ground oven) while having their hair removed by scorching on the red-hot stones. There is no notion of animal rights.

For people located within Lihir but originating from elsewhere, such as other Papua New Guineans and citizens of other countries, there is an abstract recognition of shared humanity in the sense of 'all being equal in God's eyes'. Despite this emphasis on shared humanity, if immigrants are viewed as taking benefits away from Lihirians by being treated as equals, they become the subject of gossip, ridicule and sometimes open hostility. Thus, when Tolai women are more successful in selling goods at the market there is resentment despite Lihirians apparently having equal opportunity in access to the market. This is also the case, for example, when Lihirians observe the discrepancies between the lifestyle of expatriates living in large air-conditioned houses and their own life in villages (Hemer n.d.a). In a sense, Lihirians see these as instances where people from other places are acting in an immoral fashion towards Lihirians, thereby justifying the gossip and hostility that ensues. Lihirians have an expectation that outsiders will conduct themselves in a moral way, and this includes acknowledging that Lihirians have preference in the hierarchy of rights to benefits arising from mining operations.

## Moral conduct: emotion and sentiment

Catholicism on Mahur has created a new universe of appropriate conduct in interpersonal relations, and has altered the connotations of some emotion terms. This was made most clear to me when I asked people to place emotion terms and related words into groups.[9] Some people grouped terms much as I had expected: terms for anger, terms for love and caring and so on. However, one woman, Kupulie, made a group of terms on the basis that they were involved with Christianity. These terms now carry a connotation of Catholicism—terms such as *leimulien* (love), *madanis* (compassion), *tandanis* (regret), *akne* (praise), *nornor* (belief, faith, trust), *sio* (respect) and *sekan* (T.P. to shake hands; to greet in friendship; to have agreement and be on good terms).[10] Young reports a similar occurrence for Kalauna, where the term *nuakabubu*, meaning compassion, sympathy and kindred feelings, has come to be associated with Christianity:

> In recent generations it has become encrusted with Christian sentiments, emphasising 'loving one's neighbour,' mutual help and disinterested giving ... [and now] evokes an entire moral ethos. (Young 1999:106–7)

*Leimulien* has been translated as 'love' in relation to Christianity in Lihir and while this may be one of its meanings, when I began to ask about the different uses of this word, it became clear that it has wider application. The word is a conjunction of the root word *le*, meaning 'to want', and the suffix *mulien*, which means 'to follow' (as in *kemulien* 'I will follow'), *leimulien* literally translating as 'the desire follows'. The root *le* is used in speech all the time: 'I want to go to the beach' (*Yo **le** no ka to kuen*), 'I want to drink coconut juice' (*Yo **le** no yun lmues*). The words *lemuli* (a verb) or *leimulien* (a

[9] I had made up a list of emotion terms used on Mahur and other terms involved in interpersonal relations like trust, respect, praise and so on. I had written terms on pieces of paper and I asked people to put them into groups of related terms on the basis of similarity.

[10] I was only able to do this questionnaire with six people. Very few people on Mahur are literate in the Lihir language. Mostly the purpose of this test was to give me an idea how people would group emotions rather than to be a comprehensive study (such as Epstein did [1992]).

noun) carry these connotations of wanting, so that you can say in Lihirian: *Yo leimuli a sospen ki wa*: 'I like/love/want your saucepan.' One can *lemuli* a spouse (love or sexual desire), can *lemuli* eating yams (like, enjoy), *leimuli* a piece of clothing (admire or desire), or even *leimuli* people to come to a meeting (want or need).

In relation to Catholicism, the term *leimulien* has come to mean to mean love in the sense of non-sexual, non-desiring love, despite Neuhaus's original translation that specified that *leimulien* was 'sensual love' (1954:18). This is love for God, love of your children, love (but not sexual desire) of a spouse. With this has come a high value placed on *leimulien*: it now carries the moral weight of being 'good' in Christian terms.

In the case of Lihir it is very difficult to know how the use of terms has changed over time due to the lack of an ethnographic record prior to about 1980. However, the differences in usage of terms in the context of *lotu* and in everyday life give clues as to changes in their meaning. Sometimes a term is used in *lotu* that is little-used in everyday life; or in *lotu* it has a narrow meaning which has a high moral value (like *leimulien*).

Another word, *maten*, was also translated by Neuhaus (1954) to mean love.[11] The 'Morning Prayer' states *yo maten wa* ('I love you'). While this term '*maten*' is not used very often in *lotu* (in favour of '*leimulien*') it is used in a very different context to its use in everyday life. Father Neuhaus, in his grammar of the Lihirian language, translates *ermaten* as mutual or reciprocal love (Neuhaus 1954:164). The prefix '*er*' denotes joint action or feeling. I have had *maten* (or *mden*) translated for me as meaning 'to covet' (the most frequent translation) or 'to like the behaviour of another so much that you copy it'. Unlike the word *leimulien*, the term *maten* seems not to have acquired positive moral value from its use in *lotu*, probably due to the ambiguity of the term and its connection with coveting what belongs to another, such as

[11] All translations for *lotu* of prayers and the like were done in the dialect of southern Niolam, the area around the main mission station, Palie. This is slightly different to the dialect of Mahur. *Maten* is pronounced *mden* on Mahur.

a spouse. I deal with the 'jealousy' (*eremsu*) that arises from such coveting in Chapter 5.

There is a third way of expressing love that is not used at all in *lotu, a ling sa ktetan*. I was told that this was probably the most appropriate way of expressing the sort of love that Christianity most often referred to: love of a brother, child or of God. Being in the form '*a ling sa*' means that this expression refers to actual bodily feeling rather than a state of being, as is implied by the '*yo sa*' form. Perhaps this tie to bodily feeling led to the rejection of this term by missionaries as an appropriate translation for Christian love. This particular form of expressing love has gained little positive moral value with Christianity in comparison with the terms *leimulien* and *maten*.

Some other terms relating to emotions or conduct have undergone similar processes. *Nornor* was translated to mean belief or faith in God/Christianity. Yet *nornor* only approximates the Western idea of belief in Christianity or God. In everyday usage *nornor* translates best as trust (or possibly faith), in the sense 'to believe (*nornor*) in ....[someone]'. Belief in the existence of God is virtually never in question in Lihir, the issue being one of trust in God.

The moral universe of Mahurians has also been restructured through the use of Tok Pisin in *lotu*. Some services were conducted entirely in Tok Pisin, some were entirely in the local language, while the rest were a mixture of both. Most services took their form from the *Yumi Lotu* book published in Goroka (in PNG) in Tok Pisin (1985). This book gives a list of prayers, orders of service (for ordinary services, funerals, services for the sick and so on) and hymns. The Bible used in Lihir is also in Tok Pisin.[12]

There are a number of emotion terms in Tok Pisin that have particular significance for Mahurians because of their association with *lotu*. Perhaps the

[12] The parish priest during 1998, Father Steve, requested that confessions be in Tok Pisin, despite the difficulty this caused some older people who could understand Tok Pisin but were unable to speak it. These people were often older women who had not been exposed to Tok Pisin through travelling, schooling or employment.

most important is *laikim* (to like or love). People were often implored by priests and catechists in services to love their parents, neighbours and God and were told that He loves them. Another emotion or sentiment that is emphasised in *lotu* is *hamamas*, which is a translation of terms such as happiness, rejoice, joy and exaltation. I rarely heard people refer to themselves or others as happy or joyous (except infants) either in Tok Pisin or in the local language (*a ling sa ngat/a ling sa gas*). People do not express their happiness in words, nor present it as something to strive for as it is in some Western cultures ('the pursuit of happiness'). In the context of *lotu*, however, the term *hamamas* was often used in prayers and hymns, and was portrayed as a reward for a good life here on earth or as the appropriate reaction to Jesus' resurrection (*Yumi Lotu* 1985:17).

The importance of both Tok Pisin and Lihirian terms being associated with *lotu* is that these concepts have come to carry a new morality. They signify a belief system that is seen by Mahurians as explicitly 'good' (*sa puet*). Flinn, in her paper about Pulapese identity and Catholicism (1990), argues that the Pulapese have used Catholicism to 'buttress contentions that they exhibit good, traditionally valued behaviour' (Flinn 1990:223). Flinn states that the Pulapese have found that Catholicism resonates with many of their own core values, such as sharing and cooperation (ibid.:222). Primarily for the Pulapese, Catholicism has reinforced and strengthened concepts such as '*tong*' (love, mercy, compassion) (ibid.:228).

For Mahurians the situation seems a little more complex because, as I have outlined above, Catholicism has emphasised certain aspects of terms such as *leimulien*, *maten* and so on while alternative meanings of these terms (such as sexual desire, coveting) are used in different contexts. Whether these concepts (like love, compassion and so on) were highly valued before the arrival of Catholicism is pure speculation, however, as discussed above, Mahurians have declared the values of Christianity their own through the story of Tgorous declaring peace.

## Moral conduct: relations of gender and sexuality

In adopting Christianity as their own, Mahurians have seen changes in the perceived morality of forms of conduct related to the family and to sexuality. Particular forms of emotional conduct have been promoted as moral, and sexuality has largely being constructed as dangerous, as is the case for *leimulien* being seen as asexual and associated with the family rather than with sexual desire. Partly the impact of these changes is speculative, given the lack of an ethnographic record prior to missionisation. However, it is apparent that changes to gender relations have occurred, and Mahurians are not completely at ease with them.

### *The family*

Catholicism has placed great emphasis on the family as the building block of society. Many sermons I heard in Lihir dealt with particular aspects of family life, such as loving your spouse and children or being faithful and trusting your spouse. Discussions in the community often highlighted similar issues but generally turned on particular examples of poor moral conduct in relation to the family, such as a mother allowing her child to become malnourished, a wife neglecting a garden, or a husband spending money inappropriately.

The ideals of family life are taught to couples prior to marriage through the 'family enrichment' program, run by Catholic Family Life teachers. This covered a series of topics such as appropriate behaviour for a husband and wife, the use of the ovulation method of contraception, and rearing children. Couples could also ask for extra advice from the Family Life teachers after marriage to counsel them with marital difficulties, or refresh them in aspects of the program.

The form of family promoted through Catholicism was the nuclear family rather than the lineage. It was clear that Catholicism as taught on Mahur endorsed the idea of a family with the husband as head and teacher of children, and the wife as supporter and hard worker. While Lihir has quite strong cognatic leanings in terms of inheritance, this form of the family was still at odds with ideas of lineage, with *mduan* (MB) as a key teacher of children and with male residence in the *rih* (men's house).

The form of the family constructed in accord with Catholicism is patriarchal—the husband and wife are both essential to the unit but are not equal. Men make many of the decisions about use of resources such as money, land and pigs, and are physically able to impose their will if necessary. Women do a much larger share of the work of the household (nurturance), as Chapter 2 argues. It appears that this patriarchal gender balance may mimic the situation prior to missionisation, and certainly men are comfortable with this situation. However, women are often not, and below I detail ways that women are taking up new roles through Christianity.

### *Sexuality*

The family is viewed by Mahurians as the appropriate place for sexuality if it is expressed in the suitable form of love between spouses conducted mainly for the purpose of producing children. Marriage is seen as a regulator of sexuality and as its only proper context; outside of these boundaries, sexuality is destructive and dangerous. Mahurians preached the virtues of waiting for marriage before having sexual intercourse, yet as I documented in Chapter 1, many of the couples married in church in 1998 had already conceived (and borne) a child.

Catholicism forbids the use of contraception other than the ovulation method, and Mahurians mostly followed this decree. Women who raised the idea of contraception were said (amongst other things) to want to have affairs that then would not be noticeable as there would be no possibility of pregnancy. The concept of detaching sexuality from conception in the marriage relationship appeared incomprehensible for most Mahurians.

Lihirians can be quite prudish about issues surrounding sexuality. For example, scenes involving kissing or lovemaking on videos were fast-forwarded,[13] and one Australian female visitor to Mahur was urged to keep sections of her body covered (above her knees). Most young Lihirian women wore a *laplap* (sarong) and either a polo neck shirt or a *meri* blouse; certainly women were not seen in trousers or shorts, nor anything skimpy. This control of the body can be seen as standing for control of morality, as Eves (1996a:*passim*) suggested was the case for the missionising program of the Methodists on New Ireland—unruly bodies were seen to indicate uncontrolled morals.

Uneasily coexisting with this prudishness were bawdy jokes and actions. People would tell a young girl to show off her vagina to embarrass her, men joked about other men's anatomy, and women in the gardens would speculate on people's affairs, body shape and size, or hypothetical sexual situations. Despite the aspect of prohibition in matters of sexuality, jokes and comments were common. In the past there was the *tolup* ritual of Lihir that involved the growth of girls into young women. In the New Ireland culture Babae (a pseudonym), the rites and feasts involved with the equivalent of *tolup* are quite bawdy in nature, with women exposing themselves (Fergie 1985; 1995). The existence of such rituals in the past suggests that Catholicism has introduced prudishness about sexuality. Sexuality is now moral conduct only in the very narrowly defined situation of the family.

### *New roles for women*

Within the realm of the church, women on Mahur have different roles than those they take in the household or in ritual life. Women on Mahur very rarely take leadership roles, they do not speak in most meetings or in village court sessions and they are not the controllers of land. There were only two women resident on Mahur who worked for the gold mine in 1998, compared with quite a number of men who did so (about 20 in 1998, and even more during the construction phase). Women on Mahur generally do not run businesses

[13] A few times during my fieldwork period on Mahur, movie nights took place. People paid a very small fee to enter an enclosed area and watch a video shown on a television screen powered by use of a generator.

such as contract boats or trade stores, instead they spend most of their time having children, raising them, growing gardens and feeding pigs.

In the past this may have been somewhat different. The demise of the women's rituals called *tolup* occurred fairly recently. These were not only the context for displays of sexuality, but also of women's power. During *tolup* rituals young women are said to have received teachings about womanhood, and were fed well before emerging some time later. At this time, older women could prowl the village and attack men, especially their cross-cousins (*koko*). For the New Ireland culture of Babae, Fergie describes the similar *vevene* ritual as a context where women take over men's spaces, and exert their autonomy (Fergie 1995).[14] However, the last time the *tolup* rituals were carried out on Mahur was in the late 1970s, this cessation leaving women of Mahur with little context to display autonomy or leadership.

*Tolup* also provided women with pigs and shell money that were their own property and could be used in exchanges by them. It is difficult to know what this entailed, but certainly now there is no institutionalised way that women are given pigs or shell money in order to use them as full participating transactors in their own right. They can acquire them, but there is no way that these are endowed with special status as 'the woman's pigs that her husband cannot use'.

Where this picture changes is in relation to the church. Catholicism has given the women of Mahur a chance to take on new tasks that give them a different profile in the community. In the context of ordinary church services, women often lead the singing (certain people do this as they are known for their good voices), begin the service with a welcome and statement of the theme of the service for that day, do Bible readings and stand at the front of the church to receive the offering. Women are quite visible and audible in the context of church services. While there were only male catechists on Mahur in the late 1990s and 2000s, people spoke of Bertha Slarau, a female catechist who died shortly before I arrived in the field (about 1994).

[14] Babae is a pseudonym created by Fergie.

The Virgin Mary is a very important figure in Catholicism in general, but especially so on Mahur. This mimics what Hermkens argued is the case elsewhere in Papua New Guinea (2007a). One of the first things a person notices on arriving on Mahur is that each hamlet has an altar, many including a statue of the Virgin Mary with her arms outstretched (Our Lady of Perpetual Succour) (see Figure 13). These altars are the sites for worship when the statue of Mary tours the village for two weeks each August, and they are also for each hamlet group to worship should the desire arise (impromptu worship in the evenings was a common occurrence).

The popularity of Mary can also be seen in the group 'The Legion of Mary', which is a spiritual group that 'marks' (signifies, follows) Mary. It is a worldwide group, introduced to Lihir by Father Steve Boland. The group has a hierarchical structure, with groups at village level, island level, Lihir as a whole, and so on, all the way to Rome. The work of Legion is to care for the souls of people, to help people deal with their troubles, and to counsel people (when asked) to restore good relations between them.

The Legion of Mary provides a context for women to take leadership roles. Each group at the village and island level has a president, vice president, treasurer and secretary. Women occupied half of these positions on Mahur in 1997–99.

The Catholic, United and Pentecostal churches of Lihir have also partially provided a context for a pan-Lihir women's association called Petztorme ('work together'), created as an initiative of the mining company's community relations program in the early 1990s. This organisation has representatives for each of the villages in Lihir, and meets regularly. Petztorme has organised various projects designed to benefit women in Lihir, such as running a plant nursery, collection of aluminium cans, and operation of the market at Londolovit. Monies from these projects were used to buy a car to improve transportation for women, such as when they wish to take foodstuffs to sell at the market. There were also plans in 1998–2000 to buy a boat to improve transportation for women of the outer islands, although these plans did not eventuate (see Macintyre 2003 for a fuller discussion of the initiation of Petztorme).

At the Annual General Meeting of Petztorme for 1998, Joan Saet (Kunaye village representative) said '*bipo wok bilong yumi i givim pik*' (T.P. before, our [the women's] work was to feed the pigs). She said that now they were fighting to be 'somebody' (English term used) and that they would '*provim long ol man olsem mipela i 'someone'*' (T.P. prove to the men that we are someone). Women in Petztorme do see it as their job to improve the lives and social standing of all women in Lihir.

Catholicism is thus a context where women take leadership roles, and where they are explicitly questioning their status in Lihir. However, this new autonomy is not expanding beyond the boundaries of *lotu* to everyday life, and does not have the support of the men of Lihir. Whenever men speak of Petztorme they do so to criticise its lack of achievements, and the inability of women to coordinate activities effectively. Men point to the market area (administered by Petztorme) and say that it is dirty or has a lack of variety of foods. They also point to the failed purchase of a truck by the group, or to the possible misuse of funds by the Petztorme executive, citing these examples as evidence of the general incapacity for women to carry out projects (see also Macintyre 2003:126–7). A few men suggested that they hire a man to sort things out and run the organisation.

There is certainly a lack of male support for any changes in the roles of women that may lead to a change in power relations between men and women. This becomes most apparent when men do support projects aimed at improving women's lives. Only those projects that help women to carry out tasks of the household gain any support, such as better methods of cooking, sewing of clothes and health education. Improvements to these aspects of life simply help women to carry out tasks that are seen by both men and women as their domain, rather than challenge the status quo. These tasks do not involve leadership skills, women speaking in public, and do not involve women moving into areas that are viewed, particularly by men, as the domain of males (such as business). These projects do not generally result in women obtaining money, and so do not improve women's capacity to participate in the new economic activities in Lihir (see Hemer n.d.b about the case of gender relations and the Tutorme Sewing Centre).

With Catholicism have come changes to the perceived morality of particular forms of conduct. Here I have discussed the transformations to what is locally understood as moral conduct in relation to family, sexuality and women's roles. Yet, as argued, these are not simple changes, wholeheartedly accepted, but rather there is some ambiguity about them: nuclear family conflicts with ideas of the lineage, prudishness about sexuality conflicts with bawdiness, and women's new roles are met with criticism. This is not to say that the values of Christianity are a veneer or are in competition with values of *kastam* or the past. Instead, Lihirians live with contradictions in their perspectives of exactly what is moral conduct, and use these values to navigate the seas of relationship.

## Christianity and Lihirian personhood

Christian morality places an emphasis on relations between people, and between human beings and God. In Lihir it was particularly emphasised in church that people should be loving and kind to one another, should be generous with their fellows and compassionate to those in need. Catechists emphasised relations within the family, and that people were in a relationship with '*God Papa*' (T.P. God the Father). Moreover, Christianity included people from other clans and areas as part of the changing ideas of virtue, suggesting that all people were part of the moral universe of Lihirians. Catholicism on Mahur widened the world of relations.

While I have concentrated largely in this chapter on the relational importance of Christianity, on the other hand Catholicism also emphasised that each person was an individual, with particular talents given by the Holy Spirit that a person should use. In a course run by the Church for the young people of Kuelam village, people were told that they did not have to be like everyone else and did not have to do things they did not want. This idea was attached to a catch-phrase '*mi no yu*' (T.P. 'I am not you', to be said when someone tried to get a person to do something s/he did not want to do), which was bandied around for over a week after the course had finished. Catholicism on Mahur also taught that salvation was a personal choice and responsibility, that individuals committed sins (with the help of Satan), and that sins could be absolved by personal repentance and confession.

Catholicism on Mahur thus evoked forms of personhood both relational and individual. There is no simple move from a relational Melanesian personhood to a modern individual one here, as is sometimes suggested through studies of the coming of Christianity (see Mosko 2010; and the responses to his paper, Barker 2010; Errington & Gewertz 2010; Knauft 2010; Robbins 2010). Catholicism has introduced some aspects of individuality that were absent before, and emphasised others such as personal will (persons should not be swayed by others to do wrong) yet has also highlighted relations between people of moral responsibility and communion.

These links of relationship, communication and moral responsibility have been the subject not only of this chapter, but also of the first section of this book. Lihirians navigate relationships through ideas of kinship and clan, marriage, namesakes and friendship. Relationships between members of, and within, households are the context for nurturance in all its forms (*ertnin, owo, pniari*). The centre point of all these relations is the person, who is both subject and creator of relationships in Lihir, while Christianity is one moral context for conduct of persons and relationships.

In the rest of this section of the book I explore issues of conflict on two fronts: conflicts relating to moral conduct between persons and conflicts based on notions of perceived inequality arising in connection with the development of a gold mine. Conflict in Lihir is concerned with matters of personhood and relationship. Key for my argument are the responsibilities and rights a person has as a member of a household or group, and also how conflicts entail emotion concepts in Lihir. Conflicts are conceptualised as inherently moral and so also implicate Christianity, as discussed in this chapter.

# 5

# Conflicts of moral conduct and the individual

## Introduction: a case of unresolvable conflict

The later months of fieldwork I spent embroiled in a conflict between my closest informant and friend on Mahur, Kupulie, and her oldest sister, Woklik. In part, my presence triggered the conflict, which made me very uneasy. Kupulie and two of her sons had moved to sleep on my verandah at the occasion of an old woman's death and burial in Lalakam, the hamlet where I lived.[1] Kupulie's move and quite lengthy stay was met with hostility by her older sister, and brought about Kupulie's departure from Mahur to live in Samo village on Niolam with other relatives at the end of my fieldwork period in Lihir.

Kupulie and her sister Woklik were part of a household in the hamlet Liabanis, neighbouring Lalakam, which for most of the period of my first fieldwork comprised Woklik, two of her daughters with four children between them, Woklik's son Soklas, who came and went, and Kupulie and her three

[1] During the mourning time, *mbie*, people in various relations to the deceased move to stay at the gravesite until they are released by a feast. I discuss *mbie*, and particularly the case of this old woman, in Chapter 7.

sons. None of these women were married, and so Woklik, being the oldest, was effectively head of the household. Having sore knees, she was unable to go to the gardens, and stayed near the houses minding the children during the daytime. Her eldest daughter was heavily involved with church work, so the work of gardening and carrying food and firewood fell to Kupulie and Woklik's other daughter, Niezkuenkuen. They went to the gardens every other day without fail, and if either felt unwell the work of harvesting enough food for a minimum of four adults and seven children was left to one person.

When Kupulie moved to my verandah she became part of the household mourning (*mbie*) the old woman's death:[2] her labour was used to support those people in Lalakam and the food she collected was pooled for consumption in this household. It is little wonder, then, that this loss of labour and food caused tensions between Kupulie and Woklik.

I first became aware of the conflict when Kupulie said that Woklik had been gossiping about her, claiming that she was only spending time on my verandah so that it would be easier to meet men for secret affairs. At this time the *mbie* was still continuing, and Kupulie stayed on my verandah. The conflict seemed minor, and Kupulie, though angry at the aspersions, felt no need to return to Liabanis to placate Woklik. During this time I had a friend from Australia visit for two weeks, and when the *mbie* was finished by a feast, Kupulie stayed on the basis of making sure that my friend was well-looked after.

The gossip continued. I heard it mainly from Kupulie and others of my hamlet who reported that Woklik felt that Kupulie was forcing me to devote food resources to her three children by staying on my verandah. Kupulie began to be very critical of Woklik, saying that she was only upset by the loss of Kupulie's labour because she was lazy (*pkapuez*).

When my Australian friend left Lihir, Kupulie moved back to the neighbouring hamlet. Members of my hamlet greeted this with annoyance, not

[2] See Chapter 7.

directed at Kupulie but at Woklik. They said that she had forced Kupulie to return with her complaining, and expressed the view that Kupulie should have stayed in Lalakam for the rest of my fieldwork time (another three months).

Kupulie's return did not, however, improve relations with her sister, and Woklik remained angry with Kupulie, being *mus* (sulking). She would not speak to Kupulie unless absolutely necessary, and would not share betelnut with her. She also would not give food to Kupulie's children if Kupulie spent the day in the gardens. Kupulie and her children often came to visit me at night and if they returned much after dark, Woklik's married son Peter would lock the children out of the men's house (where they normally spent the night).

Very slowly over the next three months relations improved until Kupulie and Woklik were sharing food and speaking. Yet Kupulie said that as soon as I left she would go to visit her nephew Martin (ZS) at Samo village as he had been asking for her to do so. On the day I left Mahur, Kupulie and two of her sons joined me in the boat and travelled to the main island. After bidding me farewell at the airport, she moved to her nephew's hamlet in Samo village, and had not returned to Mahur by the end of 2004. I found out that she later moved to the New Ireland mainland and then to Rabaul, before returning to Mahur after some years absence. Her oldest son Kandel stayed on Mahur to complete his primary schooling and planned to move to Samo at the end of 1999. During 1999 he spent more time with his *mduan* (MB) in a hamlet neighbouring Woklik's, telling his mother that Woklik did not feed him properly. Kupulie commented to me that her son had become thin over the year, indicating poor social relations and a failure of nurturance.

## Moral conduct and conflict

The situation described above is one of the many instances of moral conflict between close relatives I observed or heard about during my stay in Lihir. Even before I knew people or understood the language, I witnessed an instance of moral conflict. However, directed by dominant trends in the anthropology of disputation, at the time I mistook this simply for an instance of conflict over resources (in this case, a well). Since that time, Banks has argued that 'resource' conflicts are actually about conflicts around identity (2008). At the time, it took me many months to realise that moral conflict between close relatives in Lihir was common, and was worthy of serious ethnographic analysis.

While the anthropological study of violent and political conflict is well developed, the study of conflict between close relatives in particular is rare. In Western societies this has been termed interpersonal conflict, but this term carries connotations about the nature of persons and their relationships that I do not wish to assume. There are a number of bodies of literature in the anthropology of Melanesia that address conflict. There is a long tradition of the study of violent conflict in Melanesian anthropology, particularly in relation to the Highlands of Papua New Guinea, that addresses the issues of warfare and aggression (see for example, Berndt 1964; Hallpike 1977; Meggitt 1977; and more recently Dinnen & Ley [Eds] 2000; Harrison 1993; Henry 2005). Harrison (2006) has recently reviewed conflict on a national or ethnic level. Conflict in more subtle forms such as sorcery and witchcraft has been the subject of research, particularly in terms of its individualistic, sometimes anti-social nature (for example, Knauft 1985, and the collection edited by Stephen 1987). Issues of political competition, exchange and status rivalry are another trajectory in Melanesian anthropology (for example, Godelier 1986; Godelier & Strathern [Eds] 1991; Modjeska 1982; Young 1971). Conflict over resources, labour and, in particular, mining is the subject of a growing body of research and writing (for example, Banks 2008; Kirsch 2007; Koczberski and Curry 2004). Additionally, the anthropology of law and dispute resolution, begun in Africa with Gluckman (1955; 1965) and later Gulliver (1979), was developed in Melanesia with reference to land disputes and village court cases (for example, Epstein [Ed] 1974; Goddard 2005).

These various bodies of material offer broad insights into conflict in Melanesia, and provide clues as to the forms that conflict may take within a society. This material suggests who comes into conflict and how (or if) conflict is resolved in particular situations and cultures. However, more integral to the study of moral conflict between close relatives are ethnographies about emotion in a culture, which often have some material about anger, jealousy and shame in the context of personal or close kinship relationships. The prime example is *Never in Anger* (1970), in which Briggs gives a rich account of hostility among the Utku Eskimos, both in terms of the lexicon and the various gestures and communications, or lack of them, that convey a coolness or distance in social relations. In the Melanesian context, Schieffelin's work on the Kaluli (see especially 1977; 1983) and Epstein's work amongst the Tolai (1992; 1999) provide nuanced accounts of key emotions such as anger and shame that are core elements of disputation.

There are two edited collections which deal specifically with disputation, the first being *Disentangling* (Watson-Gegeo and White 1990), primarily concerned with discourse and conflict. The other, *Understanding Disputes* (Caplan 1995), has articles on issues such as the role of mediators (Parkin 1995) and the fact that dispute resolution rarely implies a restoration of social harmony (Moore 1995). In addition, there has also been research into the importance of reputation and the impact of gossip on social relationships (Bailey 1971; Gluckman 1963). This literature on emotions, disputation and gossip explores some elements relevant to moral conflict between close relations, yet few of these studies examine this type of conflict in a systematic way, exploring its implications for social relations in general. Moreover, this material is often not related to Papua New Guinea or Melanesia.

In this chapter I argue that individual desires, personal values and propensities or habits are often at the base of conflicts between close relatives in Lihir. As previous chapters demonstrate, there is a tension in Lihirian personhood between an ideal of relational behaviour and the individuality that is often practised, and this finds expression in conflicts between close relatives.

While they are part of the arena of social conflict in Lihir, I devote little space to court cases, mediations and negotiations involving land disputes or political conflicts about leadership in this chapter (but see the discussion in

Chapter 6). I begin my discussion here with the role of talk in conflicts in Lihir, before moving on to consider the involvement of bodies in disputes, and finally the importance of a notion of 'self' in Lihirian personhood and its role in disputation. Ethnographies of emotion that deal with conflict often do so through an analysis of the role of talk and discourse in disputes, this being a very important aspect and perhaps the easiest way of observing disputes.

## Conflicting talk

The most insightful material for thinking about conflict between close relatives, as mentioned above, is the anthropology of emotion. Ethnographies scrutinising emotion generally do so with reference to language and discourse: particular emotion terms, their usage, the politics of language, and how language shapes people's perception and categorisation of the world (for example, Abu-Lughod 1986; Abu-Lughod & Lutz 1990; Lutz 1988).

Particular emotion terms and their usage are the subject of much of Rosaldo's ethnography of *liget* (passion, anger) and *beya* (knowledge) (Rosaldo 1980). Levy, in his studies of Tahiti, develops the terms hypo- and hyper-cognition—being the lack or abundance respectively of particular terms for an emotion (Levy 1984). Heider, on the other hand, criticises the focus on individual words for emotion, arguing that this ignores the role of phrases and metaphors for emotion, and neglects the study of how various terms are more or less central to the category of a particular emotion (Heider 1991:92). He studies not emotion terms but clusters of terms and how such clusters relate to one another. Most anthropologists of emotion, however, agree on the fundamental importance of lexical and discourse analysis.

Talking is one of the great pastimes in Lihir, whether in the context of meetings, talking while working, or in late night fireside chats. There is a large vocabulary to describe different forms of talk or vocalisation, the most important being *tetnge* (to talk or chat during the day) and *panpan* (chatting at night). Talk with negative connotations can be classed as *puersie* (criticism: often directly to the person), *tetnge piel* or *tireh* (gossip: particularly of the malicious type) and *ertoneh* (slander or to abuse a person). While there is not a highly developed art of oratory in Lihir, and many feasts pass with few announcements or speeches, the ability to talk in front of groups of people is seen as a skill or gift that some people have more than others.

Besides formal contexts such as meetings, Lihirian people live highly verbalised lives. People are rarely told to be quiet, and unless work or walking is particularly strenuous, they will chatter or break into song on a path or sitting in a hamlet. Yet talking simply for the sake of it is not valued, and is dismissed as *maus wara* (T.P. verbal diarrhoea). If people have nothing particular to say they will sit or work in a comfortable silence.

Gossip (*tetnge piel/tireh*) is perhaps the most important form of 'talk' in conflicts. Very early in fieldwork I was told by a woman that *tetnge piel* was a destructive but very common part of life in Lihir. Her view was that it should be banished from Lihir, but she was unable to think of a way to do so. She said that malicious gossip had led to her sisters beating her for things she had not done.

Gossip is critical both in starting conflicts and as a means of perpetuating them. Gossip by a third party can lead to people thinking badly of the person who was the focus of such gossip, and can start conflict. For example, a husband may became jealous if he heard from gossip that his wife was having an affair. In other cases, parties to a dispute gossiped about each other, perpetuating the dispute, as in the case of the conflict involving Kupulie and Woklik.

Gossip in Lihir is seen as the province of women—men are said not to engage in *tetnge piel*. One of the major problems with the continuation of Petztorme, the women's association in Lihir, is said by both women and men to be the divisions between women that are maintained through gossip. This suggestion of the inability of women to cooperate is maintained in other contexts: at feasts where food is given to groups of four or five people, women are said to have to divide the food into equal portions before consuming any of it to avert gossip over unequal shares or greediness. Thus, gossip is posited as the opposite of equal and open cooperation, and the ascription of this characteristic to women excludes from them the possibility of being a united force.[3]

Gossip was raised as a problem throughout the time of my fieldwork. People who gossip a great deal are viewed negatively: two sisters were contrasted to me in terms of one being a renowned gossip while the other was not; she was trustworthy. One woman, in describing her mother to me, explained that she had been a good woman, one who did not gossip, and would walk away if people were gossiping about others in her presence. Given this value judgement of those who gossip, it is somewhat surprising that people are still judged negatively on the basis of such gossip—and yet judged they are, and sometimes with violent consequences.

Gossip in Lihir is not simply integrative or a mechanism of social control, as has been argued by some anthropologists for other contexts (for example, Bailey 1971; Gluckman 1963). While outsiders to a community can be excluded by not understanding the relations between people and the history of such relations, gossip in Lihir is represented by Lihirians as malicious rather than a force that draws a boundary around a united group. It undercuts social relations rather than reinforcing the relations of those people within the group and the exclusion of others. As Brison argues in relation to the Kwanga in Papua New Guinea,

> gossip, as a means of communication par excellence through which people can avoid responsibility for their words, has an intrinsic tendency to distort the truth, cause alarm, and escalate conflict. (1992:240)

Talk is crucial to conflicts in another way through the importance of arguments (*erzmuer*). *Erzmuer* can be variously translated as an argument,

[3] This is perhaps part of the basis of excluding women from most of the organisations that deal with the gold mine on Niolam, such as the landowners' association (LMALA) and the umbrella company (LAKAKA), and the very late inclusion of women in the local government (NLLG). However, the low status of women has more complex routes than simply the common view that women are incapable of cooperation.

where the conflicting dialogue is mutual, or as a harangue, tirade or 'telling off' of one party by another. *Erzmuer* implies and arises out of anger (*lil tua*). One person said to me that a person first experiences *lil tua* (lit. inside is hard/powerful) and then argues (*erzmuer*). There is no notion of controlling or hiding anger in Lihir, and most people I asked said they would get angry (*erzmuer*) even with an important person or leader; if not, they would not hide anger but direct it to something else (such as hacking at houses with a bush-knife or throwing plates).

*Erzmuer* most commonly occurs in the form of a parent reprimanding a child for various misdemeanours, such as not performing chores when asked (cooking, laundry, sweeping) or being '*bikhet*' (T.P. arrogant, a 'show-off', not following household rules). *Erzmuer* is part of the socialisation of children into the demands and responsibilities required of them as members of a household. In this situation, *erzmuer* occurs between people who are not equals, and consequently *erzmuer* is unidirectional: from the parent to the child. Children very rarely answer back, as doing so is most likely to result in physical punishment.

In other cases *erzmuer* is bi- (or even multi-) directional, such as occasions when the situation is not a tirade but an argument between a number of people. These exchanges often involve talking or even yelling (more rarely), and occur between siblings, spouses, friends, and children.

In a more veiled way, conflict can be carried out through the medium of joking or *eretek*. While some jokes appeared to be just in fun, a selection of them had hidden barbs directed at particular people, whether these were present at the occasion of *eretek* or not. One specific instance was joking directed towards a man who acted as a leader in a capacity beyond that which people felt he was capable of or deserved. Another old man joked about this leader's testicles being used as floaters for a fishing net. Joking in this way can be used as a subtle method to undermine someone while avoiding direct conflict of the kind described above.

Gossip, joking and arguments are aspects of conflicts that are carried out through the medium of talk. These are forms of talk that initiate and perpetuate discord. However, disagreements are not limited to the verbal sphere. To further investigate disputes it is essential to move beyond talk to other elements in conflict, such as the role of, and impact upon, bodies. According to Lihirians, emotion is not simply a communication or discourse: emotions exist at a bodily level, and in certain circumstances they can kill.

## Bodies in conflict

As discussed in relation to notions of the person in Chapter 3, in Lihir what we may term 'emotions' are referred to in two different ways. First, there is the '*Yo sa* …' form, 'I am …(angry, afraid, etc)', which describes a person in a state of being. Then there is the form '*a ling sa* …', 'my inside is … (hard, churning, etc)'. It is this second form, with its grounding in the body, that concerns me here.

Conflicts in Lihir are based in *lil tua*, or anger. The phrase '*lil tua*' refers specifically to the inside of the body being hard, tough, energised or powerful: anger in this case is seen as a bodily state, and, when asked, people said it was not simply linguistic convention but that their bodies were in this state. There were consequences of being in this state too often, with those people who were often angry said to be frequently ill and to age more quickly than others. To 'prove' this statement Mahurians would point to a number of people who were often angry, and who looked old beyond their years: knowledge about the effects of anger is grounded in particular bodies.

People said that when they experienced *lil tua* they express this rather then repress or control it. It seems that Papua New Guineans see repressed or concealed anger as problematic, rather than expressed anger (see, for example, Rumsey 2008; Robbins 2004). Unlike the case argued by Briggs for the Utku Eskimos (1970), or by Belaunde (2000) for the Airo-Pai of Peru, Lihirians often perceive anger as justifiable and very rarely view *lil tua* by itself as amoral or depersonalising. Belaunde states:

> No matter the circumstances, amongst people who regard themselves as relatives and truly human, anger is always purposeless and amoral. (2000:210)

> An angry person quite simply is not a true person or a kinsman, but an enemy, a monster, a predator. (ibid.:209)

In contrast, Lihirians do not view *lil tua* as shameful unless it results in consequences such as severe violence or sorcery. These are viewed as possible but not necessary consequences of anger.

As stated above, *lil tua* can be expressed through verbalisation, that is, through arguments and tirades. *Lil tua* can also be displayed through violence (*ersas*), and often is. *Ersas* takes a number of forms. Children are regularly punished using physical force. Sometimes this takes a stylised form, where a parent, grandparent, older sibling or other caregiver makes the child stand with his/her hands outstretched and receive a number of switches with a stick. At other times a caregiver hits a child with a hand, a broom (made of the midribs of coconut leaves) or anything else that is within close reach. Such beatings are expressly to teach a child proper behaviour and to punish offences. As with physical punishment in Tonga, children who cry after a beating are often hit until they cease crying (Morton 1996:193).

Age-mates occasionally engage in physical fighting, but this seems quite rare: I heard of about three cases in a one year period involving men of Kuelam village. In each of these cases the fighting was between men and was about women, and was exacerbated by alcohol.

Fighting between drunken men on Niolam has become quite common since the beginning of construction of the mine, precipitated by the now-ready supply of alcohol. In Lihir, like other areas of Papua New Guinea, there is an idea that alcohol produces changes in behaviour, with a few people characterised as happy and dancing while drunk while most are seen as typically angry and violent (cf. Macintyre 2008; Marshall 1979). Alcohol is generally blamed for actions while drunk, and people are rarely taken to court or held responsible for behaviour influenced by alcohol. Young men get into fights, smash things, or try to climb into women's houses while drunk, with all these actions often excused on the basis of alcohol. It is possible that with the emphasis in Lihir on moral relations with others, aggression between age-mates is normally suppressed, and alcohol allows expression of this aggression without risk of consequences (Macintyre 2008). Some men even claim that they drink *in order* to precipitate arguments that they would feel ashamed about (T.P. *fil sem*) if these occurred while they were sober. One such case occurred on Malie Island when young men got drunk in order to confront and fight with men of another clan who had beaten one of the senior men in their own clan.

Women do occasionally engage in violence against other women (see Wardlow 2006:86–7). People told me that the violence between women was something to see. Often they would tear one another's clothes off and roll on the ground kicking, screaming and punching. There is little doubt that women can do serious damage to one another, as was the case when one woman was beaten by her sisters as they had heard gossip about her poor morals. She was left bruised and with a probable dislocated jaw.

Male and female violence is viewed differently, with more negative connotations to women's aggression. Male aggression, while not valued in the way that calmness and quiet assuredness is, is seen as a natural part of male confrontation in meetings and court cases. The ability to verbalise anger and express public criticism is part of male 'debate'. Aggression in women, on the other hand, is trivialised and seen as bad behaviour. Men, when drunk or angry, are something to be afraid of, whereas female aggression or violence is seen as a spectacle: just another occasion of women being unable to cooperate. Female violence, like gossip, is seen as anti-social (an expression of non-relationality), whereas males will join in and support one another in fights, thus declaring even violence and anger as a social domain for men.

However, on occasions male violence is viewed as being abnormal and out of control. In October 1997 on Niolam, a man from from Londolovit village murdered a man from Masahet Island with a bush knife. There had been a conflict between men of Londolovit and Masahet after a love triangle resulted in a man from Londolovit receiving a broken jaw in a fight. When people from Masahet pulled ashore in boats to go to work the next week, Londolovit men ambushed them, killing one. Most Lihirians, for whom such violence is abnormal, met this event with shock and horror. In particular, people were appalled at the use of a bush knife, which nearly severed the man's head from his body. Some people believed that this indicated a complete breakdown in law and order, and fled to the hills fearing retaliation and complete war. However, negotiations commenced almost immediately to resolve the issues. Thus, male violence is perceived as a force that can in certain circumstances become completely asocial and uncontrollable.

Violence also occurs in the context of marital relations, where husbands beat wives. Almost any infraction by a wife can justify her receiving a beating from her husband. The most common causes of such violence are said to be the husband's jealousy (*eremsu*); he would hear gossip that his wife was interested or had been meeting with another man, and would respond with violence. In the year before I arrived on Mahur one of the school teachers had hit his wife over the head with a shovel, cracking her skull. He did this on the basis of gossip he had heard about her relations with another man. While he wasn't Lihirian, the people with whom I spoke saw his reaction as meaningful in terms of their own ideas of the relationship between jealousy and violence.

Wives may also be hit when they are considered to be lazy (*pkapuez*): they do not go to the gardens often enough, they do not cook food properly, or they allow a baby to become ill. They are hit when they are '*bikhet*' (disobedient or wilful—they don't listen to their husbands). Violence in this sense is a physical comment on the moral failings of women in particular. Given this list of infractions where violence was seen as an appropriate response, wives must be hit often, yet while I was there I personally saw and heard only a few cases of actual violence. However, the doctor at Londolovit hospital said that he saw at least two cases per week of injuries he suspected were the result of domestic violence. Since the women involved did not wish to discuss the origin of their injuries, it is impossible to say whether these were the result of beatings inflicted by husbands, uncles, brothers or even sisters. People all said domestic violence occurred, and if the beating was mild, women often saw it as justified. This clearly accords with the understanding more generally in Papua New Guinea that while unprovoked violence is condemned, violence in general is condoned, even by police. This equates to very high rates of violence against women (Eves 2010a; Gillett 1990; McLeod and Macintyre 2010). As with the Kove, women in Lihir saw violence as problematic only if they felt it was excessive in relation to its trigger, rather than viewing violence in any form as unconscionable (Chowning 1985:81–2).

Such violence is beyond the realm of talk, occurring at a bodily level. Conflicts engage the body, and they have an impact on that body. Anger particularly goes beyond discourse, if not in the form of violence, then in another way of expressing conflict: *mus*.

*Mus* is the absence of talking, and is best translated as sulking. People who are experiencing *lil tua* will often express this through *mus* rather than violence. People who are *mus* do not talk to the person who is the cause of their *lil tua*, and will not share food with them and often not with their children. This refusal to share food is a refusal of social relations with that person, because, as I explained in Chapters 2 and 3, food sharing is critical to good social relations, and a person who appears thin is often judged not as being ill but as having poor social relations and neglectful relatives.

*Mus* may last a few hours or days and even weeks, as was the case with Woklik described above. When I asked how you know when a person is no longer *mus*, I was told that a person would begin to greet you again, would share betelnut, and, as with Kupulie and Woklik, would begin to feed your children again. People said that there was nothing you could do to precipitate the end of another person's *mus*. There is no notion of apologising for one's wrongdoings in Lihir[4] and so *mus* just gradually dissipates over time.

[4] Outside of the context of *tandanis* [regret] in confession.

Like gossip, *mus* was generally regarded as gendered, as a characteristic result of *lil tua* in females. Some people agreed that men could also be *mus* but said it would often go unnoticed as the men would leave the area to visit friends in the men's house. *Mus*, in this account, is directional: towards the person who is the cause, and it was assumed that for men this would be a woman.[5] Children can also be *mus*, and the ability to exhibit *mus* behaviour was a sign that the child had developed understanding, often about the time of the development of speech.[6]

Apart from anger in conflicts, illness is another dimension where discords have an impact on the body. Illness is called *mniat* in Lihir, and linguistically it is seen as an outside force that attacks the person '*a mniat e se yo*' ('an illness attacked me'). People who are ill do not go to the gardens, instead resting in their own or a neighbouring hamlet. People go to the aidpost quite willingly for relatively minor ailments, and suggested I do likewise (for example, for a minor skin burn, headache or cold). However, people often avoided the aidpost for more serious complaints, and rarely finished a course of antibiotics, malaria tablets or injections.[7] In addition to the aidpost, Lihirians often seek the aid of traditional healers, who use various remedies and taboos on food to cure people, and in cases of very sick or aged people a group will hold a short Catholic Church service and prayers to ask for the help of the Virgin Mary.[8]

A number of times Lihirians explained their illness to me in retrospect as being due to conflicts with close relatives in their lives. Kupulie, whom I discussed in my case study at the beginning of this chapter, was very ill for many weeks in February and March (months before the conflict described)

[5] No one said that men would be *mus* with other men, though I never asked this directly.
[6] The child most often characterised as *mus* was a young boy, who was said to have learned it from his grandmother, who often looked after him.
[7] The aidpost is staffed full-time (almost) by a nurse, and is stocked with bandages and basic medicines for the most common ailments of malaria, tropical ulcers, respiratory illnesses and diarrhoea. If it is unable to adequately deal with an illness, the person is referred to the sub-health centre on neighbouring Masahet Island or to Londolovit hospital on Niolam.
[8] It is not my aim here to give a comprehensive account of ideas of illness in Lihir. This is simply a small excursion to provide context for my discussion of illness and conflict.

with a mysterious 'pain in her side'. This pain was said by the nurse to possibly be appendicitis, but the pain did not proceed to any acute phase (that is, needing surgery) and nor did it respond to pain alleviating drugs or antibiotics. Kupulie was unable to go to the gardens or do any major household chores such as laundry or cooking. Mostly she ate and talked very little, and slept a great deal. When members of the community realised how ill she was they held a couple of short church services to ask for her to be healed. Eventually she began to take on more household tasks until it became apparent she was well once more.

Months later, and in the context of the conflict between her and Woklik, she explained to me that her illness earlier had been the result of conflict between her and Woklik, who was at that time gossiping about Kupulie. She said that she and Woklik had argued in the past, and so she had gone to stay with her sister at Namatanai on the New Ireland mainland. Movement seems to be one of the major strategies for resolving—or simply avoiding—conflict.

Another woman explained to me that she had been ill due to the conflict she was having with her husband. She had been very angry with him in a way she later felt was unjustifiable, and had wanted to hit him. Afterwards she had wanted to commit suicide, she had not slept, and her head had ached. This clearly connects with the idea that concealed anger can cause bodily illness, as Robbins reports for the Urapmin (2004).

Conflict in Lihir is also seen to cause illness and even death through the medium of sorcery. While sorcery is not seen as the cause of all or even most deaths as it is in some areas of Papua New Guinea (for example, Counts and Counts 1985; Knauft 1985; Young 1971), it is still an important factor in some deaths. Mouth cancer is always attributed to sorcery, carried out by bespelling betelnut, pepper or particularly the lime that is then given to the target. At least one case of mental illness was attributed to sorcery, and the strange behaviour of a young man (interpreted as illness, and cured in this case) was seen as the result of sorcery.

Motives for sorcery were given as jealousy over someone else's good fortune (termed *lil tua* [anger] in this case; *eremsu* is reserved for sexual jealousy) or due to competition between (potential) leaders. When one of the leaders of Nawus clan died, the most senior man alive in the clan was accused of killing his rival by sorcery. He denied it and swore his honesty on the Bible, and so the matter was dropped. Competitions waged between sorcerers are also posited as a cause of illness or deaths: this was said to be the cause of one woman's death, who was the wife of one of the most renowned sorcerers in Lihir. I was told that another sorcerer lost in a power competition with him, and ensorcelled his wife in revenge as a way of showing that he was powerful despite his loss.

Sorcery also can lead to violence and death by more circuitous routes. In two cases I heard about, sorcery was the root but not the direct cause of deaths. The first occurred in World War II, when a sorcerer and six young men were killed attempting to open a sea mine that had washed ashore at Kuelam village. The story now goes that the sorcerer was dying from 'revenge magic in his liver' and chose to take people to the grave with him. In the second case, a man who was a renowned sorcerer was murdered in the 1980s to prevent him from causing any more deaths after he was found guilty of sorcery by a bamboo divination (*rorie a suak*).[9]

Bodies are as much the site of conflicts and emotions as talk is a medium for these aspects of relations. Far more often anger (*lil tua*) was read from gestures (or lack of them) than it was spoken about. The lack of food or betelnut sharing, movements to other areas of Lihir, illnesses and even violent chopping of firewood are all indicators of anger that is practiced rather than verbally expressed. Of course, these practices were interpreted for me through language that categorised and named these events, yet Lihirians do not relate simply through words. Much emotional practice and conflict occurred at a non-verbal level, particularly through the body.

[9] This divination involves empowering a length of bamboo, that will then 'run' (with a group of people holding it but not determining its movement) and direct its journey to the place where the sorcerer resides.

Root causes of most conflicts, however, are to be found neither at the level of the body nor in the context of verbalisation. Disputation arises from moral obligations and responsibilities that Lihirians have as persons, that is, conflicts arise from particular conceptions of appropriate conduct of persons and their relationships to one another.

## Persons in conflict

A critical basis of moral conduct in Lihir is inscribed in the notion of *sio*, best translated as respect. *Sio*, like respect, is something that is accorded another person or people, evidenced through appropriate behaviour and speech directed to that person or carried out in his or her presence. *Sio* was often mentioned in connection with behaviour in the presence of leaders (*a toe*) and general attitude towards them. One man said to me that people should work hard and get shell money to give to leaders as this is a sign of respect (*sio*) and allowed leaders to have 'standing' (*sio*) in the community. One must also respect one's kin. Sisters were unable to talk about their affairs or sexual matters within hearing of their brothers out of respect for them. The children in my hamlet were told by their parents to leave me alone when I was working—to have respect (*sio*) for me. Respect draws boundaries of acceptable conduct in relationships.

Conflicts arose when it was believed that appropriate respect was not accorded to another person. As Barker notes, 'ethical dilemmas, as entailed in everyday conflicts ... provide a strategic point of entry for the study of the key value orientations of a culture' (2007:1). One woman's sister berated her as she had taken that sister's basket to the gardens rather than make herself a new one. Others interpreted this conflict in another way, considering both sisters to be in the wrong: the first had not respected her sister's property and had been too lazy to make a new basket, while the second should not have berated her sister (showing a lack of respect) but instead should have been willing to share the use of her basket.

The example of the two sisters illustrates a second point, that lack of respect can be both the cause of disputes and the result of arguments. On one occasion there was physical fighting between male *puelkan* (same-sex cross-cousins), which was due to them both being interested in the same woman. Each man felt the other should respect the *puelkan* relationship and give up their interest in the woman. Thus, a perceived lack of respect was the cause of the fight but the fight itself was also evidence of disrespect. This fight contradicted the ethos of cooperation, friendship and joking between *puelkan*. This instance was one where a conflict between relatives drew in other members of the kin group. The fight led to a clan discussion and later a feast, complete with pork, to restore relations between these men and to pay each other for the breach of respect that this fighting entailed.

Other conflicts are based on the failure to fulfil obligations and responsibilities as a member of a group or household. As discussed in relation to the concept of *piot*, personhood in Lihir subscribes neither to a version of Western rugged individualism nor to a solely relational constitution of the person. Rather, personhood in Lihir shows features both of individual desires and autonomy, and social relationships that define the person in terms of membership of various groups (kinship, household, and so on). Most of the conflicts I witnessed or heard about centred around the tension between these interrelated dimensions of personhood or about contrasting obligations to various people or groups.

In the case of conflict between Kupulie and Woklik described at the beginning of this chapter, each conflicted with the other in terms of her relationship to the household and the neglect of the responsibilities that being a member of a household entails. These are termed *pniez*, meaning work, obligations or responsibilities. This term is similar to the English term 'duty,' in that it cannot be separated from the moral obligation to carry out these tasks. Kupulie and members of the household in Lalakam felt that this was the implicit meaning of Woklik's attack on her: that Woklik was angry and gossiping because she felt that Kupulie was being remiss in her relationship to their household.[10] On the other hand, Kupulie complained about Woklik in terms of her laziness, her unwillingness to cook for the household or do any work for the household other than babysitting. For both sides of this dispute (at least, all the interpretations I heard of it) the conflict was about obligations one has as a member of a household, and the denial of these by behaviour that in Western notions could be termed selfish.

Selfishness (T.P.: *selpis*) was not a term that was ever applied to situations and behaviours like those described above. Lihirians have a term *yienkeh*, which refers to a person who thinks only of him/herself in relation to food, in other words, not to share. It is this term that Lihirians translate as *selpis*, best translated as 'greediness'. There was also the term *tbusor*, which describes a person that does not want to help when work is being done, the emphasis being more than simply laziness but also the lack of regard of those others doing the work. Finally, there is *yiekehlik*, a person who only thinks of him or herself. This final term is perhaps the best term in Lihirian to fit the behaviour of a person who does not put the responsibilities s/he has to the household or kin group before his/her own autonomy or desires. I never heard anyone in particular described as *yiekehlik*, even though individualistic behaviour was continually an issue and the most common reason for interpersonal conflict in Lihir. *Yiekehlik* is a term describing quite extreme anti-social behaviour, and as this is quite rare, a variety of more moderate terms are used. As described in relation to the nature of personhood in Lihir (Chapter 3), there are many terms that can be applied to people who exhibit behaviour that is individualistic, such as *pkapuez* or *a kuil pong* (lazy person: what Kupulie called Woklik), *yienkeh* (greedy), *kasi lolon* (doesn't listen, arrogant) or *pniel* (thief).

During the dispute between Kupulie and Woklik, members of my hamlet redefined Kupulie's behaviour in terms of her obligations to help me in my research, thus making her conduct not selfish but morally acceptable. In

[10] I was unable to discuss with Woklik her views about this conflict. She spoke only the local language and at this stage in fieldwork I would have needed a translator. In addition, I was firmly aligned with Kupulie in this conflict, and so talking with Woklik at the height of this dispute would have been difficult.

Lihir, various factions to a conflict interpret and reinterpret disputes in order to cast a person's conduct as morally reprehensible or as virtuous in terms of satisfaction of obligations to differing parties.

Conflicts within households were fairly common during the time I spent on Mahur. I spent much of my time with seven households, and it is about these that I can comment.[11] In a number of cases, the same conflict recurred throughout the year I was present. In the hamlet where my house was built, Lalakam, there was a continuing, low-level conflict between Lolot, the only adult female in the household, and Kuir, her *kasien* (MZS). Kuir was the widowed father of many children, his wife having died several years before I arrived on Mahur. None of his children lived with him, not even the youngest who was only about five years old. These children were in the care of various other relatives, and were spread over the four islands of the Lihir group. People viewed this as remiss or inappropriate, believing that Kuir should have kept them together on Mahur, with the oldest of the children making gardens to support the younger ones (Kuir's oldest son was married with a number of children of his own, living on Mahur). Instead, Kuir lived as a member of Lolot's household, and contributed very little to that household. Kuir did no work in the gardens even though Lolot's husband was away working on the main island for two of every three weeks. He did very little cooking, collecting of firewood or coconuts. Nor did he mind the children. However, each day he received food that other members of the household had planted, tended, harvested and cooked.

Lolot was quite angry (*lil tua*) about Kuir's behaviour. She said he was lazy (*pkapuez*), and so would occasionally finish all the food in the pot before he arrived for the evening meal: a refusal of sharing food. Once or twice she upbraided him (*erzmuer*) but this did not cause him to change his behaviour. The conflict was sustained at a low-level of resentment and gossip, but Kuir was tolerated in the household.

---

[11] Interpersonal conflicts within households rarely became known to people other than frequent visitors, close neighbours and kin of particular households, and thus I generally knew nothing about the instances of conflict in other households.

However, since my main dissertation fieldwork in 1998 there has been a reassessment of Kuir's behaviour. When I returned in 1999 I was told that Kuir had become *nglo*, or mentally ill: Mahurians said he had continued his other behaviours but had also become violent. In Chapter 3, when discussing concepts of *nglo*, I stated that the behaviours that make a person *nglo* are antisocial but when considered by themselves do not constitute *nglo*. Kuir is a case in point: lack of work around the house is simply *pkapuez* (laziness), lack of care for children is *yiekehlik* (selfishness), and violence is just violence. However, in combination these behaviours constitute *nglo*. The addition of violence to Kuir's previous individualistic tendencies prompted people in the village to view him as *nglo*, rather than as a person acting in a morally reprehensible way. In being classified as *nglo*, Kuir was seen as not completely in control of his actions. This suggests that there is a point where behaviour becomes so unacceptable morally that people cannot conceive of someone intentionally acting in that way, and so behaviour gets defined as *nglo*, or as the result of sorcery.[12]

Sometimes conflicts over responsibilities to the household were more short-lived, such as when Lolot was very angry (*lil tua*) and directed a tirade (*erzmuer*) at her husband when he spent a number of days of his week off, and much of his earnings getting drunk, on Niolam while Lolot waited for him on Mahur with their seriously ill infant.

Conflicts between close relatives, then, are about perceived failures in moral conduct, and this differentiates them from conflicts based in political or exchange rivalry. Though I mentioned above conflicts involving sorcery, those that arise from competition between rivals are not moral conflict as it concerns me here. There are two main issues: first, a lack of respect (*sio*) between persons, and, second, conflicts arise in the tension between individual desires and the responsibilities (*pniez*) of relationships. Moral conflicts between close relatives are expressive of individualism that is at the heart of Lihirian sociality. When

[12] Such as the man who opened a sea mine killing himself and young men in the process. He was viewed as not completely in control of his actions, but acting in response to sorcery affecting his liver.

people sulk, move to another place or refuse to conform to what other people want, they are acting in ways that indicate they do have a 'self' at their core which can resist social pressures despite ideals of moral conduct.

Strathern's argument that the Melanesian person is relational, or composed of relations with others, leaves little space for conflict. If persons always act in terms of others, how does conflict arise? Perhaps this statement refers also to action carried out in terms of relationships of anger and conflict, but Strathern never makes this clear. In fact, it appears that she ignores aggression and conflict, apart from men beating women to make them act in a certain way. Macintyre argues that Strathern's and Battaglia's views of personhood are romantic, focusing on 'solidarity, cohesion and benign social relations' (Macintyre 1995:30). As Chapter 3 mentions, at one point in *The Gender of the Gift* Strathern allows space for alternate conceptions of action in Melanesia by suggesting that people may be able to act as their own cause (1992). That Melanesians can act as their own cause suggests that Strathern may conceive of possibilities for selfishness and individualism that are not elaborated throughout her text.

The sorts of moral conflicts described here support the view that individuals can reject their social and relational obligations when they perceive them as unjust, when they find them personally distasteful, or when they see them as not in their own interests (Macintyre pers. comm., describes similar moral conflicts between close relatives). Personal conflicts were concentrated on specific antagonists. While these could draw in others, thereby publicly acknowledging the relational implications of argument between particular people, the centrality of the antagonists as individuals who were responsible for their actions was the basis for all forms of eventual resolution—whether it took the form of withdrawal, migration, confrontation with victory for one party, or reconciliation.

In the context of conflict, people in Lihir act in terms of themselves, as well as numerable others, who often have competing claims on the person. Does the person act on his own desires to keep his pay for alcohol, does he share it with his household for rice and kerosene, or should he give it to the clan to help them purchase a pig for a feast? Each option is valid, and each may lead to conflict of the sort described above. It is this form of conflict, about individual desires and responsibilities, that leads to my final section in this chapter, about the separation of conflict between close relatives and wider social groupings.

## Personal or social conflicts?

I suspect that the reluctance of many anthropologists to study the kinds of conflicts explored above is based on the idea that this form of conflict is not suitably 'social,' that is, it is more amenable to psychological analysis. Anthropologists who do study conflict between close relatives tend to be those who have already ventured into the realm of the psychological: those with interests in ethnopsychology and emotion. Such a reluctance is based on assumptions about the separation of the personal and the social that does not necessarily hold in many societies.

In Lihir, given the tension between the ideal of relational behaviour and the lived practice of autonomous conduct, conflicts between close kin have a tendency to draw in wider groups (for example, lineages or clans) or the household depending on whom the conflict initially involved. For example, while I was on Mahur there was a conflict surrounding the possible marriage of a woman to one of two men. This dispute began about a year before I arrived, and was a long-term issue. A young woman, Mary, was promised some years earlier to a particular man, Nates, to be married at a later date. While initially she agreed to this match, she later withdrew her agreement and had an affair with Kiapten, conceiving a child. Sometime around the birth of her child she decided she no longer wanted Kiapten, but wished once again to marry Nates. This was the situation when I arrived on Mahur in November 1997. Kiapten said he loved Mary and his child and wanted to marry her. She, instead, wished to marry Nates, who still wished to marry her. Other members of the community despaired of her behaviour and the matter remained unresolved all year despite a number of meetings with the families involved.

When I returned to the field in June 1999 I found that there had been a number of clan meetings and court cases, resulting finally in a sitting of the full court (with five Magistrates present drawn from a number of villages in Lihir) to resolve this issue. What appeared to me to be a private matter of a love triangle had become a community concern.

The full court heard evidence that both men wished to marry Mary and that she wished to marry Nates, even though she had conceived a child with Kiapten. The court then decided that Mary would marry neither of them, as this was bound to cause much trouble for the community in the future. The two men were warned not to talk to Mary or go to her house at night, and she was to encourage neither of them, at the risk of a one thousand Kina fine or six months in jail. In this case, then, relationships between community members, and the future safety of the community, was put before the desires of individual members of that community. This conflict between close relatives became a social concern.

The case above was not the only example where conflicts between individuals were interpreted in terms of their positions as group members, or were resolved by group intervention.[13] Arguments between members of the same lineage, like the one mentioned above of the *puelkan* who fought, were frequently interpreted as a lineage concern. Disputes between women were rarely in my experience managed by lineage meetings, but those concerning men often were. This is because it was conflicts that crossed household boundaries that involved lineage meetings, and it was generally men who disputed across household and immediate kin boundaries. In crossing such boundaries, these disputes become issues not just for those who are in conflict: these quarrels implicate wider social groupings. Disputes around marriages draw a number of lineages or clans into negotiations, as in the situation above.

---

[13] In the case above I am not suggesting it is resolved in any final sense.

The case of the murder of the man from Masahet discussed with respect to violence and conflicts, was one where a conflict escalated not just to involve kin or clan but to involve entire villages. What began as a love triangle, with two men competing in their desire for a particular woman (in other words, wanting her for themselves or individualistic behaviour), evolved to include other kin in a fight resulting in the broken jaw of a Londolovit man, and eventually the death of a Masahet man who was linked to the conflict through his Masahet island residence. This was certainly a situation where this person was viewed relationally, or as a member of a particular group, rather than as an individual.

Simple division of conflicts into those that are 'interpersonal' or involving close kin and those that are social is impossible in Lihir and, I would assume, in many other contexts. While I have not chosen to examine 'political' conflicts or land disputes here, I shall touch on these in the next chapter, which discusses the growing feelings of inequality and hostility in the context of the gold mine on Niolam. Many of the conflicts in the next chapter turn on a person's position as a member of a particular group, in other words, on relational aspects of personhood rather than the individualistic nature of most of the conflicts of this chapter. These two chapters are like mirror images, this one about conflicts due to people having a core self, and acting according to it, while the disputes in the next chapter are about people's position as members of classes or groups. The conflicts discussed in the two chapters look very different, the ones here more intimate whereas those I now turn to involve social clashes. However, I do not imply contrast them as social versus personal conflicts, because Lihirians do not oppose the social and personal. Instead, both types of conflicts are equally social but have different mechanisms and causes. As highlighted, too, conflicts that may appear to have certain characteristics such as individuality, can evolve to include wider groups.

# 6

## Perceiving inequality: social relations, mining and conflict

The development of a large gold mine on Niolam, the main island of the Lihir group, has seen many changes in Lihir, both negative and positive. Increasingly Lihirians perceive these changes as the cause of growing inequality between various sectors of Lihirian society. Both Lihirians and some outsiders working at the mine (both Papua New Guinean and Australian) condemn what they see as the development of a 'class-based' society. Perceptions of inequality are largely based on the distribution of funds gained from the mine, particularly those of compensation and royalties, as certain individuals and groups are now seen as having gained funds through no effort of their own.

Since mining began in Lihir, conceptions of social equity have been largely expressed in terms of economic equity. This inequity is not perceived as a necessary or unavoidable result of the development associated with mining, but is viewed as the result of the actions of persons in Lihir. The economic gains of some people are viewed negatively in comparison with notions of the moral acquisition of economic benefits, primarily through work. Traditionally, gains obtained through the work of feasting were redistributed. The prestige of older men relied on their redistribution of the pigs and shell money acquired through their position as leaders. Many older men have benefitted as a result of the activities of mining are not distributing these gains. Their actions are being judged by other Lihirians as opposed to morally valued generosity, instead being viewed as greedy for breaching these ideals of redistribution (cf. Kahn 1986:39–44 on ideals of generosity and censure of greed and gluttony). Thus, the perceived growing inequality resulting from the mine is seen as ensuing from the immoral conduct of persons who act with only themselves in mind.

The characterisation of the present as one of growing inequity posits a past where social relations were based on equality and redistribution rather than hierarchy. When conflicts now arise around resources, Lihirians criticise the way the conflict is carried out, who the parties to the conflict are, and how the dispute is resolved. In referring to such disputes, Lihirians contrasted conflicts in the 'mine affected areas' with places such as Mahur, where conflicts are conducted and resolved according to customary practices. In these perceptions, Mahur appears as a representation of the past in the present, a type of 'living fossil'.

My interest is not so much in the details of conflicts resulting from the presence of the mine but on the nature of these conflicts. What are the key issues that arise in these conflicts, and how is the process of disputation changing? In Chapter 5 I explored conflicts between close relations, which often develop as a result of tension between the ideals of relational conduct and the lived experience of individual practice. The conflicts I deal with in this chapter also result from these tensions, but in a different way, being centred on ideas of equality between people (relational) and the destructive power of greed (individual). In the case of these conflicts, it is groups that are in disputation or are considered to be greedy, marking these conflicts as different to the disputes discussed in Chapter 5.

## Mining in Lihir

The major gold deposit called Ladolam was discovered on Niolam in 1982, but it was a few years before mining became a possibility. Negotiations were prolonged as all parties were mindful of the problems that the Bougainville Copper mining project faced in the late 1980s. Eventually, in 1995 approval for the mine was arranged between Lihirians and the Papua New Guinean Government and construction began later that year. This was completed in June 1997 and production began just a few months before I arrived in Lihir in November.

From 1997 to 2005 the Lihir Management Company (LMC), a wholly owned subsidiary of Rio Tinto Plc, managed the mine for Lihir Gold Ltd, the owner of the gold resource. Following this, Lihir Gold owned and operated the mine itself, before being bought out by Newcrest Mining Ltd in 2011. These changes are of little relevance to Lihirians who simply call LMC, Lihir Gold or Newcrest the '*kampani*'. What is relevant is that they have little control over the operations of the mine or its profits. The mine is large, and as of 2012 there was an estimated 80 million ounces of gold to be mined until about 2023 with processing continuing for at least a further decade. The mine itself is located in the Luise Caldera, a dormant volcano on the north-eastern side of Niolam. The processing plant is located adjacent to the mine on Malom (or Marom) Point. The village of Putput 1 had to be relocated south of this point, which had been the site of their village. To the north of the processing plant is Kapit village, the site for part of a growing stockpile—which is slowly filling in much of Luise Harbour. About 20 kilometres further north is Londolovit village and the site of the township by the same name. This area was once a plantation, and is now the site for the LMALA[1] office, the LMC offices for Community Relations and Business Development and the Provincial Government Office, as well as two supermarkets, two banks, a hardware store, and numerous smaller shops and businesses. A few kilometres

[1] LMALA: Lihir Mining Area Landowner's Association.

further north is the airport, located on the plateau above Kunaye village. The people there now tell the time by the roar of the many plane flights arriving and departing each day.

This area, from Putput on the eastern coast to Zuen, the village just past Kunaye on the north coast, is labelled the 'affected area' in the Integrated Benefits Package (IBP) negotiated by the mining company and Lihirians. In 2000 the closest island to this area, Malie, was also labelled as 'affected', as it had customary rights to make gardens and collect materials such as sago and bamboo near the villages of Kunaye, Zuen and Kapit. Through the construction years and the initial years of production, these areas (with perhaps the exception of Malie Island) received large amounts of compensation: for relocation, for dust coming off the road and the quarry, for destruction of plants and gardens due to mining and road construction, for the area taken up by the airport and so on. In addition, many of the executives of land blocks in the Special Mining Lease area live in these villages, and they receive compensation and royalty payments.

The rest of Lihir, unofficially labelled the 'unaffected area', has still been significantly altered by the arrival of the mine, but the people of this area have received very little money in the form of compensation. A ring road has been constructed around Niolam that has made mobility much easier, and with the mine have come a few hundred cars and trucks, many owned by Lihirians. During construction a large percentage of the adult males of Lihir were employed at the mine (about 2000 of a total Lihirian population of about 8000 at the time), meaning that they were unavailable for gardening, house-building, church attendance and the like.[2]

[2] Since the development of the mine, many villages have benefited from wharves, improved resources for schooling and health care, improved transport by road, sea and air, more employment and business opportunities, and improvements in the form of water supplies. Negatively, there are problems with alcohol and drunkenness, increasing law and order problems (assaults, theft, marital discord), and issues with migrants, in addition to the problems discussed in this chapter with reference to the distribution of benefits.

It is the differential impact in Lihir that bothers many (if not most) Lihirians, rather than simply the negative consequences attributed to the arrival of this gold mine. It is these perceptions to which I now turn.

## Perceiving the present

### *Criticising inequalities and social class: hostility and gossip*

People in Lihir now commonly deride what they perceive to be the growing inequality between various groups of Lihirians. Educated Lihirians refer to this in English as the growth of a 'class system,' while non-English speakers made statements such as '*mipela i no wankain nau*' (T.P. we are not all the same now) or '*sampela man i go antap*' (T.P. some people are upwardly mobile/at the top of a hierarchy), or in a mixture of Tok Pisin and English, '*mipela i no ekwal nau*' (we are not all equals now). Generally, such comments referred to economic inequalities between areas of Lihir: the 'affected areas' versus the rest of the island group. In some contexts, though, it could refer to particular persons who had benefited from the mine's presence, especially those older men who were acknowledged controllers of areas of land and who were therefore the recipients of money from compensation or royalty payments.

The mine has affected certain areas of Lihir more acutely than others. Those villages between and including Zuen on the north coast to Putput on the eastern coast of Niolam have suffered the most disruption and received the most benefits. That is the basis of compensation: it is paid for various losses and disturbances. However, many Lihirians outside the affected areas do not see it this way. The negative impacts on places such as Putput and Kapit are not readily visible to many people in Lihir who do not experience them, while the benefits, seen in relocation houses built by the mining company and cars bought from compensation money, are what is obvious.

There are a number of points on which others in Lihir criticise those people living in the 'affected areas'. There is a perception that these people receive money for little or no reason. Most people in Lihir seemed to feel it was fair that the people relocated from Putput and Kapit villages had houses built by the mining company, and were compensated for lack of access to their traditional men's house sites, damage to graves, economic plants and garden sites. However, most people also felt that people of Putput village had been given what they deserved and the claims they continue to make on the company are based in greed and laziness. While I do not agree with Filer and Mandie-Filer when they comment on the 'envy and resentment of villagers living further away from the "affected area", who are inclined to lump all "Putputs" together as a bunch of idle, greedy snobs who deserve to have their houses burnt, their cars wrecked, and their daughters raped' (1998:6), Lihirians living away from the immediate vicinity of the mine are angry about what they perceive to be the undeserved windfall given to those in the 'affected areas'.

The general objection made by people from outside the affected areas is the failure to share benefits in circumstances where it is considered normal. An example is the 'money for dust': each household in Putput, Londolovit and Kapit villages received K100 per month during 1998 and 1999 to compensate for dust that became airborne from the road and from large trucks that accessed a quarry near Putput village. In the household neighbouring mine on Mahur lived the mother of a woman who had married a man in Putput. Her daughter in Putput had borne a son to another man before being married, and she left him in the care of her mother on Mahur. What angered her mother, aunt (MZ) and sisters was her relative wealth and her unwillingness to share this with them, especially given they were caring for her child. She received this 'money for dust' as well as income from her husband's job, and lived in a relocation house, yet contributed very little to the upkeep of her son.

Since the beginning of production of gold by the mine in 1997 there have been new criticisms directed particularly at residents of Putput, Londolovit and Kunaye villages for what other Lihirians see as inappropriate and undeserved demands for more money. Members of Putput village have closed the processing plant on a number of occasions, one of the longest lasting closures being of two days in July 1998. In addition, there were threats to close the airport on a number of occasions by members of Kunaye village and at least one actual closure. Furthermore, the company has been involved in protracted discussions with the people of Londolovit many times since construction. All these occasions involved claims for more money from the company, and some of the Putput and Londolovit claims have resulted in new settlements and compensation.

Lihirians from other areas gossip about (*tetnge piel*) and criticise (*puersie*) the actions and supposed motives of the people of these villages on a number of fronts: first, on the basis of the improper use of *golgol* (T.P.: *gorgor*; taboo markers), which are used to shut down areas such as the airport or the plant site. This *golgol* is a particular plant of the ginger family (*Zingerberaceae*) that is tied somewhere in an area to place a taboo on the site. In contexts other than the mine they are used on trees to preserve fruit for later use, or more importantly in this case, on pieces of land to declare disputed ownership, to stop work and inform of the need for negotiation. In the history of mining in Lihir to date, the company has heeded the messages of golgol, stopping work and negotiating with those who have placed *golgol* at the site. Just as the construction of the airport was finished, the owners of the land closed it for a few days by placing golgol on the runway. The company abided by these *golgol* and negotiated with those involved (Bainton 2011).

The use of *golgol* in relation to the mining project is criticised as not following the customary usage: of being based in improper motives such as anger and greed rather than as peacefully signifying the need for talking and negotiation. One man on Mahur told the story of Tgorous to illustrate this point. Although use of the *golgol* as a taboo marker is common throughout Island Melanesia, some say he invented the use of *golgol* when he tied a piece of this plant to a bamboo pole and used it to taboo warfare, to bring the age of peaceful relations. This man portrayed Tgorous as having altruistic motives that are in sharp contrast to perceptions about members of the 'affected area' as interested only in themselves.

Second, people of the 'affected area' are criticised for their desire and need for money. They are sometimes mocked by people from other areas as being unwilling or unable to make decent gardens to feed themselves (a criticism mostly directed at the people of Putput); instead they must rely on money from compensation or earnings from the mine. Survey work on the nutrition of people in Putput showed that they often eat garden food, and eat store bought rice in the same frequency as people on Mahur (about one third of meals involve rice). Instead of buying all their food, the money is used to supplement an often poor diet in Lihir with sources of protein such as tinned meat and fish. On the other hand, when people believe that those of affected areas do not rely on money to survive, they then criticise them for being greedy: if the money isn't absolutely necessary they should not ask for it, or instead they should distribute it to others. Whether being portrayed as being unable to take care of themselves or as greedy, money is an important part of negative portrayals of people of the 'affected areas'.

There is, then, an insistent and growing perception of inequality between the 'affected areas' and the rest of Lihir, which is expressed through criticism and gossip about the actions and motives of people especially of the village of Putput but also of the other villages closest to the mine. This criticism by people outside of this area portrays people of the 'affected area' as a homogenous group who are concerned for themselves only (selfish: individualism), who are greedy and who get things undeservedly rather than through morally virtuous work.

In addition, there is a view that the distribution of benefits is inequitable and favours older men. The mining company leases areas of land held under customary tenure amounting to roughly 2700 acres, for which the residents of the 'affected areas' receive compensation. These lease areas were divided into 140 'blocks' of varying size, and for most of these blocks a single 'block executive' was then named, though some blocks remained disputed or have more than one executive. Some executives have claims to more than one block, so there are only 90 block executives for the 140 blocks. These men (and they are almost entirely men) have received compensation for damage and destruction as the mine has continued to progressively use land in the lease areas. With the advent of royalties the number of block executives has increased somewhat, with the proceeds from some blocks being divided among claimants, yet there is still only a small proportion of the population who have any claim to an income from blocks (Filer and Mandie-Filer 1998:3–4).

The aim of having block executives was that these people would be holders of money received from the mining project, who would then redistribute it to members of the clan, or use it on clan-based projects, as was the role of senior men in the past. There is little or no evidence about the extent to which the senior men have carried this out, but the non-executives complain that little redistribution is occurring and that 'executives' (which usually means those who are signatories to the bank account into which payments are made) are using the money as their own. Where it is redistributed, this is generally to other senior men in the clan, who do not pass it on to their younger brothers, nephews, sisters and so on.

It is this system of payment of benefits to executives that prompts perceptions of inequality. In a LMC research report on the perceptions of Lihirians about issues associated with mining, 40 per cent of those surveyed were unhappy about the distribution of royalty and compensation payments, either because they were not redistributed outside the mining area or because they were not distributed to the elderly or the young (that is, the middle-aged kept it). It was women in the 36 to 49-year-age group, and men at any age over 36 years who were most dissatisfied with the distribution (LMC 1999:12). While the block executives were senior men (over the age of 36), these satisfied men formed a small proportion of the men of this age group. In my own experience, it was men who were not employed by the mine or the contracting companies (that is, they had no other source of income), and who were from the 'affected areas', who were most vociferous about this. These inequalities based on the distribution of money by age and gender had little currency with people on Mahur, who were concerned primarily with the distribution of money by area (that is, affected versus non-affected) in Lihir.

People in Lihir perceive their island group to be divided between those who have received benefits from the mine and those who have received little. This distinction is made primarily on the basis of spatial distribution of payments (compensation and royalties) and housing assistance, but particularly within the 'affected areas' a distinction is developing between block executives (generally senior men) and others (often younger men). Perception of these inequalities is met with worry about the increasing divisions in Lihir, and also with much hostility, criticism and gossip. Whether hostility (*lil tua*) is directed at those who receive money and benefits on the basis that they are from a particular area, or whether they are 'block executives,' other Lihirians are critical because they are receiving money and benefits on the basis of their membership of a particular group, and sometimes because they are not redistributing those benefits to others. People in places such as Putput receive benefits because they are 'Putput-ers' but then ignore their other connections such as those of lineage and clan. Relationships based on area, seniority and immediate nuclear family are taking precedence over (sometimes to the exclusion of) clan and kinship relationships.

### *Money and greed*

In the section above, I made reference to the perception that continuing claims made by those in the 'affected areas' on the mining company for compensation is based in greed. Lihirians are increasingly employing the concept of greed to characterise relationships both between Lihirians and the mine, and between Lihirians themselves. Greed (T.P.: *gridi*) for Lihirians refers to wanting (and generally getting) or keeping things that one does not need or is not entitled to, and, in the context of mining in Lihir, it is a concept that is used with great frequency: by Lihirians against other Lihirians and by white employees of the mining company about Lihirians, but very rarely in reference to the activities of the mining company itself. Greed is a charge of individualism, a failure of responsibilities to a particular group (be it family, clan or household).

Lihirians use the concept of greed in two main contexts, first, as discussed above, to refer to the actions of various Lihirians in their attempts and sometimes success in gaining more money from the mining company. These extra settlements are seen as evidence of the greediness of the people of these villages.

Perhaps of more concern for many people in Lihir is greed that directly affects other Lihirians: being greedy about the property or money of other Lihirians. It is one thing to be greedy to receive more money from a mining giant, which to many Lihirians appears to have endless resources and finances. It is another thing, and far more destructive to Lihirians, to covet things of a neighbour or clan member, particularly when that desire is for another's land.

The magistrate in Kunaye village (part of the 'affected area') expressed his worry to me about the divisions in Lihir society that were being caused by greed for money: '*bipo kastam i pawa, na nau mipela i bruk bruk nabaut long toea*' (T.P. 'In the past *kastam* was our strength but now we are divided by money'). He said that cases of land disputes are not so much becoming more frequent as they are changing in character. Now people dispute not just between clans over pieces of land but within clans. Not only that, but when there are cases of disputes between clans, these seem much more heated than in the past. He explained that people know that they do not have a claim on the land, or have a very slight claim, but said they claim the land anyway, in the hope that they will earn money from it some day. In some cases this means that two clans dispute ownership of a piece of land. In other cases, conflicts arise between brothers (close or more distant) or between uncles and nephews (MB/ZS) who dispute their relations to a now dead controller of the land. The magistrate of Kunaye was angry about this turn of events and worried about what would happen in the future, expressing that everything was now going wrong: '*I no moa kamap gut nau. I no olsem taim bilong tumbuna. I senis nau.*' (T.P. 'Nothing is right now. Its not like the time when our ancestors were living. Its changed now.')

### *Alcohol and social divisions*

With the advent of the gold mine, drunkenness has become a problem in Lihir that is increasingly being perceived as socially divisive. Workers at the mine spend some or all of their pay on alcohol for themselves and their friends, resulting in binge drinking lasting minimally hours and often days. Driving while drunk is the cause of an increasing number of accidents on the island. Furthermore, alcohol consumption is associated with rowdy behaviour, damage to property and violence against people, as well as the use of wages on beer rather than household necessities.

More interesting, though, is the perception that drunkenness results in violence generated by resentment of emerging inequalities, such as those discussed above. While in June 1999 many people with whom I spoke felt that problems caused by alcohol were actually decreasing, with less violent actions within villages,[3] people felt that alcohol consumption was very dangerous given the amount of hostility and resentment between areas of Lihir. Clement Dardar, the chairman at that time of the Nimamar Local Level Government (NLLG), said that people 'have that little bit of hatred there' (tapping his abdomen; speaking in English). This hatred is based on the division between the 'affected' and other areas of Lihir. He explained that people can fight those in their own clan now, and felt that the clan system would break down under pressure of divisions of inequality. 'When that happens,' he said, 'Lihir will be ruined.'

In the perception of many Lihirians, then, the real problem with alcohol is not car accidents or increased domestic violence, but that when drunk, the resentments people feel will be expressed in violence towards members of

[3] Incidents reported to police involving alcohol were actually increasing during that period, suggesting perhaps that people were becoming accustomed to problems in the village due to alcohol.

one's own clan, eventually leading to the breakdown of what is seen by many Lihirians as the basis of their society: the clan system. Normally suppressed, the anger felt towards people as members of particular groups (such as those of the 'affected area' or 'block executives') is manifested under the disinhibiting effects of alcohol. As stated in Chapter 5, some men claim that they drink intentionally to precipitate arguments that they are unable to execute if sober. Lihirians, like many other Melanesians, believe that men are not responsible for incidents that occur while they are under the influence of alcohol.

## Perceiving the past: visions of egalitarianism

In perceiving the present as being wrought by spatial and distributive inequalities that are met with hostility, criticism and a lack of restraint in violent behaviour (exacerbated by alcohol), the past is thereby presented as the mirror image: a time of equality and egalitarianism. In particular, this refers to the time just before exploration and the development of the mine, when Lihir had been transformed from a group of people who were 'warring cannibals' by the Catholic and Methodist churches, to model Christians who loved their neighbours and lived in harmony.

There is a growing literature about both 'the past in the present' and the past as seen through the lens of the present. Marshall Sahlins's work is perhaps the most notable example of the former approach, dealing with how understandings of the past inform interpretations about and actions in the present, for example, his work on the apotheosis of Cook in Hawaii as the God Lono (Sahlins 1981; 1982; 1985; 1995). The second approach, examining views of the past as context dependent on the present situation of interpreters, is critical for an understanding of history as dependent upon the observer (for example, Dening 1992; 1995; Friedman 1992; Keesing 1982; Neumann 1992).

In lived experience, though, it is sometimes difficult to ascertain whether the past is being represented in terms of the present, or whether the present is being contextualised through the past. In Lihir, for example, there is the case of the TFA (*Tutorme* Farmers Association),[4] an association concerned variously with improving agriculture in Lihir, providing a strong work ethic based in Christianity, or waiting for cargo to be brought by the ancestors. The story of the TFA now states that the original leader of the cult, Theodore Arau, predicted the current situation in Lihir: that gold would be found and a township would arise at Londolovit. This gold would be the cargo from the ancestors, and people would become rich. Some in Lihir say that the present has been interpreted in terms of the past: that when the prospectors and mining company first arrived Lihirians interpreted their presence in terms of the TFA, assuming they were ancestors bringing cargo. Other Lihirians suggest that the predictions of the TFA have been reinterpreted (or totally revised) in light of the present situation of the mine. Perhaps it is better to conceive of the relationship between past and present as neither exclusively one or the other, but as both the past and the present being continually renegotiated in light of the other.

Lihirians are certainly reinterpreting the past in view of the changes that have occurred in relation to the mine in the last few years. As discussed in relation to Christian morality, Lihirians refer to the past as having a number of distinct episodes: during the pre-contact phase, when they were at war with one another, they lived scattered throughout the bush. People could not walk around without fear, but at the same time they were said to maintain relationships with their clan both in other areas of Lihir and neighbouring islands such as Tabar, Tanga and the New Ireland mainland. Then there was the contact time where recruiting was common and people fled to the mountains to avoid signing contracts as labourers. Those who did go brought back trade goods. This was also the time of German and later Australian administrations, but about this Lihirians said (and remembered) little. Nor did they speak of World War I, their memories being restricted to World War II. Missionisation signifies another episode of Lihirian past, and stories abound of the changes to living arrangements, burial arrangements, the arrival of schooling and church

[4] See also Chapter 4.

teaching.[5] It is this time that figures most prominently, not as 'the past' but as the 'almost present;' a direct opposite of what is now occurring in Lihir, of what Lihir is becoming. People seem to be straddled across the boundary of this 'almost present', especially on Mahur.

In the island group since the advent of mining, the past and present are located spatially as much as they are located temporally. The main island, with its mix of 'affected areas' and less affected ones, represents the present. This is a present that comprises money, better housing and cars, as well as social problems and growing inequality. From the central place located perhaps at the mine, or maybe the space from Londolovit (the town) to Putput, the impact of the mine radiates outward becoming more diffuse. In this spatial schema, Mahur, the northern most island of the group, appears as an embodiment of the past, a living fossil.

### *Mahur as the living past*

When I first arrived on Mahur it was with two women who had spent time on Mahur when they were younger (having moved later to Samo village on Niolam) and another woman, Denitha, who came from Hurtol village on Niolam and had never been to Mahur. After a few days Denitha told me that she had been afraid to visit Mahur due to the perception that Mahur was a place where the people followed *kastam* (customary law/practices) closely, where they knew sorcery and where strange things happened. She told me that a story had circulated in her area that there had been a dead man floating on a raft out near Mahur. While obscure, the tale of his presence was linked to magical practices. In this tale, Mahur seems connected with the dangerous past before the age of Christianity.

More generally, though, Mahur is linked to the valued practices of the era post-missionisation and pre-mining. Mahurians see themselves as expert gardeners, able to produce large yams as well as the surplus that is necessary

[5] Lihirians were brought to the beach from the plateau to live, and burial arrangements were changed from burial at sea or in men's houses to public cemeteries and six-foot-deep graves.

for the feasting that occurs between about April and November throughout the island group each year. As argued in Chapter 2, techniques of gardening seem to be a little different on Mahur. Mahurians who had settled at Samo continued their tradition of excellent gardening, and members of Samo village bought yams from them for feasts, a practice which would have been very shameful on Mahur. Given changes on Niolam in the context of mining that mean that much male labour has been withdrawn from gardening, the differences between Mahur (which has relatively few males working at the mine or with contractors) and Niolam are becoming more striking.

In feasts, Mahur is also seen by many Lihirians to be following customary practice more closely than Niolam. In July 1998 I witnessed a *tunkanut* feast at Samo village.[6] At one point, men chose to eat rice rather than the tubers and pork that were also available. Some people sold betelnut just outside the feast area. The feasting was also delayed a number of times by rain, and on the last day of the feast there was much drunkenness, which somewhat spoiled the dances. When I described this feasting to Mahurians they derided the changes that were occurring on Niolam: rice and drunkenness at feasts, the sale of betelnut to guests which should be plentifully supplied free by hosts, and the lack of successful rain magicians.[7]

To some extent there is a widening divide between Niolam and all three of the outer islands. When a mortuary feast took place on Malie Island later in 1998, rice was excluded from the major feasting, and drunkenness was prohibited on threat of fines and expulsion from the island during the feasts. There was no problem with the weather, and all food and betelnut was free. While all the outer islands (and Kunaye village on Niolam perhaps due to its close ties with the outer islands) pride themselves on their ability to hold 'proper' customary feasts, Mahur is emphasised by many Lihirians as being more conservative than the others in terms not only of feasting but also of magic and sorcery. Thus, the spatial distance is construed also as a marker

[6] The last feast to take place in the series of mortuary feasts that occur for people.

[7] See Chapter 8 for further discussion of mortuary feasting, including this one in particular.

of change, with distance from the mine both explaining and indicating the conservation of *kastam*.

Feasts provide a context where ideals of equality are upheld. When the ground ovens are opened, the food is taken out and lined up on slightly raised platforms made of leaves (*pke sniol*), separated into types of tubers. The pigs (if there are any for the feast) are placed at one end of the platform, generally with the yams closest to them and then mami and sweet potato. Betelnut and tobacco are placed at one end. The pork is carved by a man, and then the distribution begins. For some feasts the food is divided first into clan piles, and then given out to individuals (a distribution type called *mniase*). In other feasts the food is given out directly from the main platform to groups of three to six people (called *pniari*). Women take great care to ensure that food is divided equally, and for this reason they divide the food between the three to six women before eating anything. Men, who get their food separately from women in the grounds of the men's house, will eat first, and then divide the remains to take home among the three to six people eating from the one pile.

While the distributive hierarchy is maintained, the emphasis is on equal shares: yams are the highest prestige, and there are generally the least of these at the feast, so when the small pile has one chunk of yam this will be cut into pieces based on the number of recipients. If anyone gets less this will be the dealer of the food, who will forfeit their piece to give to a visitor (*wasir*; such as me or people from other islands at the feast). Children are not given less food than adults. Thus, when shares are not equal it will be because someone forfeits some food rather than someone being given less.[8]

Apart from the context of feasting, Mahur (in comparison to most of Niolam) appears as a living fossil in other ways. There are no cars on Mahur. During my time in Lihir, only a few men from Mahur went to work, and those

[8] Note the difference between this way of distribution and that adopted for benefits of the mine such as compensation money and housing. In this distribution, people are judged as being more or less needy or deserving and are given things on that basis, whereas the distribution of food at feasts I saw on Mahur emphasised equality.

who did had a two week on one week off roster, meaning they came back to Mahur with some of their wages and helped in the gardens. Drunkenness is rarely a problem on Mahur, except for the few men who, when they finish their fortnight's work, get drunk and come back to Mahur to continue drinking with other men. Despite the small number of men working, there is not a division between those with income and those without. Workers on Mahur have used the money earned to build permanent houses and have put some into clan businesses, feasting and into the construction of the churches. Money is being redistributed on Mahur in a way that does not appear to be occurring elsewhere in Lihir, a way that is interpreted as being according to *kastam* (customary practice). Mahurians also pride themselves on the proper treatment of visitors (*wasir*), which is to take them into the men's house or hamlet area, and meet their needs for food, betelnut, tobacco, drinking coconuts and good conversation (*pniari wasir*). This practice appears to be declining on Niolam, or is being replaced with the hospitality of store-bought biscuits and soft drinks (see Chapter 4).

The emphasis by Mahurians (and the other outer islands of Lihir) on work to provide sustenance, whether this be through labour-intensive gardening techniques or through paid employment, is in contrast to perceptions of the people of the 'affected areas' as gaining something for nothing. Unlike the situation for Wewak people described by Gewertz and Errington (1999), the 'have nots' in Lihir are not generally harshly evaluated. Through the SWIT organisation (Sepik Women in Trade), women of Wewak declared that opportunities were open to all who worked hard, thus effectively declaring that women who did not succeed brought this upon themselves:

> Poverty hence became not simply an overwhelmingly difficult and unfair life circumstance with which women must somehow cope; it became a matter of degree directly reflective of personal character and worth. (Gewertz & Errington 1999:58)

On Lihir, the continued reliance on subsistence agriculture meant that those people who did not have money were not viewed as morally bereft as long as they continued to work in their gardens. Rather than being positively morally evaluated on their position in terms of money and what they had, Lihirians were valued for their work (*pniez*), be it paid employment, gardening or a range of other skills (fishing, canoe building and so on).

### *Disputation on Mahur*

Mahur is seen also as following *kastam* in regards to the resolution of disputes about land and resources. A number of disputes occurred while I was on Mahur, most at the time of clearing gardens, between September and November. In a number of cases a *golgol* was placed at the site of a newly cleared garden to question the rightful ownership of the land. Usually these disputes were solved quickly and easily at a village court session where older men shared their knowledge of the transactions and feasts were held for owners of the piece of land. The current rightful controllers of the land were then decided upon, and *lil malum* (harmony) was restored to relationships.

More complicated disputes seemed rare on Mahur, the one example being ownership of the land on which the aidpost in Kuelam village was built. A young man of Nzol clan had a possibly valid but ambiguous claim to inheritance of the land through the performance of *kastam wok*. The aidpost was important to the community, and forced relocation of it would have caused serious disturbance to its function, at least for a considerable time. This dispute was made more difficult by the community's dislike of the nurse and her husband at the time.

The aidpost dispute was further complicated because the nurse and her husband were unable to place a *golgol* on new building work being carried out by the young man, as the land belonged not to them but to the government. In the view of the nurse's husband, they would need to receive permission from the government to place a *golgol* on their behalf. This delayed recognition of the dispute in any formal way and prevented proper negotiations from occurring.

There were a number of court cases about the aidpost, in which knowledge was produced: about the sale of the area to the government, about where the boundaries of that area lay, about how the young man's father, Tukan, came to occupy the land between the aidpost and the escarpment wall, about who cleared the area for the aidpost, and about promises made to the young man about his inheritance of the land given the performance of appropriate *kastam wok*. Various solutions to the dilemma were canvassed, including the wholesale removal of the aidpost to another area (in the Nawus plantation) or removal of the young man to another hamlet (possibly forcibly by Royal Constabulary). In fact, the debate fizzled out, while the dispute did not. The young man finished building his new house, and the new section of the aidpost was built in that area. With the departure of the aidpost worker and her husband to another aidpost in late 1998, the young man and the aidpost returned to a state of fairly pleasant coexistence.

Conflicts about land on Mahur, then, either have relatively simple solutions that identify the appropriate controller of land according to *kastam* (as disputes are generally about ownership and not land boundaries), or disputes are left to simmer and possibly fizzle out as the situation changes. It appears, then, that Mahurians can tolerate some level of unresolved conflict and strife within their community when disputes are too complex to be easily solved, and maintain cordial relations despite this. I will return to this point later in relation to conflicts in the affected areas.

The rendering of Mahur as the past in the present, as a living fossil, has particular repercussions. In perceiving Mahur in opposition to the present, which is characterised as a time of inequality and increasing hostility and social division, Mahur is portrayed by Lihirians as a bastion of *kastam* and of egalitarianism. Yet this perception hides many inequalities on Mahur itself, and ignores less dominating voices that speak of the relationship between the past and the present, between areas of Lihir and between individual persons.

## Hidden inequalities

What is missing from this perception that dichotomises past and present in space as egalitarianism versus inequality? In positioning Mahur in opposition to the inequalities developing in the island group, the inequalities inherent in social relations on Mahur itself are ignored. Despite ideals, inequalities abound on Mahur: for example, between the leaders and other men, between households, and between men and women.

Studies of inequality have generally concentrated on finding the principle locus for the production of inequality, many following an economic model which suggests that inequality arises out of the relations of production (Modjeska 1982; compare Kelly 1993:1; 510 *et passim*). Hence, the bride service model of Collier and Rosaldo suggests that because marriage organises relations of production then it is the locus of inequality (Collier & Rosaldo 1981). Kelly, on the other hand, defines inequality more broadly as 'social differentiation accompanied by differential moral evaluation' (1993:4), which allows him to discuss other forms of inequality. He argues that the Etoro social system, an ethnic group in Papua New Guinea, is mostly economically egalitarian, and that it is 'virtue, moral superiority and prestige rather than material advantages that are unequally distributed' (Kelly 1993:26).

In Lihir it is the current distribution of economic benefits and the power to control the distribution of these that captures the attention of most people. These are not the only inequalities with an economic base, as I argue below. Current discussion of inequalities highlights a very particular range of inequalities: those that are arising in the context of mining, while concealing inequalities in other contexts.

### *Inequalities of leadership*

Leaders in Lihir (*a toe*) are generally senior men who are controllers of the land of the local clan segment, who speak well at gatherings, who have knowledge of the transactions and boundaries of the land, who are not easily angered and who have knowledge of magic to control the weather, improve crop growth and so on. As discussed in Chapter 5, leaders should be accorded respect (*sio*), partially entailing giving them shell money (*a le*), so that they have standing in the community. People should not refer to their heads or teeth, and to do so would signify a distinct lack of respect. Leaders should be able to rely on other clan members to contribute large yams as well as money (both shell and Kina) to buy pigs for feasts.

Leaders, then, are not viewed as equals. Rather, they expect and are given special treatment. Their superiority is generally viewed not as problematic, but as deserved and being for the betterment of the clan. When their superiority seems undeserved, people are quick to undermine the position of these leaders. Thus, the man on Mahur who fancied himself as a leader was derided in private as being a man only of talk rather than action, and a man who was aging faster than his years. Given that his superiority was viewed as undeserved, Mahurians treated his position with joking and barbed criticism, which had the effect of undermining his claims to authority.

In recent years leadership has become more complex, as Lihirian men become 'caught between the burdens associated with tradition and modernity' (Bainton 2008a:206). Men juggle commitments to *kastam* and kin, and to employment and business. These entail different orientations to personhood with more or less emphasis on individualism.

Young men are accorded little standing in Lihir relative to leaders and senior men, instead being the workforce for the communities of which they are a part. Young men on Mahur perform communal tasks for people in the village, such as clearing gardens in small groups, cutting timber in the forest and building houses, as well as catching pigs for feasts and then butchering them. A young man's worth is measured on how willingly he carries out such tasks: a *zik puet* (good or virtuous man) is one who works hard for other people rather than one who complains, is lazy or spends his time getting drunk. Young men are not equals of senior men, rather they constitute their work force.

### *Gendered inequalities*

In perceiving Mahur in opposition to the inequalities of the present, the subordinate position of women is ignored by most Lihirian men, as is their quiet resentment of their position. Women on Mahur do most of the work of gardening, including some clearing, planting, tending the plants, weeding and harvesting. They do most of the cooking, laundry, sweeping and minding of children, and spend their 'leisure' time fishing or weaving mats and baskets. When serving food they serve themselves last, and if anyone misses out on food, it is the women. In times of shortage, women often eat one meal less than everyone else a day—that is, when food is scarce and people eat only two meals a day, women eat only one—and if there is not enough protein or greens to satisfy everyone, women miss out, eating plain rice or tubers.

At feasts, raw food is divided between the men and women, and it is the men who get the biggest yams and the largest share of food. Men also receive the largest pigs. Men's and women's food is generally cooked in separate ground ovens, and it is the men's oven that is generally completed first (with the women's up to an hour later). The ovens are opened at the same time, with the men's just slightly before the women's, meaning that their food is generally better cooked than the women's. The men's distribution is done first, and the men have time to eat their fill and then casually rest before leaving, while the women barely have time to distribute food, pack it into baskets and leave, re-cooking their food later in their own hamlets. Feasts, therefore, quite often represent the work of women, both in gardening and in the peeling and cooking, and the sociality of men.

The position of women relative to men can be read from their bodies: in general, women in Lihir are shorter than men, and are much thinner once they marry and have children. This is partly attributable to the fact that they bear (many) children. Once one child is weaned, another is often on the way. Yet it is also due to the arduous work that women undertake, their missing out on protein, greens or entire meals, and the fact that unless they are very ill they do not rest or see the nurse (in contrast to children and men).

Women rarely complain about the inequities they face, and men do not seem to notice the hardships that women suffer. One man did complain that his wife had too much work, but that was on the basis of her having to look after three of her sister's children as well as her own, not simply because the work that women do daily is excessive. Occasionally women expressed to me that they thought it was unfair that men got the best food, that this *kastam* was unjust, yet they also felt themselves powerless to change it (see also Hemer 2011b and Macintyre n.d. about the position of women in Lihir).

### *Household inequalities*

In reference to neighbouring Tanga, Foster argues that there are inequalities between households based upon differential access to coconuts for making copra:

> inequalities in the distribution of coconuts give rise to inequalities among households that are uneasily marked by the image of lineage solidarity projected in mortuary feasting (*kastam*). (Foster 1995:88)

Foster ties the differentiation of households entirely to the intensification of commodity relations on Tanga following World War II. In arguing that the household is tied to commodity production while it is the lineage that is tied to the more egalitarian *kastam*, Foster effectively denies the possibility that customary practices could have been the basis for non-egalitarian relations.

This argument is in direct contrast to that made by Newton for the Orokaiva (1985), and by Carrier and Carrier for Ponam (1989), both ethnic groups in Papua New Guinea. Carrier and Carrier describe the changes in Ponam society since colonisation, particularly the impact of remittances made by migrants. They argue that:

> As the outside world expanded and as the economic importance of Manus itself for Ponam decreased, islanders lost their ability to control significant sources of wealth … Consequently no group of villagers was

> able to control wealth to the exclusion of others, and relations among villagers became more equal. (Carrier & Carrier 1989:25)

In other words, significant sources of inequality existed prior to colonisation, and centred on the control of productive resources.

Newton performs a fine-grained analysis of household inequality among the Orokaiva, considering not only income from copra, but also remittances and other sources of money, other forms of wealth such as number of pigs, tapa cloth, betelnut trees, clothing, plates, pressure lamps and so on, in addition to other measures such as health status and consumption patterns. Inequality between households is not only viewed in terms of monetary values but also status, with some households having members with high status jobs and many modern goods while others have larger gardens and many more pigs (Newton 1985:199–220).

My observations on Mahur accorded much more closely with Newton's analysis of household inequality than with Foster's. A number of households had members that worked to gain an income, yet these were not automatically superior to households that had more pigs, larger gardens, or a member with a prestigious job such as Area Catechist. Household inequalities would appear to have predated the development of the mine. However, as argued in Chapter 2, households on Mahur can rarely be seen as corporate bodies, instead being particular configurations of relations. It was only in particular contexts that differences between households became important, such as when children in a household went hungry due to lack of money and small gardens, or a particular household had a lack of betelnut to give guests or kerosene to light lamps. These inequalities were generally perceived in terms of shortcomings of particular members of the household (lazy wife, squandering husband and so on) rather than of the household as a corporate body.

Inequalities like the ones faced by households, younger men on Mahur and especially by women in Lihir, in general are ignored in the tide of criticism about the changes occurring in the context of the mine. In seeing Mahur as a living fossil, a representation of the past as a time of egalitarianism, inequalities like those discussed above become invisible and so unaddressable.

## Imagining the future: restoring harmony

The perceived inequalities developing in the Lihir group have been met with changes primarily aimed at equalising people and restoring harmony. Above I described court cases in the affected area that have occurred both within and between clans. Those within clans have been mostly brought by younger members of the clan as attempts to gain access to money via ownership of land or machinery used by the mine. One case in Putput Village was resolved by giving younger men a share in the machines owned by their senior relatives.[9] Resolution in this case was not based on principles of *kastam*, which would decree that the younger men would have to do *kastam wok* for the senior males and only inherit when the senior men died, but on the basis of restoring good relations and harmony between these men. Whether the younger men's claims were based on ideas of equality with their elders, or on greed for money, depends on who was asked.

In cases between clans, land in the 'affected areas' has often been divided between the parties who are in conflict rather than being given to the party who has the best claim for it based on knowledge of the history of transactions and *kastam wok* done for the piece of land.[10] These cases, too, are solved with recourse to ideas of equality and harmony rather than notions of who has the best claim based in *kastam*. Cases are solved as quickly as their complications allow, and are not left to simmer as are those on Mahur. It seems that people in the affected area cannot tolerate unresolved disputes as do Mahurians.

It is somewhat perplexing that in attempting to restore equality Lihirians do not resort to solutions based on *kastam*, which is inherently associated with life before the divisive impact of the mine. Instead, equality is being restored

[9] Clans own some machines (for example, tip trucks and bulldozers) that they leased to the mine and so earn income.

[10] Land in these cases is often a source of income, such as land that contains coronous rock used in making concrete in Lihir.

(for that is how they see it, as restoration rather than creation) by resorting to innovative solutions to land and resource disputes. When I pointed this out, that new solutions to conflicts were being found, one man explained that Lihir had changed, '*mani i pulim tingting*' (T.P. money has changed people's reasoning), and that the solutions to disputes had to change too. His response implied that while Lihirians wanted things the way they had been, they had to find new solutions to these new issues.

This accords with a point made by Jackson in regards to the possibilities of compensation in the context of resource developments as restoring the balance that existed prior to the development. Jackson argues that compensation cannot 'restore a pre-existing balance' but that the 'best it can hope to do is create a new mutually acceptable balance' (1997:108). It seems that Lihirians would agree with Jackson, and are looking for a new balance.

In perceiving the present as one of increasing inequality resulting from the presence of the mine, Lihirians develop a cultural critique that demands action. Restoring equality implies a re-establishment of social relationships in the face of the individuality that is greed. However, in positioning Mahur as a representation of the golden age of the past, inequalities inherent on Mahur are rendered invisible, and excluded from this process of cultural critique. The solutions now being found, then, relegate problems of the inequality of women, of households, and the inherent age hierarchy to imperceptibility.

Conflicts arising in relation to the presence of the mine do not turn simply on the increasing individualisation of Lihirian personhood, though this is partially an issue in many conflicts. The presence of the mine, and the modernisation of Lihir in terms of money, wage employment, access to goods, television, and telecommunications (and so on), has not just seen the rise of an individualistic personhood. Instead, people are assessed on their relations with or membership of particular groups emerging in the context of mining, be these based on location (affected area) or ownership status (block executives). These are evaluations of persons based on their relational status as members of particular groups. Yet the criticisms directed at those persons are most often accusations of individualism, such as greed. Often particular persons in a group (a village, or block executives) are singled out for gossip and condemnation, which attacks them individually. Thus, the conflicts developing in relation to the mine often rely on relational definitions of persons to make them liable for disapproval, yet charge them with individualism when moral ideals of relational behaviour are not realised. The particular form of Lihirian personhood has retained both its individualistic and relational aspects, though these are now being cast in different hues (such as spatial relations rather than of kinship or clan).

Lihirian personhood has undergone a number of changes in recent history, with relations of morality being emphasised in the context of Christianity as well as individual responsibility for salvation and sin, and new forms of individuality and relationality emerging in the context of mining and modernisation. Personhood is affected by internal and external influences, and changes over time. Finding an ideal 'Melanesian personhood' is problematic because it ignores these transformations—it is ahistorical.

# PART III

# LOSS AND ITS TRANSFORMATIONS

# 7

## Dying, grieving and forgetting

To now, this book has been concerned with the nature of persons in Lihir and their relational and emotional connections to one another. In Part 3, 'Loss and its Transformation', I ask how persons in Lihir un-become. What is the meaning of death in Lihir? In what ways are relationships transformed or continued between the living and the dead, and how are relationships at stake in particular contexts such as feasting?

During my fieldwork I was perplexed by the nature of grief in Lihir, which to me seemed unaccented. There was little crying at death, people did not give eulogies, and there were no mourning taboos or obvious markers of mourning (for example, black or torn clothes, dirty appearance). People did not speak of grief as a lengthy process. They did not speak about managing their own grief or about grief as pathological. Was this apparent lack of grief a matter of lack of expression or of experience?

The nature of grief implicates understandings not only of emotions but of personhood and the attachments between persons. If personhood in Melanesia is relational, with persons the objectification of relations, then when someone dies grief should be severe and should affect the very nature of others who were in relationship with the deceased. The death of a member of the community should not only leave a space in relations but should affect the definition of all persons who were in relationship with that person. This does not seem to be the case in Lihir, as I discuss below, and this has implications for the nature of personhood.

## Grief and mourning

Death, burial and mortuary ritual has been a consistent part of ethnographies written about groups in Papua New Guinea. A brief look at indexes of many Papua New Guinean ethnographies show references to mourning taboos, burial practices and so on. Brison (1995; 1998), Leavitt (1995) and Schieffelin (1976) emphasise the value of local cultural practices in providing an outlet for strong emotions, and discuss the experience and resolution of grief in the long term. Yet apart from these analyses, there is little material on the emotional context of death, beyond description of the immediate and obvious crying at the death and burial.

Many researchers have seen grief primarily as the preserve of psychology, and it has been defined most often in terms of emotional and physiological reactions internal to the person. For example, grief is 'the emotional response to one's loss' (Stroebe, Stroebe & Hansson 1993:5), 'the state of pain, discomfort, and often mental and physical impairment that in most persons follows the loss of a loved one' (Lindemann 1963:703, cited by Kamerman 1988:66), or 'the process of thoughts, feelings, attitudes and physiological responses within a person during bereavement' (O'Connor 1991:260). In other words, grief has been seen as a universal psychological process.

Mourning, on the other hand, is generally used to refer to the public behaviour and expression of emotion: '[m]ourning represents those public behaviours and ritual expressions of grief which a society deems appropriate and helpful for a person to practice during bereavement' (ibid.). Mourning 'denotes the actions and manner of expressing grief, which often reflect the mourning practices of one's culture' (Stroebe, Stroebe & Hansson 1993:5). Mourning in these terms refers to the *expression* of grief, while grief is the *experience* of loss.

For anthropologists and psychologists alike this has been a useful distinction. It allowed a division of labour: anthropologists should deal with mourning while psychologists study grief. The problem I see with such an approach is maintaining this sharp differentiation, which is based on the opposition of culture and individual psychology as well as a public/private dichotomy. That anthropologists do use these distinctions can be seen from a curious reversal of these definitions by Wellencamp, who defined grief as 'the expression of distress following a loss' and mourning as 'the conscious and unconscious psychological processes set in motion by a loss' (Wellencamp 1988:486). In a later paper, however, Wellencamp defines grief in the same way as before, but defines mourning as 'the overt, public expression of loss' (Wellencamp 1991:119).

Starting with these definitions of grief and mourning pre-empts the research that can illuminate the nature of grief in other societies. Hence, here I do not subscribe to these definitions. Anthropologists should not begin by assuming that mourning is the expression of grief following a loss, and restrict themselves to the analysis of this alone. We can claim as validly as psychologists the ability to study the experience of others.

In this chapter I attempt to avoid this universal/relative dichotomy by defining mourning as those customs that are deemed necessary following a death, including burial, funeral services and the mourning period. It could be used to refer to various taboos on washing and particular foods, as well as wearing torn or black clothes. Mourning customs may be an expression of grief and loss, or sympathy with the bereaved, or they may be neither. Grief refers to what have been viewed as individual, private emotions as well as publicly sanctioned sentiments, in addition to physiological responses such as poor appetite and sleeping patterns and depressed immune system. This definition does not rely on a public/private distinction, nor does it assume the roles that culture or individual psychology play in reactions to bereavement.

As stated in the Prologue, studying grief in Lihir proved to be more difficult than I expected, especially early in my doctoral fieldwork. As my relationships deepened over time, however, people began to speak more about reactions to loss, first in the context of the lost boat and later about reactions to deaths or losses in the abstract. I also carefully observed reactions to both expected losses (the deaths of older people) and unexpected tragedies (another lost boat with multiple deaths, a teenager killed by lightening). Even after more than three years of fieldwork and many visits to Lihir, people rarely speak at length about their own emotional reactions to personal losses. It is difficult to say with certainty what people's particular experience of loss entails, however my research has uncovered some of the assumptions made by Lihirians about the experience and nature of grief, and the expression of grief.

I begin this chapter by relating the story of the death, burial, mourning and grieving for an old woman named Sion, interspersing this material with discussions about the nature of death, funerary rituals and mourning in Lihir. I discuss deaths due to malnutrition in detail, as these seemed an anathema to me in a place with a surplus of food and an emphasis on Christian morality. I chose to write the story of Sion here as her name was a link with my life in Australia, which, for me, gave her death more meaning.[1] I witnessed her final breaths, the only death I personally witnessed, and she was buried in Lalakam, the hamlet where my house was built on Mahur. Sion was the sister of one of my closest informants in Lihir, Ngalparok. I also chose her death because it is a bipolar opposite to many studies of death that take the funerals of middle-aged men as 'typical'.

---

[1] Sion is the name of the daughter of Deane Fergie, my Honours supervisor. Deane did her fieldwork in New Ireland, where the name Sion was used. This name, Sion, was imported to Lihir from there. It seemed fortuitous to me on my arrival on Mahur that the family who took me in and gave me land to build a house had a woman named Sion as a member.

### *The death of Anna Sion*

*Sion was over 70 years old and already blind when I arrived in Lihir in November 1997, and over the next seven months underwent a slow decline into illness. By May she was unable to go to mass even when the priest visited. On 13 June she had her final communion, with Father Steve going to her house, conducting a short mass and giving her communion. While she was no longer eating or able to turn herself by then, she was able to make the sign of the cross and bid the priest good afternoon. I was told by Kupulie that Joe, Sion's classificatory son (ZS), arrived from Londolovit where he worked (at the gold mine on Niolam) on the Wednesday before her death. Joe saw Sion and sat down and cried and cried, and then got up, got back in the boat and went back to Londolovit. I was also told that Sion had died on that Wednesday, but her daughter Panis had called and called for her, and she had come back. Kupulie, who related this story to me, was annoyed with Panis and said 'Why did she call? They can't do anything together now; Sion can't work now.'*

*On Monday 15 June I went to the main island for a quick shopping trip, and while there I met Sion's brother, Ngalparok, on the beach, waiting for a boat to travel back to Mahur. He had been away from Mahur for a little while visiting people on Niolam. He said he had seen Sion in a dream on Sunday night, and she told him she was just waiting for him before she would die.*[2]

[2] Over the course of my fieldwork I came to realise that some people are known for their predictive dreams, and Ngalparok was one of these people. Dreams are also important in composing new tunes and dances, and in learning magic. People in Lihir also believed that some dreams were simply about nothing, or due to thinking too much about something before bedtime.

*On Wednesday 17 June I had intended to go to Niolam to meet with my doctoral supervisor, who was arriving from Australia that afternoon. I rose early, packed my bag, and walked to the wharf at Liato hamlet. I noticed that there was a large group of people at Sion's house in Liematon hamlet: her daughter and husband, her son Ziklala the head catechist, her other son Landeu and his wife and children, my close friend Kupulie (classificatory grand-daughter), and others. Kupulie said that it would not be long until Sion went.*

*I looked through the window and noticed Sion was having trouble breathing, so I decided to stay on Mahur. I joined the group of people waiting in Liematon, and while we waited Kupulie and Sion's daughter-in-law (SW) Prekbel told me a story. On the previous day Sion's son Kuir had gone into the house to turn his mother. Then he went outside and washed his hands really well. After this, he went and cut some pieces of cardboard and put them up his nose to block the smell (T.P.: '*Em i suim hap katon long nus bilong en*'). The three of us laughed at his behaviour, with Kupulie wondering out loud who had looked after Kuir as a child. Then we shushed one another—the atmosphere during this waiting was not sombre.*

*We were all being quiet so that Sion could die: whenever she heard some noise she would awake. Kupulie said they wanted her to die because her left leg was already dead (with gangrene) and smelled bad. At this point she started Cheyne Stokes breathing (where breaths are deep and very widely spaced). Kupulie and Sion's daughter Panis went in to check on her, and when they laid a hand on her she took another breath, so they left unobtrusively again. Sion's son Ziklala went in to sit by her, and she took another breath. We all stayed absolutely silent, barely breathing ourselves for a long time. Finally*

*Kupulie went in to straighten her leg, and her grandson Linus (SS) went and checked her for a pulse. There was none, and he folded her hands across her stomach. It was 7.30 a.m. Then we did a very short service, with Ziklala blessing her with water.*

## Causes of death (*muet*) in Lihir

Of the nine deaths that occurred on Mahur while I was in the field, for only two of these was sorcery considered a probable cause: there was relatively little speculation about deaths. There were many factors that were considered as causes of deaths that occurred both while I was there, and of deaths in the past. For the deaths of four children, two were attributed to neglect, one to malaria and the other to meningitis. This was not the attribution of nurses but by Mahurians themselves. *Sotwin* (T.P. lit. short wind; short of breath, which could be asthma, emphysema or pneumonia) is a common cause of death, and the death of an old man was attributed to this, as was the death of Sion's sister in 1992. Both Sion and another old woman were said to have died just because they were old, and these deaths were marked by a lack of attempts to seek medical treatment or to keep the person alive.[3]

Mahurians have the service of an aidpost in Kuelam village, and a Community Health Worker treats them there for illnesses such as malaria, tropical ulcers, boils, and colds with antibiotics, dressings, pain relief and malarial drugs. Western medical knowledge is used in conjunction with 'traditional' medicine, often in the form of particular plants crushed or heated and applied to the body. Some illnesses are seen as incurable by Western medicine, such as sorcery cases and spirit attacks (by a *tndol*, T.P. *masalai*), which must be cured by traditional healers if at all.

[3] See Counts & Counts 1985 on the passivity of acceptance of the death of persons due to old age.

In cases of death (or illness) involving mouth sores or cancer, sorcery is always suspected, as corrupting the betelnut, pepper and lime for betelnut chewing is considered an easy way to cause such afflictions. Sorcery was also suspected in the case of a man who married a woman from Pinikindu (mainland New Ireland) and had returned for a visit to observe his daughter's wedding: he got malaria that rapidly became severe, causing him to become delirious before he quickly died.

While not explicitly made by Lihirians, there was always a distinction between what a person died of, and why they died. Thus, a child may die of malnutrition, but she died because of the lack of support for her parents by others, or the mother and father wanting another child too soon. There is a commentary around death about people's responsibilities to one another, and the state of people's social relations.

### *Malnutrition and personhood*

There were four separate cases of malnutrition on Mahur during my fieldwork, one involving twins, and two of these leading to the deaths of the infants involved. In a total population of 800, this indicates a very high rate of malnutrition in infants. Given that there is no shortage of food or water on Mahur, this level of malnutrition was quite extraordinary. All the people with whom I spoke knew that babies could be given coconut juice to supplement breast milk if this was in short supply (as was often the case with twins), and all knew that infants could be fed mashed or pre-masticated bananas, pawpaw, sweet potato and so on. This left me with the question: why were infants on Mahur dying from malnutrition?

The first and most obvious answer is that these children had some other underlying condition that made them weak or unable to take in energy from food: that they were well looked after and fed but sick from some other source. In all of these cases, medical staff saw the children involved, diagnosing malnourishment rather than other illnesses. There is a program of clinic visits by nurses and a doctor on a monthly basis, and medical staff expect all children under the age of five to attend with their mother. The medical staff told me that on Mahur the attendance rate was excellent: about 95 per cent attended. However, the weight for age ratio in Lihir was quite often low at this time, with about 40 per cent of infants and children being only 60 to 80 per cent of expected weight for their age. Thus, malnutrition needs to be seen against a backdrop of many children in Lihir being underweight.

Why is this the case? Lepowsky addressed this question in relation to the malnutrition of infants in Vanatinai and the Louisiade Archipelago more generally. She reported that infants there faced quite broad food taboos (on animal protein, fruits, greens, store-bought foods and foods classified as greasy) that contribute to their malnutrition. Following medical evidence that suggests that malaria is less severe and less likely to be fatal in those that are malnourished, Lepowsky proposes that malnutrition in infants could be a culturally adaptive responsive to lessen the harmful effects of malaria (Lepowsky 1985). However, Lepowsky also notes that malnutrition makes children more susceptible to illness and death from pneumonia, another serious and common illness for children in Papua New Guinea.

Unlike in Vanatinai, infants in Lihir do not face broad food taboos. However, they do regularly suffer quite serious illnesses such as malaria, respiratory illnesses (chest infections, pneumonia), boils, worms and diarrhoea. In addition to this, many are left in hamlets while mothers go to the gardens atop the plateau to harvest food for the rest of the family. For children who are still being breastfed, this can mean eight hours per day for about three days a week with no food except for some water or coconut juice, as mothers do not express breast milk to leave it for them. Older infants on solid foods may be fed only two large meals in a day (adult sized) with very light snacking between them. Thus, infants do not receive a continuous and moderated intake of nutrients, and there is no expectation that they should be in a state of perfect health.

Yet such considerations do not explain chronic malnutrition. Mahurians gave me various explanations about this issue. In one case of an eighteen-month-old girl who eventually died, the parents blamed this on *a tndol* (spirits, T.P. *masalai*) afflicting their daughter. Others said that the mother was pregnant once again and did not want the daughter any more, and thus did not feed her properly. In the case involving twins, people said the mother did not have enough milk (which was probably the case as the mother herself appeared somewhat malnourished). When I asked why the parents did not feed them something else, given that they were ten months old and able to take solids, Mahurians said that their kin were not helping them by giving them food and obtaining coconuts for them. In the case of the serious malnourishment of a four-month-old child, people gossiped that the mother would not stay in the hospital to help her child; yet no one attempted to make her stay there.

From the four cases of serious malnutrition, a pattern emerges of notions of responsibility and autonomy. Clearly it is seen as the parents' responsibility to feed the children in their care, and that close kin should aid them in that process. Yet when these responsibilities are not met, there is no ethic of social welfare that suggests that others should feed the children, force the mother to stay in hospital, or remove the children to care for them. In the terms of Melanesian personhood, it might be expected that failure to thrive would be met with action on the part of others:

> An agent is one who acts with another in mind, and that other may in fact coerce the agent into so acting. (Strathern 1988:272)

Strathern argues that with death, a person loses a 'part of her or himself in the relationship that has "died"' (ibid.:262; see also ibid.:292). Despite this, in Lihir we do not see agents being coerced into action by persons who are obviously malnourished and in need of help. It is difficult to reconcile this ideal of relational Melanesian personhood with the lived reality of deaths due to malnutrition in Lihir.

Malnutrition in Lihir is based on ideas about the autonomy of others. It is unacceptable to intervene in others' affairs even though gossip is common and allowed. The issue, then, is not one of personal or family privacy but that parents in Lihir have the autonomy to deal with their children as they see fit—occasionally to the point of death, as can be seen in these cases. Moreover, children have autonomy in relation to their eating habits. Older children can eat as much or as little as they wish. Resourceful children can eat meals in more than one household, and often finish the leftovers of others, while some children eat very little and do not finish what they are given. Parents do not force children to eat, and eating patterns are an area of personal autonomy.[4]

It is accepted by Mahurians that medical personnel do intervene in cases of malnutrition. Yet, parents could (and did) simply leave the hospital when they wished, or did not turn up in the first place. Authorities do not remove children from their parents in this situation as they would in many Western countries, and thus parents in Lihir retain their autonomy with respect to their children.

While both parents and children have autonomy, malnutrition in children is viewed as evidence of a failure of nurturance (*ertnin*) on the part of parents and their close kin. People assert their autonomy to the detriment of their relations with others, and thus their own (if they are children) or their children's health. Once again, there is evidence that personhood in Lihir is not simply relational but develops out of tension between individual and relational elements.

---

[4] However, in regards to gifts of foods, it is highly offensive to refuse, and people will accept and eat a little even if it is not wanted. Often it is then passed to children to finish.

### *Sion's funeral and burial*

*After Sion's death and the short service I left to take my bag back to my house (as I was no longer going to Niolam), collect my notebook and camera, and tell Kuir (Sion's S) and Lolot (Sion's ZD) of Sion's death. As I walked through the village, two boats left to inform relatives on the other three islands of Lihir. I told many people of Sion's death, and all asked when she had died (to know when to go and perform the first major prayers and service). Sion's grandson (SS) Zirmol went and found an old canoe in which to bury her.*

*I arrived back in Liematon 20 minutes later (8.10 a.m.). People were drinking tea and eating bread rolls. Sion had been covered with a white* laplap *(T.P.), and people were slowly arriving in preparation for the service. At 8.40 a.m. we had another service, which was longer, with many people attending. Much of this service was in the local language, and it included a litany, the repeat for it being 'Have mercy on Anna [Sion] and all the people on earth'.*[5]

*After this service, most women left. Lolot and her husband Iruo went back to Lalakam to clean the area of the men's house where Sion was to be buried: the grass had grown long and they would clear and sweep it. The young men stayed to prepare Sion's coffin (see Figures 14 and 15). To do so, the ends were cut off a canoe (*pako*), then boards were placed on the ends to make the coffin more rectangular, and a piece of wood was shaped for the lid. Much effort was made to clean the canoe and fill in the cracks. For Sion's coffin a cross was made out of a piece of wood and nailed to the lid, which was painted white with the cross brown. The atmosphere was again not sombre, as the*

[5] '*Marimari long Anna na olgeta manmeri long giraun.*' (T.P.) People's Christian names are always used in *lotu*, even if they are not in everyday life.

*young men played with the paint, attempting to paint children. Then all who had helped with the preparation of the coffin were fed a meal of rice, yam and tinned fish.*[6]

*At about 10 a.m. some young men carried the* pako *into Sion's house and put Sion inside it wrapped in her* laplaps *and with her bed sheet in the coffin to be buried with her. Half an hour later the* pako *was carried outside, put on the ground, then lifted and carried back inside the house. I turned to Kupulie in confusion, and she said that Peter was not happy: he wanted Sion to be buried in Liematon. I asked why and she said* 'Na yu ting husat i lukautim lapun meri?' *(T.P. And who do you think cared for this old woman?). Peter and his wife lived in the house neighbouring Sion, and over the later period of her life and especially her illness, they had been giving her food and caring for her. Sion was Peter's father's classificatory sister: a relationship called* papa wein *(FZ)/*yamung *(BS/D) and quite a close, caring one in Lihir. Kupulie said Peter was crying inside his house, and so it was decided to settle the matter before moving Sion at all. Sion's son Ziklala sat down with Peter, who had moved to sit in the doorway of Sion's house (thus barring the entry of anyone to move the coffin). They spoke a little and then lapsed into silence. Some onlookers whispered a little, and the atmosphere was tense. Then there was the sound of crying from Ngalparok, Sion's brother. Kupulie said he was upset by all the confusion, and wanted Sion buried in Lalakam next to her sister. Silence returned. Finally, after about twenty minutes Panis (Sion's D) went and intervened. She talked to Peter and Ziklala, jogging them out of silence. Then Peter stood and allowed the young men to get the coffin: he had made his point about his relationship*

[6] This included me as I was considered to be working by taking photos and asking questions. A canoe, once shaped into a coffin, is still called *a pako*.

*to Sion and his moral judgement about the lack of nurturance Sion received from some of her children. As said above, a death provides an opportunity to highlight the state of social relationships, which may not always be tied to the cause of death: for Sion's death this arose in relation to where she was to be buried.*

*At about 11 a.m. the group of people who had been at Liematon with the coffin arrived in Lalakam. Other people also began to arrive with bales of rice, packets of 2-minute noodles, and cartons of tinned fish or meat. The children of the hamlet were sent to find dry coconuts to make coconut milk for cooking the food, and other women closely associated with Sion (for example, Panis D and Yanalian SD) fetched firewood. Young men were busy building a wooden and bamboo 'bed' (bench) for people to sit on, and women wove mats (*a pke sul*) to sit on and baskets (*per*) which would later be used to put food in. Women began cooking, and we had our first meal in the burial hamlet.*[7] *This hive of activity was in complete contrast to the earlier stand-off over the place of burial.*

*At 2.30 p.m. the first boat arrived: this was Kiaplamlik's boat with some people for the burial service. Ten minutes later Kamiz's boat arrived with more rice and other food, as well as Agnes from Masahet Island, classificatory daughter (ZD) of Sion. Kupulie said to me that they were now just waiting for Joe (ZS, and 'boss' of Lalakam hamlet)*[8] *to arrive before starting the burial. I asked if they were waiting for Sion's brother Morpo to arrive from Malie Island too. Kupulie replied 'Yes', but it seemed an afterthought. At 3.30 p.m. a*

[7] Women (except me) did not eat in the earlier meal at Liematon hamlet for those engaged in the coffin-making.

[8] '*A tboh wan a puor*', literally 'big of the ground', meaning controller of the land.

*contract boat arrived with Joe and his sister Susan, and more rice and tinned food. By this time the grave had been dug and we started the service immediately.*

*The service was a Catholic funeral and burial service taken from the* Yumi Lotu *book and led by head catechist Ziklala (Sion's son) and catechist for Kuelam village, Kolie. Monica, a prominent leader in church services, called out the hymns and began them (that is, gave everyone else their note). As is the case for burial services, everyone had collected a flower or some colourful leaves, and these were placed in the coffin during the singing of* 'Klostu long yu o God'.[9]

*The coffin was then carried a short distance to be buried on the eastern side of her sister Lusbeh's grave. Joe put in a* bilum *(T.P. string bag) and Susan a mat; both were old and had belonged to Sion. Then men started to fill in the grave: Joe (ZS), Iruo (ZDH), Kuir (S), Lasum (S), Zirmol (SS) and other young men. Besnale, a classificatory brother, held the cross in place while the other men filled in the sand.[10] There was a core of young men in Mahur who always did the work at events such as burials. The addition of Kuir and Lasum in this case reflects their position as sons of Sion: generally they watched others work. At the actual burial there were no women (besides me) present, and there was no crying (see Figure 16).*

---

[9] This hymn (*Yumi Lotu* book No. 264) is sung to the tune of 'Nearer my God to Thee'.

[10] Besnale was one of the men on Mahur who enjoyed being a part of the action and helped where he could. This was restricted by his health problems of a weak heart (diagnosed by doctors), and thus rather than doing strenuous activity such as shovelling dirt, he held the cross.

## Funeral services and burial on Mahur

Funeral services on Mahur are taken from the *Yumi Lotu* book of Catholic services and hymns, and are always conducted by a catechist. This may be the catechist of the village, or if he is away or in the gardens, a catechist from a neighbouring village will be summoned. News of a death spreads quickly throughout the three villages of Mahur, and generally about one third to half of the population of Mahur (300 to 400 of 800 people) will attend each funeral, including children of all ages who are not in the least sheltered from the reality of death. Even in the case of a death of a two-month-old child, about 200 people attended the funeral service. Funeral services are conducted in a mixture of Tok Pisin and the local language, and comprise a combination of prayers, a reading from one of the gospels, a short sermon and about three hymns. Generally during the third hymn people place flowers in the coffin.

Unlike many places in Papua New Guinea (for example, Foster 1995:106–8), in Lihir there is no prescription that certain people must cry (*tenden*) at a death or burial, or that crying must occur at all. At the death of infants often only the mother cried, although in one case an older sibling did likewise. For old people sometimes their children would cry, or their sibling's children or grandchildren. It was for people in their prime that most crying occurred, and this was said to be due to the 'shock' (*rbet*) that accompanied such deaths. Men very rarely cried, though some men, such as Joe, were known as people who cry. There was never any gossip about a certain person either crying or not crying at a death.

Such crying was just that: crying loudly rather than keening or mourning songs. Generally it did not contain any words, though for one death which was unexpected, the daughter of the dead man kept crying out for her father, 'Papaaaaaa …'. Unlike neighbouring Tanga and nearby (pseudonymous) Babae, there are no questions addressed to the deceased about why they left, or what the person should do without them (Fergie 1985:237; Foster 1995:107–8). Such crying is generally brief, occurring when the person first dies, when someone arrives from elsewhere after the person has died, or after the funeral service before the coffin is actually buried.[11]

Lihirians said that they used to cry much more at deaths, but the Catholic Church had prohibited excessive crying and keening (*yehr*) at death, explaining that people would see their loved ones later in heaven (*yumi no ken krai olsem ol heden*; T.P.: 'we cannot cry like heathens', said during funeral services). Tuzin reports a similar effect of Christianity among the Ilahita Arapesh, reporting that revivalist Christians proscribe crying at death (Tuzin 1989:207n13).

Prior to the funeral service the body is placed on a bench at the front of the men's house where the deceased will be buried.[12] A coffin is usually made from an old canoe (*pako*), or, in the case of infants, from pieces of timber. The deceased is then dressed in good clothes, wrapped in new *laplaps* and laid in the coffin, which is then placed back on the bench of the men's house. At this time a cross (*bolo*; T.P.: *kruse*) is also made with the person's name and often the date of death. For the funeral service the coffin is placed on the ground in the men's house enclosure. Someone stands holding the cross, and people gather around the coffin. The chief mourners, such as sons, daughters and the spouse, do not necessarily stand closest to the coffin or behave differently from anyone else at the funeral service. Due to a taboo on women not being able to enter the men's house enclosure of their husband, some women, including the new widow (*a nol*), often stay outside, and participate from outside the stone fence.[13]

---

[11] In the case of the death of a young man at the hospital on Niolam, crying occurred when the body arrived back on Mahur for the burial. His death caused much 'shock' (*rbet zket*), and even young men cried at his death.

[12] This is the case unless, like Sion, the body must be transported to another place to be buried. The deceased is then simply left where he or she died until the coffin is made. I would assume that in cases of drowning or accidents that the person would be moved to a house or men's house while the coffin is made.

[13] However, the stones beside the 'Y'-shaped 'gate' to the men's house enclosure are often removed for funerals, allowing these women to enter as well. Even when this was the case, many such women chose to stay outside anyway.

While I was on Mahur all burials were inside men's houses rather than in the public cemeteries in each village. For Kuelam village the most recent burials in the public cemetery were in the early 1990s. I asked many times why there had been a change away from the public cemetery and heard various reasons, such as many people not keeping the graves clean, a fear of using the bodies in sorcery as people cannot keep watch properly, and the belief that burials in a men's house solidify a lineage's or clan's claim to that land. Cemeteries were an initiative of the Catholic Church and the Australian Administration, rather than being a Lihirian idea.

For burials, a group of young men dig the grave, taking turns to shovel the earth and drag it back from the hole. Often it was basically the same group of young men who did this for each burial: they were the eighteen- to thirty-year-olds who were hard workers. There is little ceremony in either the digging or filling in of the grave, with some talking and laughter (though generally this is hushed by others in the group), and thuds as rocks and soil land on the lid of the coffin. Nor was there any particular orientation of the body or grave in my observation, though one man said the head should not be placed towards the sea.

*Following the burial there was a meal, known as* 'tienmazien a lotu' *('to finish the burial service'). This was served in the baskets (*per*) made earlier, and consisted of rice, purple yam, noodles, fresh chicken, tinned meat and tinned fish. There was not really enough to go around (there were about 300 people present) and so the female immediate family and hamlet owners (females only: daughter, granddaughters, daughter in law, sister's daughters) did not eat.*[14]

[14] This lack of food to go around was not due to a lack of raw food, but a lack of cooked food. As is the case on Mahur where males get the best food, it was the females who missed out. Generally there is not a problem with a lack of food.

*While we were eating, Bebe (ZD), her husband and children arrived from Kunaye village on Niolam with more rice. Half an hour later Sion's brother, Morpo, arrived from Malie Island with his grown son, Nezik. Nezik was angry, asking why we had all been in such a hurry to bury Sion rather than waiting for them to arrive. It was explained about Sion's leg being gangrenous (T.P.* 'skin i sting pinis'*), which had led to a fear of illness from the bad smell.*

*Many people left at about this time: for most people this is the end of the burial and funeral for that day. Some had walked from the neighbouring villages of Lakamelen and Li, and wanted to return before it was fully dark (the sun set at about 5.50 p.m. that day, which is when people finished eating). For others, however, this was the start of a very long night, known as* 'panpan kut na kanut' *(last night of chatting with the corpse/spirit).*

### *Panpan kut na kanut*

This is the final night of socialising—chatting and eating—with the deceased. Quite often the *kanut* has not been buried, and the coffin remains on the bench of the men's house. In the case of very important people and leaders, this last night includes '*yiarngen*', which are songs composed by the deceased or including magic he knew (Bainton, Ballard & Gillespie 2012; they use the Niolam dialect term '*rangen*' for these songs). I never heard these songs performed while I was on Mahur. One of the deaths that occurred during my doctoral fieldwork was of a leader, and there was some speculation that *yiarngen* would be sung, but for unknown reasons this did not occur.

*Everyone left in Lalakam for the* panpan kut na kanut *ate again at about 6.15 p.m. There were quite a number of people, and this was partially due to many coming from other islands. After this meal I went inside my house to write up my notes, and heard people conduct another service at about 6.45 p.m. After this the community generator was collected from the school, and lights were rigged up which stayed on until about 4 a.m. By this time the place was quiet, with most people fast asleep, including about four people on the verandah of my house.*

## *Sion's* mbie

*The day after Sion's death there was a feast called* pkieslih *involving pigs and ground-oven-cooked tubers. This feast is not very common, and I saw it done twice in the context of nine deaths.* pkieslih *is a feast given either before or after burial as a consequence of the deceased being moved from the place he or she died to the place of burial. Thus, if a person dies in the hamlet where they are to be buried, or at the hospital or aidpost, this feast is omitted. The clan that relinquishes the deceased provides the pigs for this feast. In the case of Sion, she died on land of her classificatory brothers of another clan (Nielik), who had the stronger claim (in* kastam*) to having her buried in their men's house. Yet Nielik allowed her children and brothers to bury her on her own clan land (Nawus), and thus Nielik people provided the pigs, being the relinquishing clan.*

*In the case of Sion's death,* pkieslih *occurred on the first day of the* mbie *or mourning period.*[15] *This is a time following the burial*

[15] In other cases *pkieslih* can occur before the person is buried, as occurred with Azroh's death. He was not buried until the afternoon following his death, and *pkieslih* occurred on the day of his death.

*of a person where people stay in the hamlet where the person was buried, and also at the place of death (if these are different).* Mbie *generally lasts a few weeks, and involves people who are close kin of the deceased.*

*Sion's* mbie *lasted from June 18 to July 24, a fairly long time. At Lalakam, where she was buried, two of her sister's daughters and their families stayed, as well as two of her sons and their families, her brother, her classificatory grand-daughter and her children, and me. At the house where she died, Sion's daughter and family stayed, as well as her son's wife and some of their children.*

## *Mbie* participation

The crucial concepts for participation in *mbie* are *owo* and *ertnin*. *Owo* means to raise a child, either your own or one belonging to someone else. It involves all the care and nurturance that children need: feeding, teaching, clothing and so on. *Ertnin* is the nurturance given to a person (or pig), which may be in the context of illness or simply to bring them certain food they need or like (for example, fresh fish).

People say that in deciding to participate in an *mbie* you think of the *owo* or *ertnin* the deceased gave you. In this case, the immediate family has little choice but to participate in an *mbie* as generally the deceased raised them. Other people who were given *ertnin* should participate or face others' censure. In one case, a person was gossiped about because the deceased had given many fish to the person, and yet the person did not participate.

*During the* mbie *for Sion, people participating would sleep in the two* mbie *areas, but during the day would go around visiting or work in the gardens as usual. The garden produce of those involved in the* mbie *was shared communally, with the place of death and place of burial functioning as separate units. At night, people would sit and talk: the areas involved in the* mbie *became places to gather for those not involved in* mbie, *as they knew there was always a group of people there to talk to. From my observation, this talking had nothing to do with the deceased, except when there was discussion of when the* mbie *would finish.*

*Sion's* mbie *united a number of entire households and took members from others. Lalakam usually functioned as a single household comprising Lolot (a woman of the owning lineage), her husband and their two children, two of her sister's children, and her classificatory brother. During the* mbie *this was swelled by Sion's son Ziklala, his wife and a minimum of two of their children at any time (an entire household), Sion's brother Ngalparok and his grandson (an entire household), Sion's classificatory daughter, her husband and their four children (an entire household), and Sion's classificatory grand-daughter Kupulie and her three children (part of an 11-member household).*

### Mbie *and the household*

*Mbie* affects the composition of the household, as can be seen above. In fact, a new, short-lived household is created for the time of the *mbie*. As I explained in Chapter 2, one of the defining characteristics of a household are relationships of nurturance. Food is one of the key demonstrations of nurturance in Lihir. In the case of *mbie*, those present cook communally, with women going to the gardens, harvesting food and amassing it, cooking it, and everyone present then consumes it. In the case of Sion's *mbie* there was a fishing net (owned by Ngalparok, her brother) that was used to catch fish for those people in Lalakam. The household is a particular configuration of relationships, and as a death alters the composition of those relationships, so it temporarily modifies the household.

There was a communal area for sleeping, with people spread over three houses (including mine) and the men's house. People were recognised as members of the *mbie* household, and were expected to stay for the whole *mbie*. There was much complaining of *piot* if people slept elsewhere, or came from elsewhere to spend the night. However, despite supposed sanctions (such as killing a pig) for creating *piot* for participants of a *mbie*, there was a considerable amount of mobility and also a matching amount of complaint directed at those who caused *piot*.

> *Sion's* mbie *lasted just over five weeks, quite long in comparison with other cases, which were generally two to three weeks long. During the time of* mbie, *food is amassed for the feasting to finish the mourning time,* mbiektip. *Two weeks after the burial a pink pig (a European breed from a piggery on Niolam) arrived at Lalakam, where it terrorised the occupants, particularly me, for the next three weeks, eating valued plants and flowers, baskets and people's thongs. Hus, Sion's grand-daughter (DD) bought this pig as her family's contribution to the feast. Chasing this pig was considered to be the local sport of the children of Lalakam and neighbouring hamlets.*
>
> *The mood of the* mbie *was not at all sombre, in fact, it appeared that people enjoyed the chance to be part of a larger group, to have people readily available to talk with at night around a fire.*

*As mentioned in the context of conflict with her sister (Chapter 5), Kupulie was reluctant to leave the* mbie *household, and owners of the hamlet were reluctant to see her go. People also ate better during the* mbie, *with fresh fish part of the diet quite regularly, other (tinned) protein to go with rice or tubers readily available, and generally three meals a day rather than the more common two meals. At the same time, many people got tired of the* mbie *towards the end of the five weeks, and wished to go back to their respective homes. Bebe (Sion's ZD), her husband and children had come from Kunaye, and had to go back to check on their gardens every week or so, harvesting a little food while there. Her sister Lolot, who resided at Lalakam normally, found that she had to go to the bush and draw from her own gardens more often than usual to supplement the food that Bebe brought from Kunaye. Thus, while the* mbie *provided the context for sociality, by the end of the* mbie *people felt it was time for it to be over.*

*The day for the feast (*mbiektip*) to finish* mbie *was chosen by meetings of those involved in the* mbie. *Other people were then informed, seemingly by osmosis, with not much notice given before the day (most people knew about two days before it occurred). As I shall deal with this feast in the next chapter, I will just say here that it occurred on 24 July 1998 in rain and that about 300 people attended. While it is a feast that is supposed to 'send everyone back to their homes' (T.P.* salim ol i go bek long ples bilong ol*), most of those involved in the* mbie *actually took another week to slowly pack up their things and drift back to their respective villages and houses.*

## Grief (*lil wirwir*) in Lihir

Grief in Lihir is generally expressed by the term *lil wirwir* (a noun), or, more rarely, *lil tenden*. In its first person verbal form, *a ling sa wir*, this translates literally as 'my inside is turning', an expression of worry mixed with sorrow and sometimes fear, while *a ling sa tenden* translates as 'my inside is crying' and relates to sorrow or sadness. *Lil wirwir* occurs in a broad range of contexts, not simply in relation to the death of a person. In its most minor form, the term *a ling sa wir* can be used to refer to worry about an issue. Thus, one day a catechist said he was worried or grieved ('*a ling sa wir*') about people coming late to church on Fridays. *Lil wirwir* is also the term used to describe homesickness (see Chapter 3). In the case of the missing boat described in the prologue, the mother of the young boy on the boat, Kwildun, was worried (*lil wirwir* or *lil zket*) about her son and husband.

*Lil wirwir* is a term referring to the experience of loss or grief. Primarily *lil wirwir* was expressed through crying (*tenden*) and statements to the effect that a person felt *lil wirwir*. Often others made such statements about a person. People assumed that others would be feeling or experiencing *lil wirwir* in the circumstances, and also read this from small behavioural cues such as the person not going to the gardens, refusing betelnut or food (or chewing/eating only a little), and in Kwildun's case, her standing on the beach looking out to sea.

While people in Lihir said the best thing was to take a person's mind off their worry by being with them and talking about other things (see Prologue), they also said that it was important to discuss worry or grief rather than hide it. If hidden, *lil wirwir* can cause illness, and in one case on Mahur was said to be the basis for a healthy young woman's death (see the case of *ung kis* or 'bad talk' for the Ku Waru in the Western Highlands, Rumsey 2008). Friends are important in relation to *lil wirwir* because if a person is reluctant to express their worry or grief, a friend will notice the behavioural cues and will ask about the reasons for this, allowing the expression of this dangerous *lil wirwir*.

People in Lihir were said to worry (*lil wirwir*) over a death for about six months if quite severe, and less than that normally. People were perplexed when I said that people would grieve for deceased persons for two or three years and longer in Australia. On one occasion I watched a man making and painting a cross, and then helping to dig the grave for the death of an infant only two weeks after the death of his own daughter. I asked two people how he could do this. Both looked confused, and even more so when I explained that many people in Australia would find it difficult to be involved with another funeral so soon after their own loss. This made no sense to them.

I was told that people could take on taboos called *tomdom* on various foodstuffs following a bereavement. People can chose whether or not they take on taboos and the subject of these: thus if the person who died gave you yams from their garden or always brought back pig from feasts, then you would take on a taboo on yams or pig. I never saw anyone undergoing such a taboo, and everyone I asked said they had not done it. It appears that this custom is gradually being abandoned as at the death of a very important leader in 1992 no one took on such taboos. Yet one man did state that when his adopted father died he would never eat yams again; this man likened such taboos to grieving (he knew English). *Tomdom* are lifted at the second major mortuary feast called *pkepke*.

Lihirians commonly expressed what in Western terms would be seen as one aspect of grief (or a lack of it) in terms of remembering the person. When I asked if someone was still sad about the death of a daughter or spouse, they would say '*Kopue, sa nanse baliye*' (No, s/he has forgotten). This remembering was particularly important in terms of customary treatment of the dead: whether all the necessary feasts had been completed (see my next chapter). If they had, then people were able to forget, yet people stated this forgetting was in terms of '*kastam wok*' rather than forgetting altogether about the person. In other contexts it seemed that remembering (and attempts to forget) was more than simply about *kastam wok*.

In recent years there have been a number of ethnographies on Papua New Guinea that deal with issues of memory and death (for example, Battaglia 1990; 1992; Eves 1996; Kuchler 1987; Lohmann 2007; Maschio 1994). It seems that memory is a crucial way of thinking and talking about grief in many Papua New Guinea societies instead of the strong emotional focus that Western concepts of grief encapsulate. Over my year in Mahur I came to know Kiaplam as a member of the Kuelam community and also of Mahur as a whole: yet Kiaplam had been dead since 1992. All the time people spoke about his great leadership, his ability to unite the various clans and villages, his knowledge about *kastam wok*, and the amount of knowledge and stories that had died with him. They explained that if he had been alive I would have gotten some very good stories. People from all over Lihir remembered the huge *kastam* ceremony that occurred in 1987, where the *mormor*[16] were made for the first time in many years, and perhaps for the last time. They spoke of how there were so many pigs that they took to the bush and began a race of wild pigs, and about how there was so much pig that it could not be eaten and was left rotting and causing illness. They also spoke of his funeral, where they sat him on a plank, washed him with coconut milk, dressed him up and put special scented leaves and shell money on his coffin. They spoke about how he was so important that they did not bury him for four days until he was beginning to decompose. I was shown photos of his decorated corpse early in my fieldwork. They also remarked disgustedly that after his death some people had cut down all the good fruit and shade trees he had planted, and that this was not Mahurian *kastam* and would not be done again. Kiaplam certainly was a part of life on Mahur: he was remembered.

[16] *Mormor* are figures displayed at a mortuary feast. Their heads are the actual skulls of the deceased covered with clay and grass to look like human beings, and their bodies are made of wood. Some people in Lihir called these '*malangan*'. There was dispute in Lihir about whether *mormor* were used in the past, or whether these were a poor substitute for the actual *malangan* which characterise Northern New Ireland mortuary feasting, however as reported by Gifford (1974) similar figures were seen by Europeans early this century (cf. Brouwer 1980; Fergie 1985; Kuchler 1987; Lewis 1969).

Most people with whom I talked spoke of the resolution of worry over a death as a process of forgetting (*nanse baliye*), which required some action to ensure its success. Objects belonging to the deceased could remind people of him or her initially, but gradually these things lost their significance as they came to be used or owned by others, are purposely destroyed or are given away to interrupt the process of remembering the deceased (see Lohmann 2007). This was the case with a man who gave me a yam out of his garden that he had been growing for his young daughter who had died before the garden was ready. He felt unable to eat the yam as it reminded him of her every time he went to the garden.

Another way of facilitating this process is to pass on the name of the deceased. This acts to detach the name from the first person it signified, thus aiding the process of forgetting. The man whose daughter died gave the next daughter born the same Christian and local names. In many current Western contexts this might be seen as pathological behaviour: a dysfunctional attachment to the dead child, and a transference of hopes for the first child onto the second (Bowlby 1980:164). Yet in Lihir this is quite common behaviour, and is seen as an adaptive and useful way of resolving and forgetting *lil wirwir*.

Mahurians did believe that in some cases, worry about a death could be excessive, and in such cases there could be a feast conducted involving the killing of pigs to end this worry of the bereaved. This feast mimics other feasts used to end worry (*lil wirwir*). When the boat that is the subject of the Prologue was lost, people said that should people's worry be great and linger on the boat's return, then a feast could be held to end this worry. In fact, in the case of a boat that drifted to Tench Island in 1986, the survivors did a feast while on Tench Island to end their own worry. *Lil wirwir* is seen as quite dangerous, particularly when it is severe and long lasting.

Remembering and forgetting, then, are crucial ways of expressing and experiencing grief in the time after the *mbie*. People are remembered through stories, through their names and the things they own—but many of these things progressively lose their connection to the person who has died. Ritual provides a further context for the process of remembering and forgetting the deceased, and in the following final chapter I turn to the way key ritual feasts perform and transform persons, emotions and relationships.

# 8

## Relations at stake: performing and transforming personhood, emotions and relations

Like other New Ireland societies, Lihirians signify even minor events through the use of communal feasting. All life transformations and closures of events are indicated through the use of food, and there is an inability to even conceive of these events without food. For example, when the aidpost on Mahur was extended to create more space it lay unused for about two years as it was considered impossible to use the aidpost without an opening ceremony, complete with a feast, and Mahurians were waiting to jointly celebrate the opening of the aidpost with the new church in Kuelam village.

Feasting in Lihir varies from minor household meals to mark a visitor's departure, to extensive multi-day events with hundreds of guests and a great deal of food. These latter feasts are called *karot*, referring to a feast that includes the killing of pigs and the gathering of many people. These generally celebrate life-cycle events, though they may also be feasts to remove the influence of spirits (*tndol*) on persons (*niaktip*), to celebrate removal of a *golgol* (taboo marker) or to celebrate the resolution of a major conflict.[1]

As Fergie describes for the New Ireland society of Babae (a pseudonym, Fergie 1985; 1995), there is a corpus of life-cycle feasting events in Lihir that convey persons from conception to death and beyond. These include the conception/first pregnancy feast of *tektipsasie*, the hair cutting ceremony of *kiptiekoh* or *kuirkoh*, the women's puberty/initiation ceremonies *tolup*, the feast to honour elderly persons, *hararum*, and a cluster of mortuary-type feasts, *mbiektip*, *pkepke* and *tunkanut*.

In this chapter I concentrate on mortuary feasting in Lihir, returning to Sion's death. During mortuary feasting personhood, emotions and relations are publicly performed and transformed. While this is particularly true for mortuary feasts, it must be remembered that these feasts are part of a larger corpus of ritual and feasting that occurs throughout the course of life, and these other feasts may also perform and transform persons, emotions and relationships.

## Mortuary ritual in New Ireland

The practice of mortuary ritual has consumed the attention of anthropology in New Ireland, and with good reason: these events take months of planning, consume vast amounts of pigs, garden produce and wealth in both shell and paper money, draw large crowds, and are the main context for the production of the now famous *malangans* (in northern and central New Ireland) as well as dances and songs. They appear as a startling deviation from everyday life in villages throughout the area.

Anthropologists have taken a number of approaches to the study of mortuary ritual in New Ireland, probably the most common viewing mortuary rituals as the context for the production of *malangans*. Such studies

[1] On Niolam, Bainton (2011:192) notes that *karat* are a particular class of feasts and are contrasted to *pkepke* feasts, rather than being a term for the entire corpus of feasting as was the case on Mahur.

focus on the form and production of *malangans*, their iconography, and their place in ceremonies (for example, see Albert 1986; Bodrogi 1987; Brouwer 1980; Gifford 1974; Kuchler 1999; 2002; Lewis 1969). Others have discussed the role of memory and forgetting in mortuary ceremonies (Eves 1996b; Jackson 1996; Kuchler 1987; also Kingston 2003 on memory and attention). Foster (1995) and Wagner (1986) have represented mortuary ceremonies as the context for leadership succession, while Clay (1986) argues that such ceremonies provide an opportunity for the objectification of male power. These last three anthropologists (Clay, Foster and Wagner) all maintain that reciprocal exchanges of paternal nurture between moieties or pairs of lineages are crucial to mortuary rituals, that the structure of mortuary ceremonies is dichotomous—of hosts and guests—and that in mortuary rituals social reproduction is performed.

In one of the more recent contributions to the ethnography of mortuary ritual in New Ireland, Richard Eves (1998; but see also Bolyanatz 2000) critiques such approaches for assuming that social reproduction is carried out unproblematically in these rituals. He argues that mortuary ceremonies provide an arena of contestation, and can be sites for the failure of social reproduction (1998:228). His analysis then explores ways that feasts are made to succeed or fail, and the importance of the memory of particular feasts. His work is part of a growing body of material that highlights the risk and struggle that rituals and performances entail (compare Howe 2000). Schieffelin has argued that:

> The burden of success or failure in a cultural performance is usually laid on the central actors, but the real location of this problem … is the *relationship* between the central performers and others in the situation. (Schieffelin 1998:203, original emphasis)

Rather than seeing ritual as predictable, it is fundamentally interactive and inherently risky (Schieffelin 1996:80). The relationship between performers and others in the situation then becomes critical for the production of memorable performances, which may become the basis for evaluating subsequent ones

(Howe 2000:67). This perspective is illuminative of the performances of Lihir feasts.

In this chapter I argue that there has been an overemphasis on the structure of feasts in New Ireland as simply dichotomous: of hosts and guests. For Lihirians, feasts were also crucially concerned with the deceased (*kanut*). *Karot* minimally have a tripartite structure in Lihir (deceased, hosts and guests), and, additionally, none of these parties are homogenous. I argue that in viewing the structure of feasts as dichotomous, the meaning of these feasts is also simplified. In Lihir in the course of these feasts, people perform and transform persons, emotions and relationships, particularly in relation to *kanut*, and feasts can conclude in the failure of at least some of their aims.

My argument diverges from those anthropologists who have proposed that ritual is a completely separate arena from everyday life, and that a different type of personhood can exist in this separate space (Foster 1995:212–7; Harrison 1985). I do agree that these rituals do highlight personhood as an issue, particularly of the deceased and the hosting group. Yet in Lihir the forms of personhood performed in ritual were not disparate from those apparent in everyday life. Even though it entails more drama and self-conscious display, I see ritual as a part of the continuum of daily life. While it calls attention to relations, emotion and personhood and can transform these, the everyday life of households, child-raising, religion, loving and conflict can do likewise.

I begin here with an account of the *mbiektip* feast held to conclude the mourning period for Sion, before moving on to discuss the performances and transformations that occur in *karot* that coalesce around death.

## *Mbiektip*: to 'cut' the mourning period

In Chapter 7 I discussed how death and the initial mourning period is experienced in Lihir. The deceased is buried with a Christian service, and then a number of people, those who wish to remember the *ertnin* or *owo* (care, nurturance) the deceased gave them, move to the burial hamlet to spend their nights. This practice is called *mbie*, and it is this time that is cut (*ktip*) by the feast *mbiektip*. This feast transforms relationships of contiguity to separation: to disperse those who moved to the hamlet from those people who normally reside there and from the deceased. It also concludes the time exclusively dedicated to mourning the deceased (*mbie*), returning people to their daily lives: a transformation from time nominally devoted to remembering and being sad (*lil wirwir*).

*Mbiektip* is a one-day feast, attended on Mahur by most people in the village where the deceased was buried as well as many people from the neighbouring villages.[2] Those attending did not appear to have any special relationship with the deceased or principal mourners.[3] Instead, most men who were not engaged in some other pressing task, and women who were not busy with ill children and who had the necessary tubers to take with them, would attend. It was seen to be somewhat disrespectful to simply stay home for no reason, and thus these feasts generally attracted some 300 to 400 people.[4]

My experience of Sion's *mbiektip* compared to other *mbiektip* feasts was very different as I stood in the position of female *hukarot* (host), rather than my usual position as female *wasir* (guest). In addition, my position was different from all other hosts or guests because I was the resident anthropologist, which exempted me from having to carry out the work associated with feasting such as building the stone oven (though I could choose to do this work if I wished).

Previously as a guest of five *mbiektip* feasts, I had experienced these as one-day events. I would arrive mid-morning like many other people, not leaving my hamlet until I had heard the yells and whoops of the men catching pigs for the feast. Even so, I would usually arrive quite early, and watch as

---

[2] I have heard that both funerals and burials, and *mbiektip* on Niolam, are smaller affairs, possibly due to the fact that villages on the main island are spread over a greater distance and seem less close-knit, and due to a high proportion of men working at the mine.

[3] Although, as explained in Chapter 1, all Lihirians can assert *some* kin tie should circumstances require it.

[4] Given Mahur had a population of about 800 people in 1998, this level of attendance is remarkable.

other women trickled into the area with baskets full of yams, mami or sweet potato. They gathered to talk, and would eventually sit down and begin to peel the tubers. Sometimes the ground oven was already lit when I arrived, and young men were suffocating pigs, ready to singe off their hair and butcher them. A few older men would sit in the men's house talking, chewing betelnut, or sewing the leaves in which to wrap the pigs. I would watch, take photos, and ask about who brought the pigs, or another of my innumerable questions. Eventually the ground oven would be ready, and the last pieces of unburned wood were removed and the stones spread out. The leaf parcels containing pig would be placed in the centre with the vegetables around them; then stones would be placed on top. Next, another layer of tubers was placed, being generally smaller mami and many sweet potato. These tubers were for later consumption in hamlets, not part of the feast, and each woman brought and cooked her own, noting exactly where her tubers were placed in the ground oven. Leaves were used to cover the ground oven, topped with old *laplaps* and pieces of canvas, weighed down with stones, logs and some sand. Then everyone would disperse to wash and sleep for an hour or two.

If the *mbiektip* was held in Kuelam village, at this time I, like many other women of Kuelam, would go to my own hamlet for a break. However, if it was held in Lakamelen village I stayed there, the twenty-minute walk to and from the next village making me nervous that I would miss something vital. After an hour or two, people would return, somehow knowing that the ground oven would soon be opened. Coconut and banana leaf platforms were quickly constructed, both within the men's house and outside, and the tubers and pigs were carried to the platforms. Men and women generally received the same number or amount of pigs (for example, men's distribution: three large pigs; women's distribution: four small ones) and tubers, though men tended to get more and bigger yams, while women got more sweet potato (considered somewhat inferior). Food distributions for *mbiektip* were generally divided into clan piles first, and then divided onto leaf plates. Boys inside the men's house would emerge while the women were eating, handing their leftovers (and the leftovers of their fathers or uncles) to their mother or sister to place in her basket and carry home. Women would then leave, as by this time it was often 5.30 p.m., only 30 minutes before sunset. Some men would also leave, while others stayed to listen to speeches in the men's house or simply to socialise. Women generally could hear (almost) nothing of the speeches occurring within the men's house enclosure, and showed little interest in them. For the female guests, the eating and packing up of leftovers signalled the end of the *mbiektip* and the mourning period for the deceased.

For Sion's *mbiektip*, held on 24 July about five weeks after her death, I was counted as a female host. During the interval an important man of the same clan (though a different sub-clan) died, which seemed to delay the feast for Sion. Allowances also have to be made for other events occurring, and the son of Sion was not only head catechist of Mahur but was involved in preparations for major mortuary feasting to be held for his mother's brother later in the year on Malie Island.

For female hosts, the *mbiektip* is much more complicated than it is for guests, with preparations starting days before the event. Two days before Sion's *mbiektip* I went to the gardens in the rain with Kupulie to cut greens to accompany the pig, while other women collected leaves to cover the mumu. Young men of the village were asked to cut firewood for the ground oven. One of the female hosts went and got tubers from her garden on Niolam (where she resided on her husband's land), while others collected them from gardens on Mahur. Some men went to get or buy pigs for the feast, and on the day before the *mbiektip* these were killed and put in a ground oven to cook so they would be properly cooked (as they were so large). That afternoon there was a small feast of tubers accompanied by fish for the men, and chicken for the women.

On the day of the *mbiektip* everyone in the hamlet was up early, including the young men who caught the pigs (and some were brought from other hamlets), and the brother of Sion, Ngalparok, who was busy trying to halt the rain through the practice of rain magic. The preparation of the ground ovens, one each for the men and women as well as one for the affines of Sion, was much like that for other *mbiektip* feasts, with the host women busy sweeping the area while the ground ovens were cooking. At the distribution, I, with a number of other host women, received a basket, but ate nothing until the other distributions were complete, women had eaten and left, and we had cleaned all the feast debris away.[5]

Visitors staying in the hamlet as part of the *mbie* household did not depart immediately following the *mbiektip*. In fact, these people were generally the hosts of this feast. In the case of Sion's death, over the week following the *mbiektip* people slowly packed their things and went back to their hamlets in Kuelam or Lakamelen village on Mahur, or to the other islands of Lihir. Far from being a one-day event as it is for guests, for female hosts this feast extends for 10 days or so. The meaning differs from a single day of feasting to show respect for the deceased in the perspective of the guest, to the view of a female host as a feast that takes much work and many resources to properly honour the deceased, and to show the lineage and extended family as a group capable of following *kastam*. In this case, the food at the burial feast was insufficient for the number attending, so it was essential for the reputation of the hosting group that guests were well served at the *mbiektip*. Given that there were nine pigs killed and many tubers cooked, this aim was achieved.

From the structure and activities at the *mbiektip*, the meaning of the feast is not clear. There are very rarely any speeches about the deceased,[6] no eulogies or statements as to the meaning of the feasting. Those gathering generally do not have particular relationships to the deceased, and do not talk about the deceased. *Mbiektip*, as its name suggests, is not an event in and of itself, but rather could be seen as a marker of the boundary between *mbie*, which began with a death, and daily life. Yet even more so than a marker of a boundary, *mbiektip* actually accomplishes this transformation: from a time

---

[5] In my basket I received 4 mami, 2 pieces of pig, 2 betelnut, 1 pepper and 4 *brus* (T.P. tobacco; often locally grown or purchased from markets). A friend visiting from Australia who went into the men's house to eat left with 2 mami, 1 piece of pig, 2 pepper and 1 *brus* in addition to what he had eaten in the men's house.

[6] I was told that these only occur in extreme circumstances, such as for people lost at sea.

and state of mourning, of remembering and *lil wirwir*[7] in the shared space and close relationships of the *mbie* household, to the daily life of more separated existence, particularly separation from the newly deceased.

## *Karot* in Lihir

*Mbiektip* is one variety of a large number of feasts in Lihir that are called *karot*.[8] These are major ceremonies involving the gathering of many people who form the audience for this performance by the hosts, and the consumption of pigs. There are three major rituals (sometimes compressed into two occasions), as well as *mbiektip*, that occur for people in Lihir towards the end of their life or after death: the *hararum*, *pkepke* and *tunkanut*.[9] Other anthropologists working in New Ireland have termed these mortuary rituals, though they have observed that they may occur while the person is still alive. In Lihir it could be argued that both *pkepke* and *tunkanut* are mortuary ceremonies, for regardless of whether the person is alive or not, he or she is termed *kanut* (deceased/corpse/spirit) and plays no part in the ritual. However, for the *hararum* the person is more often alive and quite aged, and is not called *kanut*; this ritual is a mark of respect for the person. When the person has died, or sometimes just for convenience, the *hararum* is carried out as the initial part of a *pkepke* ritual.

It is tempting to argue that in the past both *pkepke* and *tunkanut* always occurred after the death of an individual, the *tunkanut* displaying the decorated skull of the person atop a carved wooden body (*mormor*) before secondary burial. This is said by Lihirians to have been discouraged due to ideas about hygiene and sacrilegious disturbance of the dead by missionaries and the German or Australian administrations. Given that *pkepke* and *tunkanut* are generally performed when people are past the prime of their life (that is, over 50 years of age), it may be the case that in the past people generally died

[7] Even if there often did not appear to be much remembering or *lil wirwir* occurring, this argument can still apply. *Mbie* gives time and space for mourning, and it is this time and space that are being transformed, rather than the mourning itself.

[8] Also known as *karat* in differing dialects.

[9] *Pkepke* is also known as *pkekanut*, *katokatop* or *katkatup* in different dialects, while *tunkanut* is also known as *tutunkanut* or *tutunlih*.

| | | *Pkepke* | | |
|---|---|---|---|---|
| | **Day 1** | **Day 2** | **Day 3** | **Day 4** |
| Version 1 | blo ketol | zkuel *wasir* | babe | taltal bol |
| Version 2 | blo ketol | tunuiakale | ? | minien |
| Version 3 | zkuel *wasir* | blo ketol | kez na mlal | - |
| Version 4 | blo ketol | tonenie | tonenie | - |
| Version 5 | blo ketol | kez na mlal | kez na mlal | - |
| | | *Tunkanut* | | |
| | **Day 1** | **Day 2** | **Day 3** | **Day 4** |
| Version 1 | pzioz *kanut* | zkuel *wasir* | kez na mlal | taltal bol |
| Version 2 | pzioz *kanut* | ? | kez na mlal | bebe |
| Version 3 | pzioz *kanut* | zkuel *wasir* | blo ketol | bebe |

**Table 8.1: Feasts associated with *pkepke* and *tunkanut*.**

at an age before such rituals were performed, and only occasionally did the person live long enough to be present. Given the improvement in health care in the last century, many more people are living to ages at which these rituals are performed. They can be seen as vestiges of previously functional rituals designed solely to deal with death and its contingencies. However, I suggest that this view renders the past as simple and one dimensional, and just mirrors some Lihirians' views of the present as a time of decay of once resplendent, singular and unchanging 'tradition'.

Given that people may often be alive for such rituals, it is difficult to say how these rituals articulate with those for burial and mourning. The ideal sequence was once expressed to me as the *hararum* first, when the person is aged, as a mark of respect for him or her. Then the person would die, having burial feasts, then mourning period, *mbie*, followed by the *mbiektip*. Some months or years after this would be the *pkepke*, a ritual designed to remember the dead of the lineage or clan and be sad for their passing. Finally, a number of years later again, the *tunkanut* would be performed, to finish the memory of a number of deceased of the lineage or clan, to finalise inheritance of their lands, and to celebrate. I am not sure, however, how often this ideal sequence was realised in practice, with any number of these three feasts occurring before death in my experience.

Both the *pkepke* and *tunkanut* occur over about three to four days, with each day being dedicated to particular named feasts. The exact ordering and nature of each of these feasts was open to question, and I was given various orders (see Table 8.1).

The individual feasts are portrayed as accomplishing certain aims: *blo ketol* is a feast of pigs to remember the *kanut*; *zkuel wasir* means 'to give (food) to visitors'—those who have come from other places as guests to the feast. For *tunkanut*, *pzioz kanut* means 'to decorate the *kanut*' and referred in the past to the revelation of *mormor*, statues with bodies carved from wood and topped with a decorated skull of the deceased.[10]

This table is quite different from most of those found in ethnographies dealing with mortuary ritual in that it presents an image not of ideal order but of variation and choice. To me there appeared to be little difference between *tonenie*, *bebe* and *taltal bol*, for example, but for Lihirians there did appear to be differences in customary meaning and practice, and for the organisation of each ritual choices were made about the constitution of these rituals. There appeared to be no accepted, final order for the feasts within the rituals, though the people with whom I spoke about feasts would criticise the hosts or laud them on the basis of their own notion of proper customary practice. This ambiguity in the ordering of these feasts is one way that Lihirians remember and assess the success (or lack of it) of *pkepke* and *tunkanut*.

## *Karot* and emotional transformation

As *mbiektip* transforms a time of mourning to daily life, one aspect of the meaning of some *karot* is emphasising and transforming emotions. This is particularly the case for *pkepke* and *tunkanut*, which both have atmospheres highly laden with emotion. Each case accentuates distinct and differing emotional tones.

[10] *Taltal bol* means 'to cut pigs', the day these are lined up and the names of the *kanut* called out with one to three pigs representing each person; *kez na mlal* means 'to sit in a clearing', which is a day of feasting and dances. *Tonenie* means 'to give out pigs', and *bebe*, which is the last day of a ritual, involves feasting and watching dances once again.

The *pkepke* is primarily concerned with remembering (*nanse mle* or *nanse miel*) the *kanut*, and so the mood of the ceremony is supposed to be sombre (though it often is not, as the *kanut* are still alive). At least initially in the *pkepke*, there should be no dances or singing except for the mournful *yiarngen* songs. These cannot be sung unless there is someone who is properly a *kanut* (really dead). Neither of the *pkepke* I attended had these songs, which are also sung on the night before the burial of an important man and are accompanied by the blowing of the *tawil* (conch) shell. However, the mood was at least supposed to be one of remembering and being sad (*lil wirwir*).

The *tunkanut*, on the other hand, is a time to forget (*nanse baliye*) the deceased, particularly in terms of finishing the obligations dictated by *kastam* to the deceased. It is characterised by the *bel* (a women's dance) and *buot* (a dance involving both men and women, T.P. *bot*), both of which accompany the *glamuit* (slit drum, T.P. *garamut*) at night, as well as numerous dances during the day. The *tunkanut* is a celebration of life, and I was told that the nightly dances around the *glamuit* were often the context for the kindling of liaisons between young men and women that have the potential to lead to marriage.

This pair of rituals perform emotion, and achieve an emphasis on first the sadness and memory of the deceased persons who are the subject of these rituals, and then the release and celebration of life on their completion.

That these rituals emphasise emotion came particularly to my attention during Easter 1998. On Good Friday, occupants of Kuelam village performed, as Catholics do, the 14 Stations of the Cross, a procession that recalls the last stages of Christ's life from his trial to his crucifixion. This procession was accompanied by music from the *pkepke*: the mournful *yiarngen* songs, and the blowing of a *tawil* shell. Some people had blackened their hair and faces, and none wore decorations. On the previous evening, however, people had gathered and danced *buot* accompanied by the *glamuit*, before having a small feast to celebrate the time of the Last Supper. The emotional tones of Holy Thursday and Good Friday were emphasised through the performance of the music and dance of the *pkepke* and *tunkanut*, though these were done in reverse, with the *tunkanut* music and dance preceding the music of *pkepke*.

## *Karot*: performing relationships

Not only emotions are highlighted and transformed in certain *karot*, relationships may also be. In this and the following sections, I consider the performance and transformation of relationships through the practice of *pkepke* and *tunkanut* rituals. There has been increasing attention given to performance as an analytical concept encompassing meanings other than simple display:

> Performances—whether ritual or dramatic—create and make present realities vivid enough to beguile, amuse or terrify. They alter moods, attitudes, social states and states of mind. (Schiefflin 1996:59)

> Cultural performance has a power to transform both experience and social relations. (Csordas 1996:92)

While I separate performance and transformation of relationships, note that it is by making relationships visible, by drawing attention to their nature, that transformation is possible.

The structure of *pkepke* and *tunkanut* rituals is essentially tripartite, of *kanut* (deceased/corpse and subject of the rituals), *hukarot* (hosts) and *wasir* (guests). I also draw attention to the heterogenous composition of both *hukarot* and *wasir* groups. *Pkepke* and *tunkanut* are held for members of a single clan, who may be from separate subclans and lineages, and who also have a tie to the locality where the ritual is being held (that is, if someone is considered to be from Mahur and has always lived there they will not generally be included in ritual on Malie Island). The hosts are the lineage and extended family of each of the *kanut*, and thus there may be two, three, seven separate groups (up to as many groups as there are *kanut*) working together to host the event. These *hukarot* are forbidden to eat the feasting food, but, as I discuss below, these restrictions are less strict than those on *kanut*, with *hukarot* being allowed to smell the smoke of the ground ovens and light their cigarettes from firewood of the feast.

The relationship between *kanut* and *hukarot* (hosts) varies depending on whether the *kanut* is male or female. Female *kanut* are hosted by their own children, while male *kanut* are (generally) hosted by their sister's children. This difference is crucial and is mostly ignored in New Ireland ethnography, which describes in detail the relationships between hosts and guests but not those between the 'deceased' and hosts, generally glossed simply as the lineage or clan of the deceased (for example, Clay 1986:126–7; Eves 1998:236; Foster 1995:109 *passim*; Wagner 1986:194–7; but see Fergie 1995:121 for the varied composition of the hosting group for the women's ritual *vevene*). When a male *kanut* is honoured by his sister's children, and his own children choose not to commemorate him as well, they (his children) are still classified as hosts (*hukarot*) of the feast, their work being to feed their cross-cousins (FZCh), this way acknowledging the nurturance they received from their father. A female *kanut* is honoured by her own children, who in turn are fed by no one. The gender of the *kanut*, therefore, is critical to the constitution of the hosting group, whether it includes only the lineage of the deceased or whether members of other lineages are included.[11] Whenever the *kanut* is male in Lihir, it is then impossible to talk just about the hosting clan or lineage, as members from other clans are also hosts. However, these rituals are still spoken of in practice as, for example, '*tunkanut ol Nawus i wokim*' (T.P. *tunkanut* that Nawus clan is doing).

*Hukarot* perform their relationship to the *kanut* through these rituals, particularly in the final stages of both *pkepke* and *tunkanut*, when the signifying pigs of the ritual are lined up in front of the *rih* (men's house), and one of the *hukarot* then calls out who each pig is for. At this stage, people gather to watch and hear how many pigs are for each *kanut*. I was told by a few people that even if nothing else in the ritual happens, as long as these pigs are lined up and

[11] I am unclear at this time about whether the husbands and wives of hosts are also considered to be hosts given that they do work for the hosting group.

the names called, then the *hukarot* will have done enough to effect the transfer of land that is one reason for these rituals (see Figures 20 and 21).

These signifying pigs also indicate the *hukarot*'s relationship to *wasir*. These pigs are not provided by the *hukarot* but rather by certain groups of *wasir*. In preparation for these rituals, *hukarot* ask lineages to provide a pig for the feast. On some occasions these pigs are in return for those that the *hukarot* provided in the past, while for other groups these pigs are a new debt. To be successful *hukarot*, a group must be able to call in debts and create new ones. *Hukarot* choose *wasir* to be pig donors on the basis of friendship rather than any specific kin relationship. The leaders of the *hukarot* choose to create debts with those people with whom they have a prior relationship of trust and understanding (see Chapter 1).

It is through these pigs that some groups of *wasir* demonstrate (perform) their own capacities. Those groups that bring pigs present a statement about their resources to all those watching: their ability to pool resources (both cash and shell money) under the leadership of a senior man. Such groups are generally lineages or subclans. One group is asked by the hosts to provide the main pig for the feast (*a kon a karot*, head of the feast), which is generally the largest and always the most expensive pig present. To be able to provide this pig (which like all other pigs is reciprocated later) is highly prestigious.

Those groups providing pigs begin their preparation for the feast months in advance. They must gather the necessary cash and shell money and plan a voyage to elsewhere in Lihir, if not to elsewhere in New Ireland or even New Britain, to find a pig of the right size. In recent years people have been going as far as Rabaul (as well as Tanga, Tabar and Namatanai) to get pigs for feasts. In addition to the pig, pig donors must organise a dance (*ngues*) to accompany it, which is performed on the third or fourth day of the feasting. About two weeks prior to the feasting, there is *zekut*, the dress rehearsal of the dance. On this day, the pig donors have a feast of tubers and pork, the dancers perform for the people gathered, and then are paid (*ge plo a ngues*, they buy the dance) by the pig donors with tubers (called *pienbol* on this occasion) for their participation.

*Zna bol*, 'to bring a pig (to the feast)', occurs in a very particular way that is a performance of the relationships between the givers (*wasir*) and receivers (*hukarot*) (see Figures 22 to 24). The donors, both men and women, can be heard singing *nierom* (a song about catching and bringing the pig/s) before they can be seen. They come into view of the main feast area, decorated with lime, *tol* (red colouring from clay or the *bixa* plant) and leaves, carrying a pig tied to a bamboo stretcher (and sometimes another slung on bamboo poles), with the leaders of the procession carrying shell money (*a le*).[12] A greeting committee of the hosts, also decorated and carrying *a le*, meets them. The two groups run to meet each other and, planting one foot well forward, they rock back and forth in a pose of mock challenge, both groups shouting an appropriate relationship term (for example: *a buerpuelkan*, same sex cross-cousins; *a buertbon*, grandparents/children; *a buertman*, fathers/children; *a bertruan*, friends) as well as statements about the pig,[13] and often also shouting '*a ginas*' (happiness).

For *wasir* that are pig donors, the feasting of *pkepke* or *tunkanut* represents the culmination of much work: after bringing the pigs that demonstrate the extent of their resources and their ability to cooperate as a group under their leader, they can relax and watch the dances. Occasionally things do not go quite to plan, as was the case when the group providing the major pig, *a kon a karot*, on Malie in October 1998 breached the agreement they had with the hosts about the price of the pig. The agreement had been that Nzol clan of Mahur should get a pig that cost 60 fathoms of shell money (*a le*) yet when they brought it to the hosts they asked for sixty *a le* and K1000. The price Nzol had paid for the pig on Tabar was twenty *a le* and K1000, and they added extra *a le* for expenses like boat fuel and hard work. The host clan, Nawus,

[12] Occasionally there is also a man sitting atop the pig, said to be because he is a very important man of the group bringing the pig.

[13] *Saksak* pay debt; *tele* create debt of pig paid for with *a le*; *yembi* create debt of pig not paid for.

while paying this increased price, did not use this pig as *a kon a karot*, instead including it in a feast on the penultimate day of the ritual, as they felt people would not be happy to eat it when the price had increased so much. For the pig donors, this incident hardly increased their prestige in the eyes of *hukarot* or other *wasir* at the feast.

Relationships are also performed during the dances themselves, which usually consist of between 12 and 20 dancers, and some twenty or so musicians usually playing *kndur* drums (hourglass drums, T.P. *kundu*) and bamboo clappers. Some time into the dance, after their initial entrance, members of the audience walk to either a dancer or musician and throw lime, pig's blood or water over them, or slap their legs with twigs and then pay them a small amount of money (50t, K2). The people who perform this action may be male or female, young or old, *hukarot* or *wasir*, and the action is directed towards their male or female cross-cousin (*puelkan* same sex; *koko* cross sex), or a woman may do it to her brother's children (*yamun*). The audience take these interactions during performances as comical. This action is a public recognition of their relationship that occurs in no other context, and while these rituals provide a situation where this performance can occur, the relationships of these people are peripheral to the event itself. These do not particularly occur between the hosting clan/lineage and their guests (though that is occasionally the case) but they occur between dancers, drawn from any clan/lineage, and anyone at the feast. Thus, these rituals in Lihir are about more than just the relationships between the hosting clan/lineage (*hukarot*) and its audience (*wasir*).

## Transforming relationships in *karot*

It is through the performance of relationships in *karot* that relationships are transformed. This is particularly the case (and often the explicit aim) for the relationships between the *hukarot* and the *kanut*, yet is also the case for relationships between *hukarot* and *wasir*. When asked why these rituals are performed, Lihirians gave a range of answers, including finishing the debts of the deceased, transferring land from the deceased to those who were performing the rituals, and becoming leaders in the place of the deceased. All of these statements indicate an alteration of the relationship between *hukarot* and *kanut*.

In the course of life, Lihirians create and are burdened with many debts of exchange: primarily of pigs and shell money but also of nurturance. Debts of pigs and shell money are generally created through attendance at rituals such as *pkepke* and *tunkanut*. If a person is given the leg of a large pig at a *tunkanut*, then this must be exactly reciprocated at a later *tunkanut*. When a person dies leaving such debts, these can be discharged at the *pkepke* or *tunkanut* held for the person.

Debts of nurturance in the form of *owo* or *ertnin* are created through everyday life (see Chapter 2): particularly between a man and his children and sister's children, and between a woman and her children. These debts are reciprocated through attendance at a person's *mbie*, and also through acting as *hukarot* at the *kanut*'s *pkepke* and *tunkanut*. It was said to be particularly the reciprocation of debts of nurturance rather than pigs or shell money that qualified a person to gain access to, or control of, part of the land of the *kanut*.

That being said, as noted above, it is essential to the transferral of land from *kanut* to *hukarot* that pigs be lined up in front of the *rih* (men's house). In a sense, these pigs are all of the other work and cost of the *pkepke* and *tunkanut* coalesced into a single performance that transforms the relationship between *hukarot* and *kanut* from one of indebtedness to one of completion. These pigs represent a recognition and reciprocation of the nurturance of the *kanut* to the *hukarot*.

Even if *kanut* are actually deceased by the time of the *pkepke* or *tunkanut*, before their death men (particularly) or women can give a fathom of shell money to one or several people to declare that they should be the main host(s) for the rituals that later occur. However, if the ritual should not go as planned by the *kanut*, land is still passed on to the *hukarot* as long as the pigs are lined up in front of the *rih*. In a case that was described to me, a particular man gave shell money to a number of people indicating that they should be *hukarot* for the *tunkanut* to be held for him, meaning that he marked them as the future landholders and controllers. However, another man in the clan usurped these men, holding a *tunkanut* without making them aware of this and thus inheriting rights to the land of the *kanut*. This man had performed the necessary *kastam wok*, had lined up pigs in front of the *rih*, and thus disqualified others from gaining land that appeared to be more rightfully theirs.

The *hukarot* group for each *kanut* is led by a particular person, generally a man, and it is he that goes to meetings about the ritual with other such leaders, he organises his own group, and plans the resources needed, such as pigs and gardens. In doing so, this person is recognised or confirmed as leader of this lineage by the lineage themselves as well as other groups. If one of the *kanut* of the ritual was a controller of land (*a tboh wan a puor*), then through this work at *pkepke* and *tunkanut* (as well as other feasts ) this person is able to take over this role. The mantle of *tboh wan a puor* can pass from a *kanut* to one of the *hukarot* leaders through the performance of these rituals.

This aspect of the meaning of these rituals cannot be said to be the main concern of *pkepke* and *tunkanut*, as few *kanut* are actually *tboh wan a puor* or other types of leaders, and few of the *hukarot* can ever assume this role. However, *pkepke* and *tunkanut* do seem to be an important context for testing and proving the leadership skills of men. Not only the relationship between *kanut* and *hukarot* in this respect is altered, but also among the *hukarot*, and between *hukarot* and *wasir*. Let me give an example of a disastrous *tunkanut* at Samo village in 1998.

The ritual in this case was held for eleven *kanut* drawn from a number of lineages within a clan. Preparations had begun months before the event, with a *glamuit* (slit drum) newly cut and carved for the nightly *buot*. The ritual was scheduled to last four days, with *bel* and *buot* each night, daily feasting, and the major dances and feasting to occur on the final day. People came from all over Lihir for the feasting, particularly from Samo and the villages close by.

From the first day of feasting there was trouble with rain, which delayed proceedings. Lihirians practice magic that can cause or prevent rain. I was told that there is a delicate balance to be achieved at the time of a major feast: often in the week prior to the feasting rain is preferred as it calms the sea to allow easier travel for *wasir* (particularly those bringing pigs) but for the feasting time itself it is essential to have no rain. Rain during this time is seen as a sign of discord in the group hosting the ritual, and also suggests that the *hukarot* have been unable to hire experienced and successful rain magicians.

Rain led to a delay of about two days in proceedings, and *wasir* (including me) were unsure of when the final day of feasting would occur. Day three of the feast was held despite rain that threatened and eventually ruined the day. However, the *hukarot* delayed the final day of feasting until it appeared it would be fine. However, this was only the start of the problems of the *hukarot*.

On the final day of feasting *hukarot* had to ask groups to cease selling betelnut just outside of the main feast area. This sale of betelnut was considered appalling by Lihirians, as it suggested that the *hukarot* could not supply enough betelnut for the *wasir*, and contradicted the conception that all food and condiments in the feast should be freely and more than adequately provided. Following this, the dances started, and it quickly became apparent that some of the dancers and dance leaders were drunk, as were many of the other *wasir* who were simply observers. Dances also were poorly timed, and so clashed with each other. Finally, I was told that food distributions at the feast did not follow customary procedure, with both cooked food and raw pork being distributed at the same time.

Was this a successful feast? The answer to this question relies on the measure of success. I later asked if the transfer of land would have been effectively carried out through this feasting. After ascertaining that the pigs were lined up in front of the *rih*, the answer was always in the affirmative.

This means that the transformation of relations between *kanut* and *hukarot* was achieved: the debts of the *kanut* were paid, and land transfer accomplished (Hemer 2002a:264; see also Bainton 2010:183). However, the people with whom I discussed this case always went on to say that relations between *hukarot* and *wasir* would certainly not have benefited from this experience, and the reputation of *hukarot* would have suffered even among those not at the feast.

Respect (*sio*) is a critical issue in these feasts. *Hukarot* aim to display their resources and their ability to organise themselves under the leadership of a particular person. In doing so, their relations and reputation are at stake. If the ritual goes as planned then *hukarot* benefit from the performance and transformation of their relationships with *kanut*, *wasir* and even others in Lihir. However, when there are significant problems with the feasting then *hukarot* suffer, as Eves suggests can be the case: these rituals are not sites for unproblematic social reproduction (Eves 1998). Partially these rituals can be viewed in terms of the respect (*sio*) shown to *kanut* by the *hukarot* and also by the *wasir* (by attending and sometimes donating pigs and dances), and also in terms of the respect shown by *hukarot* to the *wasir*, and *wasir* to the *hukarot*.

The Samo *tunkanut* was successful in transferring land as *hukarot* showed appropriate respect (in the form of pigs) to the *kanut*. However, it failed because *hukarot* did not supply betelnut and food to *wasir* in a bountiful and appropriate manner, thus disrespecting them. It also failed because *wasir* showed disrespect to both *hukarot* and *kanut* by being drunk. *Hukarot* could have at least partially rescued their position had they acted swiftly and harshly against the drunken men—they could have been charged under ideas of customary respect. The fact that *hukarot* did not take this action simply weakened their position in the eyes of *wasir* and many others in Lihir.

Relations are at stake in the performance of these rituals. Relationships have the potential to be transformed in a positive way, or as in the Samo case, be significantly damaged. It is also the case that part of a feast may be successful, while other aspects may fail (Hemer 2002a:264–6; see also Bainton

2010:184–7). As Bainton argues, notions of what constitutes appropriate *kastam* are shifting on Lihir, and even diverge between different places within Lihir (Bainton 2010). Each feast is assessed individually as to whether it achieves enough and appears to maintain protocols about tradition. The *tunkanut* at Samo indicates that it is important to look beyond the aims of land and leadership transfer when discussing the success of particular feasts, and that in the performance of these feasts, relationships can be transformed in a negative way.

## Personhood in *karot*

With regards to mortuary rituals on Tanga like *pkepke* and *tunkanut*, Foster argues that a different form of personhood exists than in the space of everyday life. Everyday life is characterised by relational personhood based in reciprocal nurturance, while mortuary ritual is typified by force-feeding and thus autonomy:

> Tangan mortuary feasting is a collective action that gathers together a number of particular composite persons, persons differentiated from each other in terms of their particular constitutive relations. In so doing, this action temporarily eliminates what differentiates these persons, thereby creating for them a unitary identity; or, differently put, thereby creating out of them a collective individual .... The establishment of this unitary identity is a precondition for lineage replacement. (Foster 1995:216)

> The collective individuality created through force-feeding is a transcendence of relationality, an escape from a world in which relations define persons .... Collective individuals are autonomous, unencompassed by relations and hence .... outside of sociality. (ibid.:216–7)

It is apparent from my foregoing discussion about the performance and transformation of relationships in *pkepke* and *tunkanut* that it would be difficult to argue that these rituals accomplish lineage succession through the promotion of hosting lineages as completely autonomous. It is clear that *hukarot* (hosting groups) rely on other groups to succeed in the performance of a *karot*, and that Lihirians do not deny these relations. Rather, relations are the subject of performances that draw attention to the support (*erim*) given by groups of *wasir* to the *hukarot*. This is not a context where *hukarot* or *wasir* promote individual aspects of personhood, either within these groups or between them. Rather, relations which may be taken for granted at other times are illuminated through performances such as pig donation and the sham fights that accompany it, and certain classes of kin disturbing dancers.

This is not to say that individual aspects of personhood are erased during *pkepke* and *tunkanut*. Both *hukarot* and *wasir* make choices throughout the feasting that are based on individuality. People retain their autonomy: they may choose to come late to the feasting area or go elsewhere for the day, they can decide whether they wish to eat the food offered, and *hukarot* may choose not to join in to carry out the work needed to be done on a particular day.

## Kanut *and personhood*

*Kanut* represent a special case for personhood for the *pkepke* and *tunkanut*. For each ritual occasion, there were between two and 15 people who were *kanut*, and there were often an equal proportion of men and women. For all the feasts I attended and most of those for which I have details, at least one (and often more) of the *kanut* were actually still alive. Despite this, *kanut* play no part in *pkepke* or *tunkanut*; in fact, it is as though they are already dead. They eat none of the feast food, and cannot eat any food grown in the gardens for the feast. They chew none of the betelnut included in the feast, and cannot even light their cigarettes from the firewood of the feast; nor can they smell the smoke of the feasts. Instead, they are fed tubers from ground ovens not part of the feast, and eat rice and chicken. I was told that this was because participating in the feast could hasten their deaths, given that the feast portrays them as already dead in a social sense.

In actuality, the *kanut* wander around the area, apparently not avoiding the smoke of ground ovens, and chatting to people attending the feast. On one occasion a *kanut* (Moktel of Malie) cooked some mami for me as she observed that I had had nothing to eat all day, and the ground ovens weren't due to be opened till late afternoon. While movements and actions were less restricted in practice than in rule, I never saw *kanut* eating from the feast food or chewing betelnut designated as part of the feast.

In being labelled as *kanut*, those people who are the subject of these rituals are effectively construed as non-persons: that they are still alive has little meaning because they are unable to act. However, rather than argue as Sykes does, that in death the person is 'alienated from the relations which made him' (1999:163) or that the relationship between the living and dead has died (Strathern 1988:261–2), instead I contend that *kanut* are more relational in personhood than the living. In some senses, deceased *kanut* can no longer relate on their own terms to others, and cannot in general exercise their will. They largely live in the memories of others, and so are more constituted by others than they can constitute themselves. In the particular context of feasting, live *kanut* can do little except watch the proceedings.

These statements need to be tempered by the observation that deceased persons can have an impact on the living. On Mahur it was never explicitly said that *kanut* could effect the fertility of gardens or the health of the living (as is the case on Tanga; Holding 2000:pers. comm., and for the nearby (pseudonymous) Babae; Fergie 2001:pers. comm.). There was little speculation on the actions and motives of *kanut*, or about life after death beyond going to Heaven. However *kanut* can act, as was the case mentioned in Chapter 3 when a *kanut* took back his pipe, and hence they retain aspects of individuality.

It seems, then, that the particular relationship between ideals of relational conduct and constitution, and the practice of individuality, can vary over the life course. Like a person before birth that exists in relation to its mother and has little identity and no life on its own, a *kanut* is defined and lives in relation to living persons. While this is the case for all persons in a lesser sense, as argued throughout this book, adults exercise their will and individuality. The differences cannot be seen as qualitative, with infants and *kanut* as relational and adults as individual. Rather, it is a matter there being more or less emphasis on individual or relational existence.

While someone is still alive they can exercise their will and refuse to be included in a ritual. This was the case at a *tunkanut*, where one woman refused to be part of it and thus declined to be rendered as a *kanut*. At the time, she explained to me that she preferred to be included in a ritual to be done for her classificatory brother due to a close tie between their fathers. Months later when I questioned others about this instance, it was revealed that she had actually been in conflict with members of her lineage doing the ritual, and so was publicly demonstrating the state of her relationships. As she was still alive, she could exercise her autonomy and choose not to be part of a ritual, something that a real *kanut* never could do.

For *kanut*, then, these feasts are also a time when relational personhood is paramount. However, while for *hukarot* and *wasir* these rituals allow the illumination and performance of relations, and live *kanut* may return to an experience of personhood that allows greater scope for the practice of individuality, for deceased *kanut* this more relational state is permanent.

## Conclusions: person, emotion and relations

Feasts such as *pkepke* and *tunkanut* are contexts where relationships are at stake; issues such as reputation and respect are at risk in this contentious arena. Rather than being sites for the simple reproduction of the social order through the cooperation of hosts and guests, such feasts are the sites where relationships are performed and transformed, with the distinct possibility of failure. As I have shown, failure can be on a number of levels, such as failure in the transfer of land and nullification of debts or failure to succeed in creating (and performing) respect of all parties to the feast. Not only *hukarot* can fail, but *wasir* may fail in their task of being competent pig donors, dancers or simple observers.

In *pkepke* and *tunkanut*, relations are at stake against a backdrop of the evocation of emotion: sadness and memory for the *pkepke*, and celebration and release for the *tunkanut*. Partially it is the creation of these emotional moods that suggests the success of these two feasts. The Samo feast was such a debacle because the mood of celebration and release was never achieved due to the rain, betelnut sellers and drunkenness. Each of these issues is viewed by Lihirians as an expression of individualism: other rain magicians made the rain to disturb the event, people selling betelnut effectively denied appropriate relations of exchange between *hukarot* and *wasir*, and drunken people ignored their impact upon *hukarot*, *kanut* and *wasir*.

*Karot* such as *pkepke* and *tunkanut* are therefore about relationships between *kanut*, *hukarot* and *wasir*. Relationships are illuminated and altered in this context. These relationships are not qualitatively different from those of daily life, though certain aspects such as relational personhood may be emphasised over more individualistic tendencies. However given the tension between individual and relational features of personhood explored throughout this book, feasts do not always go to plan, and the gamble made by *hukarot*, *kanut* or *wasir* can result in failure. Outcomes at feasts are certainly not predetermined or assumed: relationships are truly at stake.

# Afterword

## Being Lihirian and tracing the Melanesian person

What did it mean to be Lihirian? This was the question that emerged most strongly for me during my fieldwork in Lihir. Life on Mahur continually turned on a number of key values: of respect (*sio*) for leaders, for relatives, for adults. Work or duty (*pniez*) was considered to be morally virtuous, and the proper basis for all gains of status and capital. Finally, nurturance (*pniari*, *owo*, *ertnin*) of children, visitors, pigs and gardens and its reciprocation through feasting was a constitutive component of social life. Christianity promoted love (*leimuli*) as core to families and social relationships. These key values promote the ideals of relational conduct in Lihir, ideals that fit well with relational personhood as the root metaphor of Melanesian sociality.

Yet as I have shown throughout this book, the ideals of moral relational conduct are often not met. Persons in Lihir have a sense of core self, of personality, and often act with themselves in mind. This leads to conflict and to charges of selfishness or greed, and censure of movement in the case of *piot*. Despite such conflict, people continue to practice autonomy, while others assert their relational ties through the medium of complaint and criticism.

This view of relationships requires a view of the person as an active subject, and this was my experience of persons in Lihir.

Far from the person being passive, an 'objectification of relations', the person in Lihir had a sense of self. Persons have individual conscience, and are held individually responsible when they do wrong. Shame and guilt is personalised, and while the clan or lineage may take responsibility to compensate the aggrieved person, they do not take on the guilt for the wrong-doing. This individual responsibility also applies to notions of sin and salvation that have been well accepted from Christianity.

Changes over the last century with Christianity and capitalism have not simply shifted personhood from more relational models of conduct to ones that emphasise individualism. Christianity has placed emphasis on an expanding moral universe and moral relations of conduct. Yet nor can Christianity be re-evaluated as emphasising pre-existing notions of partible Melanesian personhood. Instead, there have been layers of complexity added to the negotiations and tensions between relational and individual modes of conduct.

Being Lihirian also meant experiencing, expressing and understanding emotions in particular ways, often little explored by studies on Melanesian personhood. Some aspects of emotion in Lihir seemed familiar, such as common facial expressions and hence the ability for Lihirians to interpret my reactions to events. Lihirians' reactions to some occurrences accorded with what I expected, and were intelligible within the familiar frameworks of my own culture. Yet there were other occasions, such as the lack of relief at the return of the missing boat, that were beyond my comprehension.

Certainly there were aspects of emotion in Lihir that were culturally relative. Lihirians do not have the concept of the subconscious, and so do not believe that emotions can be repressed in the psychoanalytic sense. They do believe that people may hide their emotional reactions from others, but this is seen as dangerous to the person. Some emotions are viewed differently from others, as potentially negative. On occasions, anger, fear, worry and grief can be dangerous to people. They can cause people to age when experienced in excess, and can even kill. In certain circumstances there are forms of emotion work that can be carried out, such as distracting the person, and conducting feasts to finish people's fear or grief.

Aligned with this concern with occasions of dangerous emotions, on occasions when people act in a manner that is vastly different from expected social norms and ideas of moral conduct, this is interpreted not as being due to some variant of internally sparked emotional pathology but as an emotional or mental illness (*nglo*) caused by some form of external agency such as sorcery or spirits (*a tndol*).

Other than these extreme cases, there is not the emphasis on emotional introspection that there is in Western contexts. The lack of relief shown at the return of the boat in the Prologue needs to be seen in this context: of concern when emotions become dangerous, and yet a relative lack of stress placed on emotion in other circumstances. The reaction to the return of the boat was more about the sudden absence of worry and fear, rather than an expressive reaction of relief. Relief was not expressed as it is in the West, but rather as the absence—the *relief* of dangerous emotions.

Emotions in Lihir are fundamentally social. Rather than being about the inner person and introspection as they are largely perceived to be in the West, emotions are about social relationships. They arise in the context of these relationships even though they are considered to be bodily or existential states of the person. A person may be characterised by a lack or excess of a particular emotion—for example, an angry or a calm person—and yet emotions are commentaries on a person's relationship with others. People interpret their own and other's reactions to events that always occur in a web of social relationships. It is the triad of persons, their emotions and the relationships they navigated that constituted the experience of being Lihirian.

In understanding the person in Lihir I followed the trail of certain core values and key people in my attempt to come to grips with what it meant to be a person in this particular Melanesian context. I also tracked my own navigations and shifting relations to explore the similarities and disjunctures. The concept of *a malmalien e makil*, those echoes and scraps of detritus as indicative of a recent presence, resonated with the analytical process of this book that traces the nature of the person in Lihir.

# Bibliography


Abu-Lughod, L. 1986. *Veiled Sentiments: Honor and Poetry in a Bedouin Society*. Berkeley: University of California Press.

Abu-Lughod, L. and Lutz, C.A. 1990. Introduction: Emotion, Discourse and the Politics of Everyday Life. In *Language and the politics of emotion*. Edited by C.A. Lutz and L. Abu-Lughod. Cambridge: Cambridge University Press.

Albert, S.M. 1986. Completely by Accident I Discovered its Meaning: the Iconography of New Ireland Malagan. *Journal of the Polynesian Society* 95:239–52.

Arbuckle, G.A. 1978. The Impact of Vatican II on the Marists in Oceania. In *Mission, Church and Sect in Oceania*. Edited by L.A. Boutilier, D.T. Hughes and S.W. Tiffany. Ann Arbor: University of Michigan Press.

Bailey, F.G. 1971. *Gifts and Poison: the Politics of Reputation*. Oxford: Basil Blackwell.

Bainton, N.A. 2006. *Virtuous Sociality and other Fantasies: Pursuing Mining, Capital and Cultural Continuity in Lihir, Papua New Guinea*. PhD Thesis, University of Melbourne, Australia.

Bainton, N.A. 2008a. Men of *Kastom* and the Customs of Men: Status, Legitimacy and Persistent Values in Lihir, Papua New Guinea. *The Australian Journal of Anthropology 19*(2):194–212.

Bainton, N.A. 2008b. The Genesis and the Escalation of Desire and Antipathy in the Lihir Islands, Papua New Guinea. *The Journal of Pacific History 43*(3):289–312.

Bainton, N.A. 2010. *The Lihir Destiny: Cultural Responses to Mining in Melanesia*. Canberra: ANU E Press.

Bainton, N.A. 2011. *Customary Dispute Handling Processes at the Lihir Gold Mine, Papua New Guinea*. Paper Presented at Mining and Mining Policy in the Pacific Conference. Noumea, New Caledonia, November 2011.

Bainton, N.A., Ballard, C. and Gillespie, K. 2012. The End of the Beginning? Mining, Sacred Geographies, Memory and Performance in Lihir. *The Australian Journal of Anthropology 23*:22–49.

Banks, G. 2008. Understanding 'Resource' Conflicts in Papua New Guinea. *Asia Pacific Viewpoint 49*(1):23–34.

Barker, J. 1992. Christianity in Western Melanesian Ethnography. In *History and Tradition in Melanesian Anthropology*. Edited by J.G. Carrier. Berkeley: University of California Press.

Barker, J. 2010. The Varieties of Melanesian Christian experience: a Comment on Mosko's 'Partible penitents'. *Journal of the Royal Anthropological Institute 16*:247–49.

Battaglia, D. 1985. 'We feed our father': Paternal Nurture among the Sabarl of Papua New Guinea. *American Ethnologist 12*(3):427–41.

Battaglia, D. 1990. *On the Bones of the Serpent: Person, Memory and Mortality in Sabarl Island Society*. Chicago: University of Chicago Press.

Baxter, M.W.P. 1977. Orokaiva Rural-Urban Contacts and Attitudes. In *Change and Movement: Readings on Internal Migration in Papua New Guinea*. Edited by R.J. May. Canberra: PNG — IASER.

Belaunde, L.E. 2000. The Convivial Self and the Fear of Anger amongst the Airo-Pai of Amazonian Peru. In *The Anthropology of Love and Anger: The Aesthetics of Conviviality in Native America*. Edited by J. Overing and A. Passes. London: Routledge.

Bell, F.L.S. 1934. A Report on Fieldwork in Tanga. *Oceania 4*:290–309.

Bell, F.L.S. 1937. Death in Tanga. *Oceania 7*:316–39.

Bender, D.R. 1967. A Refinement of the Concept of Household: Families, Co-residence and Domestic Functions. *American Anthropologist 69*:493–504.

Berndt, R.M. 1964. Warfare in the New Guinea Highlands. In *New Guinea: the Central Highlands*. Edited by J. B. Watson. Special Publication *American Anthropologist 66*(4).

Billings, D.K. 1969 The Johnson Cult of New Hanover. *Oceania 40*(1):13–19.

Billings, D.K. 1987. Expressive Style and Culture: Individualism and Group Orientation Contrasted. *Language in Society 16*:475–97.

Billings, D.K. 1991. Cultural Style and Solutions to Conflict. *Journal of Peace Research 28*(3):249–62.

Billings, D.K. 2002. *Cargo Cult as Theatre: Political Performance in the Pacific*. Maryland, USA: Lexington Books.

Bodrogi, T. 1987. New Ireland Art in Cultural Context. In *Assemblage of Spirits: Idea and Image in New Ireland*. Edited by L. Lincoln. New York: Minneapolis Institute of Arts.

Bolyanatz, A.H. 2000. *Mortuary Feasting on New Ireland: the Activation of Matriliny Among the Sursurunga.* Westport, Connecticut: Bergin & Garvey.

Bourdieu, P. 1990. *The Logic of Practice.* Cambridge: Polity Press.

Bowlby, J. 1980. *Attachment and Loss, Volume III: Loss: Sadness and Depression.* London: The Hogarth Press.

Briggs, J.L. 1970. *Never in Anger: Portrait of an Eskimo Family.* Cambridge, Massachusetts: Harvard University Press.

Brison, K.J. 1992. *Just Talk: Gossip, Meetings and Power in a Papua New Guinea Village.* Berkeley: University of California Press.

Brison, K.J. 1995. You Will Never Forget: Narrative, Bereavement and Worldview among Kwanga Women. *Ethnos 23*(4):474–88.

Brison, K.J. 1998. Giving Sorrow New Words: Shifting Politics of Bereavement in a Papua New Guinea Village. *Ethnos 26*(4):363–86.

Brouwer, E.C. 1980. *'A Malagan to Cover the Grave': Funerary Ceremonies in Mandak.* PhD Thesis, University of Queensland.

Caplan, P. (ed.). 1995. *Understanding Disputes: The Politics of Argument.* Oxford: Berg Publications.

Carrier, J.G., and Carrier, A.H. 1989. *Wage, Trade and Exchange in Melanesia: a Manus Society in the Modern State.* Berkeley: University of California Press.

Carter, A.T. 1984. *Household histories. In Households: Comparative and Historical Studies of the Domestic Group.* Edited by R.McC. Netting, R.R. Wilk and E.J. Arnould. Berkeley: University of California Press.

Chapman, M. 1979. The Cross-cultural Study of Circulation. *Current Anthropology 20*(1):111–14.

Chapman, M. 1991. Pacific Island Movement and Socioeconomic Change: Metaphors of Misunderstanding. *Population and Development Review 17*(2):263–92.

Clay, B.J. 1977. *Pinikindu: Maternal Nurture, Paternal Substance.* Chicago: University of Chicago Press.

Clay, B.J. 1986. *Mandak Realities: Person and Power in Central New Ireland.* New Jersey: Rutgers University Press.

Clay, B.J. 1992. Other Times, Other Places: Agency and the Big Man in Central New Ireland. *Man 27*(4):719–33.

Chowning, A. 1985. Kove Women and Violence: the Context of Wife Beating in a West New Britain Society. In *Domestic Violence in Papua New Guinea.* Edited by S. Toft. Port Moresby: PNG Law Reform Commission.

Cohen, A.P. 1994. *Self Consciousness: an Alternative Anthropology of Identity.* London: Routledge.

Collier, J.F., and Rosaldo, M.Z. 1981. Politics and Gender in Simple Societies. In *Sexual Meanings: the Cultural Construction of Gender and Sexuality.* Edited by S.B. Ortner and H. Whitehead. Cambridge: Cambridge University Press.

Csordas, T.J. 1996. Imaginal Performance and Memory in Ritual Healing. In *The performance of healing.* Edited by C. Laderman and M. Roseman. London: Routledge.

Curry, G. and Koczberski, G. 1998. Migration and Circulation as a Way of Life for the Wosera Abelam of Papua New Guinea. *Asia Pacific Viewpoint 39*(1):29–52.

Dening, G. 1992. *Mr Bligh's Bad Language: Passion, Power and Theatre on the Bounty.* Cambridge: Cambridge University Press.

Dening, G. 1995. *The Death of William Gooch: a History's Anthropology*. Honolulu: University of Hawaii Press.

Dinnen, S. and Ley, A. (eds) 2000. *Reflections on Violence in Melanesia*. New South Wales, Australia: Hawkins Press.

Dundon, A. 2005. The Sense of Sago: Motherhood and Migration in Papua New Guinea and Australia. *Journal of Intercultural Studies 26*(1–2):21–37.

Dundon, A. 2011. DNA, Israel and the Ancestors: Substantiating Connections through Christianity in Papua New Guinea. *The Asia Pacific Journal of Anthropology 12*(1):29–43.

Epstein, A.L. 1969. *Matupit: Land, Politics and Change among the Tolai of New Britain*. Canberra: Australian National University Press.

Epstein, A.L. 1974. *Contention and Dispute: Aspects of Law and Social Control in Melanesia*. Canberra: Australian National University Press.

Epstein, A.L. 1992. *In the Midst of Life: Affect and Ideation in the World of the Tolai*. Berkeley: University of California Press.

Epstein, A.L. 1999. *Gunantuna: Aspects of the Person, the Self and the Individual*. Bathurst, Australia: Crawford House Publishing.

Errington, F. and Gewertz, D. 2010. Expanding Definitions, Contracting Contexts: a Comment on Mosko's 'Partible penitents'. *Journal of the Royal Anthropological Institute 16*:250–52.

Eves, R. 1996a. Colonialism, Corporeality and Character: Methodist Missions and the Refashioning of Bodies in the Pacific. *History and Anthropology 10*(1):85–138.

Eves, R. 1996b. Remembrance of Things Passed: Memory, Body and the Politics of Feasting in New Ireland, Papua New Guinea. *Oceania 66*:266–77.

Eves, R. 1998. *The Magical Body: Power, Fame and Meaning in a Melanesian Society*. Amsterdam: Harwood Academic Publishers.

Eves, R. 2000. Waiting for the Day: Globalisation and Apocalypticism in Central New Ireland, Papua New Guinea. *Oceania 71*(2):73–91.

Eves, R. 2010a. Masculinity Matters: Men, Gender-based Violence and the AIDS Epidemic in Papua New Guinea. In *Civic Insecurity: Law, Order and HIV in Papua New Guinea*. Edited by V. Luker and S. Dinnen. Canberra: ANU E Press.

Eves, R. 2010b. 'In God's hands': Pentecostal Christianity, Morality, and Illness in a Melanesian Society. *Journal of the Royal Anthropological Institute 16*:496–514.

Eves, R. 2011a. 'Great signs from Heaven': Christian Discourses of the end of the world from New Ireland. *The Asia Pacific Journal of Anthropology 12*(1):13–28.

Eves, R. 2011b. Pentecostal Dreaming and Technologies of Governmentality in a Melanesian Society. *American Ethnologist* 38(4):758–73.

Fajans, J. 1985. The Person in Social Context: the Social Character of Baining 'Psychology'. In *Person, Self and Experience: Exploring Pacific Ethnopsychologies*. Edited by G.M. White and J. Kirkpatrick. Berkeley: University of California Press.

Fajans, J. 1997. *They Make Themselves: Work and Play Among the Baining of Papua New Guinea*. Chicago: University of Chicago Press.

Fergie, D.J. 1985. *Being and Becoming: Ritual and Reproduction in an Island Melanesian Society*. PhD Thesis, University of Adelaide.

Fergie, D.J. 1995. Transforming Women: Being and Becoming in an Island Melanesian Society. In *Gender Rituals: Female Initiation in Melanesia*. Edited by N.C. Lutkehaus and P.B. Roscoe. New York: Routledge.

Filer, C.S. 1992. *The Lihir Hamlet/Hausboi Survey 1992*. Interim Report. Mimeo.

Filer, C.S. and Jackson, R. 1986. *The Social and Economic Impact of a Gold Mine on Lihir*. Pt Moresby: University of PNG.

Filer, C. and Mandie-Filer, A. 1998. *Lihirian Perspectives on the Social and Environmental Aspects of the Lihir Gold Mine*. Mimeographed Report.

Flinn, J. 1990. Catholicism and Pulapese Identity. In *Christianity in Oceania: Ethnographic Perspectives*. Edited by J. Barker. New York: University Press of America.

Foster, R.J. 1995. *Social Reproduction and History in Melanesia: Mortuary Ritual, Gift Exchange and Custom in the Tanga Islands*. Cambridge: Cambridge University Press.

Friedman, J. 1992. The Past in the Future: History and the Politics of Identity. *Cultural Anthropology* 7:194–210.

Gewertz, D.B. and Errington, F.K. 1999. *Emerging Class in Papua New Guinea: the Telling of Difference*. Cambridge: Cambridge University Press.

Gifford, P.C. 1974. *The Iconology of the Uli Figure of Central New Ireland*. PhD Thesis, Columbia University.

Gillespie, K. 2011. Stories, Songs and Emotion: Exploring the Power of the Sung Refrain in Lihirian Oral Literature. Musicological Society of Australia, National Conference, University of Western Australia, Perth 30 Nov–3 Dec, 2011.

Gillett, J.E. 1990. *The Health of Women in Papua New Guinea*. Goroka: Papua New Guinea Institute of Medical Research.

Gluckman, M. 1955. *The Judicial Process among the Barotse*. Manchester: Manchester University Press.

Gluckman, M. 1963. Gossip and Scandal. *Current Anthropology* 4(3):307–16.

Gluckman, M. 1965. *The Ideas in Barotse Jurisprudence.* New Haven: Yale University Press.

Goddard, M. 2005. Research and Rhetoric on Women in Papua New Guinea's Village Courts. *Oceania 75*(3):247–67.

Godelier, M. 1986. *The Making of Great Men: Male Domination and Power among the New Guinea Baruya.* Cambridge: Cambridge University Press.

Godelier, M. 1991. Is the West the Model for Humankind? The Baruya of New Guinea between Change and Decay. *International Social Science Journal 43*(2):387–99.

Godelier, M. and Strathern, M. (eds) 1991. *Big Men and Great Men: Personifications of Power in Melanesia.* Cambridge: Cambridge University Press.

Groves, W.C. 1934/5. Tabar Today: a study of a Melanesian Community in Contact with Alien Non-primitive Cultural Forces. *Oceania 5*:224–40, 346–60.

Gulliver, P.H. 1979. *Disputes and Negotiations: a Cross-cultural Perspective.* New York: Academic Press.

Hallpike, C.R. 1977. *Bloodshed and Vengeance in the Papuan Mountains: the Generation of Conflict in Tauade Society.* Oxford: Clarendon Press.

Hammel, E.A. 1984. On the *** of Studying Household Form and Function. In *Households: Comparative and Historical Studies of the Domestic Group.* Edited by R.McC. Netting, R.R. Wilk and E.J. Arnould. Berkeley: University of California Press.

Harrison, S. 1985. Concepts of the Person in Avatip Religious Thought. *Man 20*:115–30.

Harrison, S. 1993. *The Mask of War: Violence, Ritual and the Self in Melanesia.* Manchester: Manchester University Press.

Harrison, S. 2006. *Fracturing Resemblances: Identity and Mimetic Conflict in Melanesia and the West.* New York: Berghahn Books.

Heider, K.G. 1991. *Landscapes of Emotion: Mapping Three Cultures of Emotion in Indonesia.* Cambridge: Cambridge University Press.

Hemer, S.R. 2002a. *A Malmalien e Makil: Person, Emotion and Relations in Lihir.* PhD Thesis, University of Melbourne, Australia.

Hemer, S.R. 2002b. *Maternal Health Report.* A Report to Lihir Management Company.

Hemer, S.R. 2010. Grief as Social Experience: Death and Grieving in Lihir, Papua New Guinea. *The Australian Journal of Anthropology 21*(3):281–97.

Hemer, S.R. 2011a. Local, Regional and Worldly Interconnections: the Catholic and United Churches in Lihir, Papua New Guinea. *The Asia Pacific Journal of Anthropology 12*(1):60–73.

Hemer, S.R. 2011b. *Gender and Mining: Women's Associations and Women's Status in Lihir, PNG.* Invited Plenary Paper, Mining and Mining Policy in the Pacific. Noumea, New Caledonia, 22 November 2011.

Hemer, S.R. n.d.a. Pursuing the 'Good life': Contrasting Conceptions of Well-being in Londolovit Township, Lihir. Manuscript.

Hemer, S.R. n.d.b. Sensual Feasting: Transforming Emotions and Spaces in Lihir. Manscript.

Hendry, J. 1992. The Paradox of Friendship in the Field: Analysis of a Longterm Anglo-Japanese Relationship. In *Anthropology and Autobiography.* Edited by J. Okely and H. Callaway. London: Routledge.

Henry, R. 2005. Smoke in the Hills, Gunfire in the Valley: War and Peace in the Western Highlands, Papua New Guinea. *Oceania 75*(4):431–43.

Hermkens, A.K. 2007a. The Power of Mary in Papua New Guinea. *Anthropology Today 23*(2):4–8.

Hermkens, A.K. 2007b. Church Festivals and the Visualization of Identity in Collingwood Bay, Papua New Guinea. *Visual Anthropology 20*:347–64.

Holding, A. 2000. *Anatomy of Context: Issues in Understanding Tangan Views of Illness*. PhD Thesis, University of Cambridge.

Howe, L. 2000. Risk, Ritual and Performance. *Journal of the Royal Anthropological Institute 6*:63–79.

Iteanu, A. 1990. The Concept of the Person and the Ritual System: an Orokaiva View. *Man 25*:35–53.

Jackson, R. 1997. Cheques and Balances: Compensation and Mining in Papua New Guinea. In *Compensation for Resource Development in Papua New Guinea*. Edited by S. Toft. Port Moresby: Law Reform Commission of Papua New Guinea Monograph No. 6.

Jackson, S.A. 1996. Remembering to Forget: Memory, Burial, and Self-similarity in Sursurunga, New Ireland, Papua New Guinea. *Anthropology and Humanism 21*(2):159–70.

Kahn, M. 1983. Sunday Christians, Monday Sorcerers: Selective Adaption to Missionization in Wamira. *Journal of Pacific History 18*:96–112.

Kahn, M. 1986. *Always Hungry, Never Greedy: Food and the Expression of Gender in a Melanesian Society*. Cambridge: Cambridge University Press.

Kahn, M. 1996. Your Place and Mine: Sharing Emotional Landscapes in Wamira, Papua New Guinea. In *Senses of Place*. Edited by S. Feld and K.H. Basso. Santa Fe: School of American Research Press.

Kamerman, J.B. 1988. *Death in the Midst of Life: Social and Cultural influences on Death, Grief and Mourning*. New Jersey: Prentice Hall.

Keane, W. 2008. Others, Other Minds, and Others' Theories of Other Minds: an Afterword on the Psychology and Politics of Opacity Claims. *Anthropological Quarterly 81*(2):473–82.

Keesing, R.M. 1982. Kastom in Melanesia: an Overview. *Mankind 13*(4):297–302.

Kelly, R.C. 1993. *Constructing Inequality: the Fabrication of a Hierarchy of Virtue among the Etoro*. Ann Arbor: University of Michigan Press.

Kiapseni, A. 1976. *Traditional and Introduced Leadership in Lihir Christian Community*. Parts A, B and C. Manuscript.

Kidd, S.W. 2000. Knowledge and the Practice of Love and Hate among the Enxet of Paraguay. In *The Anthropology of Love and Anger: the Aesthetics of Conviviality in Native America*. Edited by J. Overing and A. Passes. London: Routledge.

Kingston, S. 2003. Form, Attention and a Southern New Ireland Life Cycle. *Journal of the Royal Anthropological Institute 9*:681–708.

Kirsch, S. 2007. Indigenous Movements and the Risks of Counterglobalization: Tracking the Campaign against Papua New Guinea's Ok Tedi Mine. *American Ethnologist 34*(2):303–21.

Knauft, B.M. 1985. *Good Company and Violence: Sorcery and Social Action in a Lowland New Guinea Society*. Berkeley: University of California Press.

Knauft, B.M. 2010. Beyond Polarization and Partition in Melanesian Anthropology: a Comment on Mosko's 'Partible penitents'. *Journal of the Royal Anthropological Institute 16*:244–46.

Koczberski, G. and Curry, G.N. 2004. Divided Communities and Contested Landscapes: Mobility, Development and Shifting Identities in Migrant Destination Sites in Papua New Guinea. *Asia Pacific Viewpoint 45*(3):357–71.

Koczberski, G., Curry, G.N. and Imbun, B. 2009. Property Rights for Social Inclusion: Migrant Strategies for Securing Land and Livelihoods in Papua New Guinea. *Asia Pacific Viewpoint 50*(1):29–42.

Kowal, E. 1999. *Children, Choice and Change: the use of Western Contraception on the Lihir Islands, Papua New Guinea*. BA Hons. Thesis, University of Melbourne, Australia.

Kuchler, S. 1987. Malagan: Art and memory in a Melanesian Society. *Man 22*:238–55.

Kuchler, S. 1999. Binding in the Pacific: Between Loops and Knots. *Oceania 69*(3):145–56.

Kuchler, S. 2002. *Malanggan: Art, Memory, and Sacrifice*. Oxford, UK, New York: Berg.

Kuehling, S. 1998. *The Name of the Gift: Ethics of Exchange on Dobu Island*. PhD Thesis, Australian National University.

Leavitt, S.C. 1995. Seeking Gifts from the Dead: Longterm Mourning in a Bumbita Arapesh Cargo Narrative. *Ethnos 23*(4):453–73.

Leenhardt, M. 1979. *Do Kamo: Person and Myth in the Melanesian World*. Chicago: University of Chicago Press.

Lepowsky, M.A. 1985. Food Taboos, Malaria and Dietary Change: Infant Feeding and Cultural Adaptation on a Papua New Guinea Island. In *Infant Care and Feeding in the South Pacific*. Edited by L.B. Marshall. New York: Gordon and Breach.

Lepowsky, M.A. 1993. *Fruit of the Motherland: Gender in an Egalitarian Society*. New York: Columbia University Press.

Levy, R.I. 1984. Emotion, Knowing and Culture. In *Culture Theory: Essays on Mind, Self and Emotion*. Edited by R.A. Schweder and R.A. Levine. Cambridge: Cambridge University Press.

Lewis, P.H. 1969. *The Social Context of Art in Northern New Ireland.* Chicago: Field Museum of Natural History.

Lihir Management Company (LMC). 1999. *Perception Report.* Community Relations Department, Mimeo.

LiPuma, E. 1998. Modernity and Forms of Personhood in Melanesia. In *Bodies and Persons: Comparative Perspectives from Africa and Melanesia.* Edited by M. Lambeck and A. Strathern. Cambridge: Cambridge University Press.

Lohmann, R.I. 2007. Mementos of the Dead: Technologies of Memory Management in a New Guinea Village (author's translation of 'Souvenirs des morts: Techniques de gestion de la me'moire dans un village de Nouvelle-Guine'e'). *Journal de la Societe des Oceanistes 124*: 45–57.

Lutz, C.A. 1988. *Unnatural Emotions: Everyday Sentiments on a Micronesian Atoll and their Challenge to Western Theory.* Chicago: University of Chicago Press.

Lutz, C.A. and Abu-Lughod, L. (eds). 1990. *Language and the Politics of Emotion.* Cambridge: Cambridge University Press.

Macintyre, M. 1995. Violent Bodies and Vicious Exchanges: Personification and Objectification in the Massim. *Social Analysis 37*:29–43.

Macintyre, M. 2003a. Petztorme Women: Responding to Change in Lihir, Papua New Guinea. *Oceania 74*:120–33.

Macintyre, M. 2003b. *The Changing Value of Women's Work in Lihir.* Paper presented at 'Women in Mining: Voices for Change' conference in Madang, 3–6 August 2003.

Macintyre, M. 2006. Women Working in the Mining Industry in Papua New Guinea: a Case Study from Lihir. In *Women Miners in Developing Countries: Pit Women and Others.* Edited by K. Lahiri-Dutt and M. Macintyre. Aldershot: Ashgate.

Macintyre, M. 2008. Police and Thieves, Gunmen and Drunks: Problems with Men and Problems with Society in Papua New Guinea. *The Australian Journal of Anthropology 19*(2):179–93.

Macintyre, M. n.d. Matrilineal Structures and Patriarchal Attitudes: Women's Health on Lihir, Papua New Guinea. Unpublished manuscript.

Malinowski. B. 1961. *Argonauts of the Western Pacific*. New York: E.P. Dutton.

Marshall, M. 1979. *Weekend Warriors: Alcohol in a Melanesian Culture*. Palo Alto: Mayfield Publishing Company.

Martin, K. 2007. Your Own *Buai* You Must Buy: the Ideology of Possessive Individualism in Papua New Guinea. *Anthropological Forum 17*(3):285–98.

Maschio, T. 1994. *To Remember the Faces of the Dead: the Plenitude of Memory in Southwestern New Britain*. Wisconsin: University of Wisconsin Press.

May, R.J and Skeldon, R. 1977. Internal Migration in Papua New Guinea: an Introduction to its Description and Analysis. In *Change and Movement: Readings on Internal Migration in Papua New Guinea*. Edited by R.J. May. Canberra: PNG — IASER.

McDougall, D. 2009. Christianity, Relationality and the Material Limits of Individualism: Reflections on Robbins's *Becoming Sinners*. *The Asia Pacific Journal of Anthropology 10*(1):1–19.

McLeaod, A. and Macintyre, M. 2010. The Royal Papua New Guinea Constabulary. In *Civic Insecurity: Law, Order and HIV in Papua New Guinea*. Edited by V. Luker and S. Dinnen. Canberra: ANU E Press.

Meggitt, M. 1977. *Blood is their Argument: Warfare among the Mae Enga Tribesmen of the New Guinea Highlands*. California: Mayfield Publishing Corporation.

Modjeska, N. 1982. Production and Inequality: Perspectives from Central New Guinea. In *Inequality in New Guinea Highlands Societies*. Edited by A. Strathern. Cambridge: Cambridge University Press.

Moore, S.F. 1995. Imperfect Communications. In *Understanding Disputes: the Politics of Argument*. Edited by P. Caplan. Oxford: Berg Publications.

Morton, H. 1996. *Becoming Tongan: An Ethnography of Childhood*. Honolulu: University of Hawaii Press.

Mosko, M. 2010. Partible Penitents: Dividual Personhood and Christian Practice in Melanesia and the West. *Journal of the Royal Anthropological Institute 16*:215–40.

Neuhaus, K. 1954. *Grammatik der Lir-Sprache in Melanesien*. Microform.

Neumann, K. 1992. *Not the Way It Really Was: Constructing the Tolai Past*. Honolulu: University of Hawaii Press.

Newton, J. 1985. *Orokaiva Production and Exchange*. Canberra: Australian National University.

O'Connor, J.A. 1991. Good Stories From There Develop Good Care Here: a Therapeutic Perspective. In *Coping with the Final Tragedy: Cultural Variation in Dying and Grieving*. Edited by D. R. Counts and D. A. Counts. New York: Baywood Publishing Co.

Parkin, D. 1995. Disputing Human Passion: the Negotiation of the Meaning of Love Among the Giriama of Kenya. In *Understanding Disputes: the Politics of Argument*. Edited by P. Caplan. Oxford: Berg Publications.

Patterson, M. and Macintyre, M. 2011. Introduction: Capitalism, Cosmology and Globalisation in the Pacific. In *Managing Modernity in the Western Pacific*. Edited by M. Patterson and M. Macintyre. St Lucia: University of Queensland Press.

Ramstad, Y. n.d.a. *Introducing Lihir Society: Kinship Roles and Human Resources.* Seminar Paper given at Australian National University.

Ramstad, Y. n.d.b. *The TKA Movement in New Ireland.* Seminar Paper given at Australian National University.

Ramstad, Y. n.d.c. *Rituals on Lihir.* Seminar Paper given at Australian National University.

Read, K. 1955. Morality and the Concept of the Person among the Gahuku-Gama. *Oceania 25*:233–82.

Robbins, J. 2004. *Becoming Sinners: Christianity and Moral Torment in a Papua New Guinea Society.* Berkeley: University of California Press.

Robbins, J. 2007. Afterword: Possessive Individualism and Cultural Change in the Western Pacific. *Anthropological Forum 17*(3):299–308.

Robbins, J. 2010. Melanesia, Christianity, and Cultural Change: a Comment on Mosko's 'Partible Penitents'. *Journal of the Royal Anthropological Institute 16*:241–43.

Rosaldo, M.Z. 1980. *Knowledge and Passion: Ilongot Notions of Self and Social Life.* Cambridge: Cambridge University Press.

Rosengren, D. 2000. The Delicacy of Community: on Kisagantsi in Matsigenka Narrative Discourse. In *The Anthropology of Love and Anger: the Aesthetics of Conviviality in Native America.* Edited by J. Overing and A. Passes. London: Routledge.

Ross, A.C. 1984. *Migrants from Fifty Villages.* Boroko: PNG Iaser Monograph 21.

Rumsey, A. 2008. Confession, Anger and Cross-cultural Articulation in Papua New Guinea. *Anthropological Quarterly 81*(2):455–72.

Sahlins, M. 1981. *Historical Metaphors and Mythical Realities.* Ann Arbor: University of Michigan Press.

Sahlins, M. 1982. The Apotheosis of Captain Cook. In *Between Belief and Transgression: Structuralist Essays in Religion, History and Myth*. Edited by M. Izard and P. Smith. Chicago: University of Chicago Press.

Sahlins, M. 1985. *Islands of History*. London: Tavistock.

Sahlins, M. 1995. *How 'Natives' Think: About Cook, For Example*. Chicago: University of Chicago Press.

Scheper-Hughes, N. 1992. *Death Without Weeping: the Violence of Everyday Life in Brazil*. Berkeley: University of California Press.

Schieffelin, B.B. 2008. Speaking Only Your Own Mind: Reflections on Talk, Gossip and Intentionality in Bosavi (PNG). *Anthropological Quarterly 81*(2):431–41.

Schieffelin, E.L. 1977. *The Sorrow of the Lonely and the Burning of the Dancers*. St Lucia: University of Queensland Press.

Schieffelin, E.L. 1983. Anger and Shame in the Tropical Forest: on Affect as a Cultural System in Papua New Guinea. *Ethos 11*(3):181–91.

Schieffelin, E.L. 1996. On Failure and Performance: Throwing the Medium out of the Séance. In *The Performance of Healing*. Edited by C. Laderman and M. Roseman. London: Routledge.

Schieffelin, E.L. 1998. Problematizing Performance. In *Ritual, Performance, Media*. Edited by F. Hughes-Freeland. London: Routledge.

Segalen, M. 1984. Nuclear is not Independent: Organization of the Household in the Pays Bigouden Sud in the Nineteenth and Twentieth Centuries. In *Households: Comparative and Historical Studies of the Domestic Group*. Edited by R.McC. Netting, R.R. Wilk and E.J. Arnould. Berkeley: University of California Press.

Skeldon, R. 1977. *Internal Migration in Papua New Guinea: a Statistical Description*. Boroko: PNG Iaser.

Smith, K. 2012. From Dividual and Individual Selves to Porous Subjects. *The Australian Journal of Anthropology 23*:50–64.

Strathern, A. and Stewart, P.J. 1998. Seeking Personhood: Anthropological Accounts and Local Conceptions in Mt Hagen, Papua New Guinea. *Oceania 68*(3):170–88.

Strathern, M. 1988. *The Gender of the Gift: Problems with Women and Problems with Society in Melanesia*. Berkeley: University of California Press.

Stephen, M. (ed.). 1987. *Sorcerer and Witch in Melanesia*. Melbourne: Melbourne University Press.

Stroebe, M.S., Stroebe, W. and Hansson, R.O. (eds). 1993. Bereavement Research and Theory: an introduction to the handbook. In *Handbook of Bereavement: Theory, Research and Intervention*. Cambridge: Cambridge University Press.

Sykes, K. 1999. After the 'Raskol' Feast: Youths' Alienation in New Ireland, Papua New Guinea. *Critique of Anthropology 19*(2):157–74.

Sykes, K. 2007. The Moral Grounds of Critique: Between Possessive Individuals, Entrepreneurs and Big Men in New Ireland. *Anthropological Forum 17*(3):255–68.

Thune, C.E. 1990. Fathers, Aliens and Brothers: Building a Social World in Loboda Village Church Services. In *Christianity in Oceania: Ethnographic Perspectives*. Edited by J. Barker. New York: University Press of America.

Trompf, G.W. 1991. *Melanesian Religion*. Cambridge: Cambridge University Press.

Tuzin, D.F. 1989. Visions, Prophecies, and the Rise of Christian Consciousness. In *The Religious Imagination in New Guinea*. Edited by G. Herdt and M. Stephen. New Brunswick: Rutgers University Press.

Wagner, R. 1986. *Asiwinarong: Ethos, Image and Social Power among the Usen Barok of New Ireland.* Princeton: Princeton University Press.

Wagner, R. 1987. Figure-ground Reversal among the Barok. In *Assemblage of Spirits: Idea and Image in New Ireland.* Edited by L. Lincoln. New York: George Biaziller and Minneapolis Institute of Arts.

Wardlow, H. 2006. *Wayward Women: Sexuality and Agency in a New Guinea Society*. Berkeley: University of California Press.

Watson-Gegeo, K.A. and White, G.M. (eds). 1990. *Disentangling: Conflict Discourse in Pacific Societies*. Stanford: Stanford University Press.

Wellencamp, J.C. 1988. Notions of Grief and Catharsis among the Toraja. *American Ethnologist 15*:486–500.

Wellencamp, J.C. 1991. Fallen Leaves: Death and Grieving in Toraja. In *Coping with the Final Tragedy: Cultural Variation in Dying and Grieving.* Edited by D.R. Counts and D.A. Counts. New York: Baywood Publishing Co.

Were, G. 2007. Fashioning Belief: the Case of the Baha'I Faith in Northern New Ireland. *Anthropological Forum 17*(3):239–53.

Wilk, R.R. and Netting, R. McC. 1984. Households: Changing Forms and Functions. In *Households: Comparative and Historical Studies of the Domestic Group*. Edited by R.McC. Netting, R.R. Wilk and E.J. Arnould. Berkeley: University of California Press.

Williams, F.E. 1928. *Orokaiva Magic*. Oxford: Clarendon Press.

Wikan, U. 1990. *Managing Turbulent Hearts: a Balinese Formula for Living.* Chicago: University of Chicago Press

Yanagisako, S.J. 1979. Family and Household: the Analysis of Domestic Groups. *Annual Review of Anthropology 8*:161–205.

Young, E.A. 1977. Population Mobility in Agarabi/Gadsup, Eastern Highlands

Province. In *Change and Movement: Readings on Internal Migration in Papua New Guinea*. Edited by R.J. May. Canberra: PNG — IASER.

Young, M.W. 1971. *Fighting with Food: Leadership, Values and Social Control in a Massim Society*. Cambridge: Cambridge University Press.

Young, M.W. 1999. Feasting Friends, Eating Enemies: Amity and Enmity in Kalauna. In *Identity and Affect: Experiences of Identity in a Globalising World*. Edited by J.R. Campbell and A. Rew. London: Pluto Press.